JAMES CHAMBURY

JAMES CHAMBURY

COLOUR LIGHT & SHADE

PAINTING IN EAST ANGLIA & BEYOND

Louise and Nicola Chambury

HALSTAR

First published in Great Britain in 2011

British Library Cataloguing-in-Publication Data
A CIP record for this title is available from the British Library

ISBN 978 1 906690 35 9

HALSTAR
Halsgrove House,
Ryelands Business Park,
Bagley Road, Wellington, Somerset TA21 9PZ
Tel: 01823 653777 Fax: 01823 216796
email: sales@halsgrove.com

An imprint of Halstar Ltd, part of the Halsgrove group of companies
Information on all Halsgrove titles is available at: www.halsgrove.com

Printed and bound in Italy by Grafiche Flaminia

CONTENTS

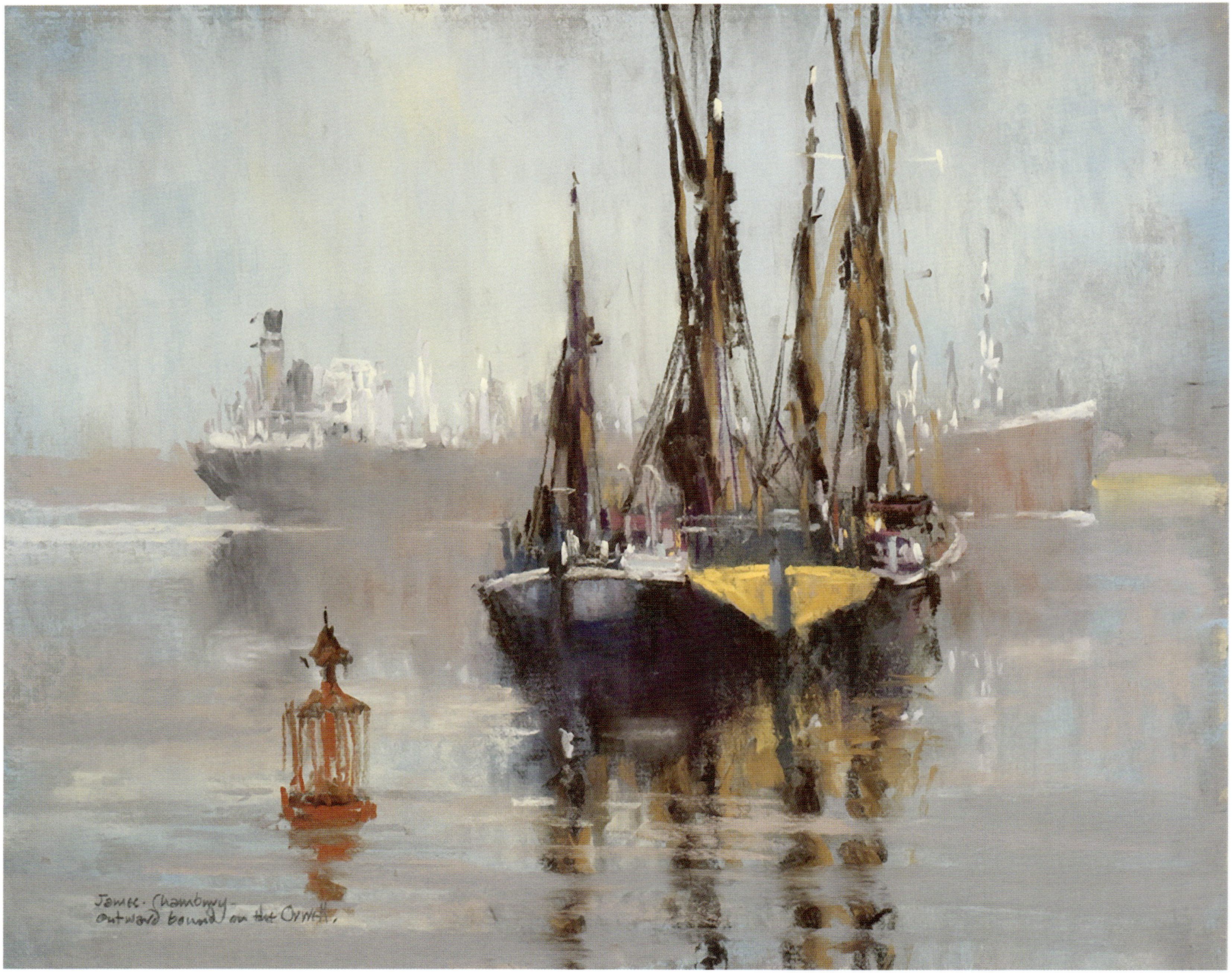

Outward Bound on the Orwell, Suffolk. Pastel 35x26cm

INTRODUCTION

Leigh-on-Sea is an old fishing village on the Essex coast, where the Thames Estuary meets the North Sea. After training and working as an illustrator and commercial artist since his teenage years, at the age of forty James took his first steps as a landscape artist sketching at Leigh-on-Sea. He had first been there as an evacuee from wartime London, when it gave him his first sight of the sea, of the ebb and flow of water over the vast mud flats and the play of light on clouds and water.

Maybe now, as a man, the uncertainty of the boundaries between sky and earth and water resonated with his excitement and fears as he looked back over his life so far and forward to the hopes the future might hold. His path to this moment had not been an easy one, but from now on he was able to create the sketches, oils, watercolours and pastels we can enjoy today.

Louise Chambury
Nicola Chambury
2011

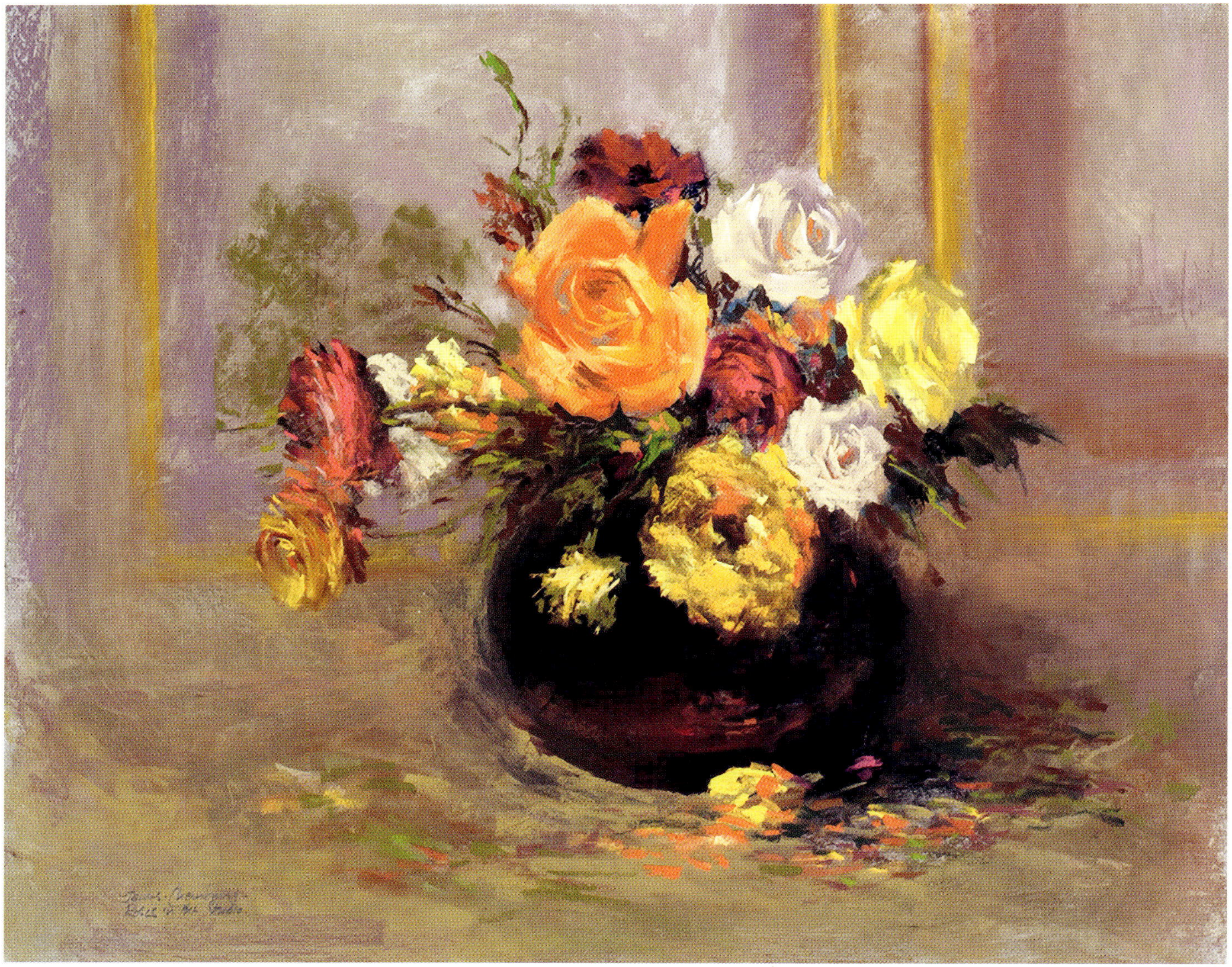

Roses in the Studio. Pastel 51x40cm

CHILDHOOD

James was born in 1927 into a large family in the East End of London. His father was an unskilled labourer, out of work for most of the 1930s. Like many fathers of that time and place he was a distant figure for his children. His mother, a talented lace maker, knitter and seamstress, took in piece-work such as hand-sewing shoe uppers and soles together. James belonged to her second family, as she already had nine children with a previous husband. He left her just after the First World War, and the oldest children had to go to the children's home in Ilford, which still operated on workhouse-like conditions. The boys and girls lived separately, and brothers and sisters never saw each other. Children left at fourteen to work as labourers or go into service. The younger children stayed with their mother, and during James' childhood there were always large numbers of people about, but his older half brothers and sisters belonged to a different generation. His mother had another four children in her second family, Joseph, James, Bill and Doreen, known as 'Sis'. In all, his mother spent thirty years having children, being pregnant twenty times and having thirteen surviving children.

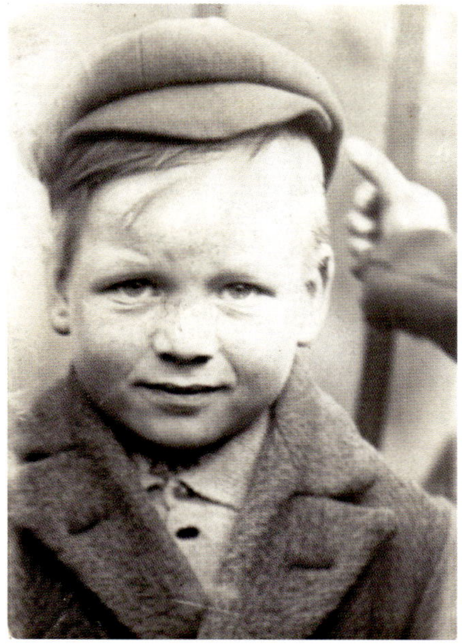

James as a child.

It was the kind of home where family background was not discussed, questions treated with a cuff and not with an answer and expectations were low. James had a keen interest in drawing from an early age, and during the wars spent hours drawing airplanes and warships. James' dream of becoming an artist was greeted not with encouragement but with disapproval.

We often wonder where talent suddenly appears from in a family. Some of James' siblings were also keen artists or skilled with their hands. In earlier generations poor children with such skills usually had to channel them into practical occupations such as a carpenter, cabinet maker, seamstress or cook. As our society has become more affluent, there has been more opportunity for such children to become professional artists or designers. Certainly James' mother and sister were both highly skilled needlewomen.

James was an intelligent boy, with an eagerness for knowledge and understanding he kept throughout his life. He passed the scholarship to go to grammar school. He could remember the teacher who interviewed him saying, "Oh yes, good with his hands, he could maybe become a dental technician." Holding out the chance of improvement as long as he remembered his

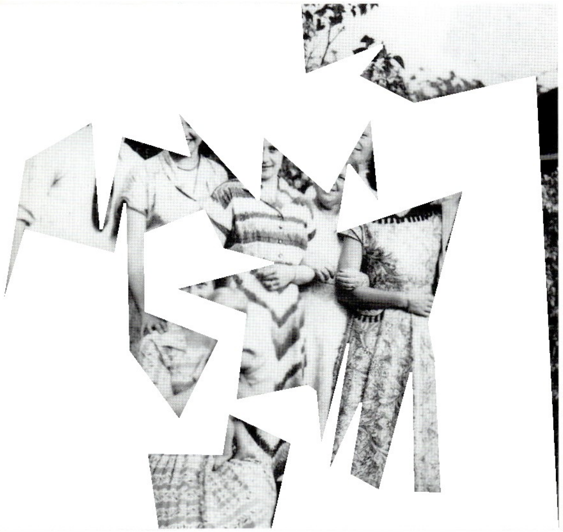

Photo of James' family taken in 1963. Left to right: James' brother Bill; his wife Joan; Doris; James' mother, Mary; James' brother Joe; James' wife Josephine; James. In the front James' sister Doreen and baby John.

place was typical of the period. His parents did not want him to go as it would be too expensive and it would put off the time when he would start earning a living. So he stayed on at elementary school. The report card from his last school reads, "Art: very good always".

James always drew, using whatever materials he could lay his hands on. Like many teenaged boys of the war years, he was fascinated by the machinery of war. Like all Londoners, he could tell the sound of an enemy plane from an allied one, and could recognize all the bombers and fighter planes from their silhouettes. He collected books and cigarette cards and drew them all the time.

The third time the family was bombed out, they moved to Hadleigh in Essex. For the first time James saw the countryside, sea and large open skies which had a significant and lasting effect on him and later inspired his art. Leigh-on-Sea was nearby and he often cycled there on his delivery bike to see the fishing boats and buy treats of cockles and whelks, which he loved all his life.

James left school while living here and found his first job, a delivery boy for a local butcher. He was always keen to tell his children, when they asked for more pocket money, that his first wage was 14/- a week (70p), and that he gave 12/- (60p) of that to his mum!

By the time he was sixteen James was a messenger for *The People* newspaper in London. In those days it was cheaper to travel into London on the early morning workmen's trains. He arrived at work far too early, and while he waited to start work he drew the Fleet Street buildings he could see out of his window.

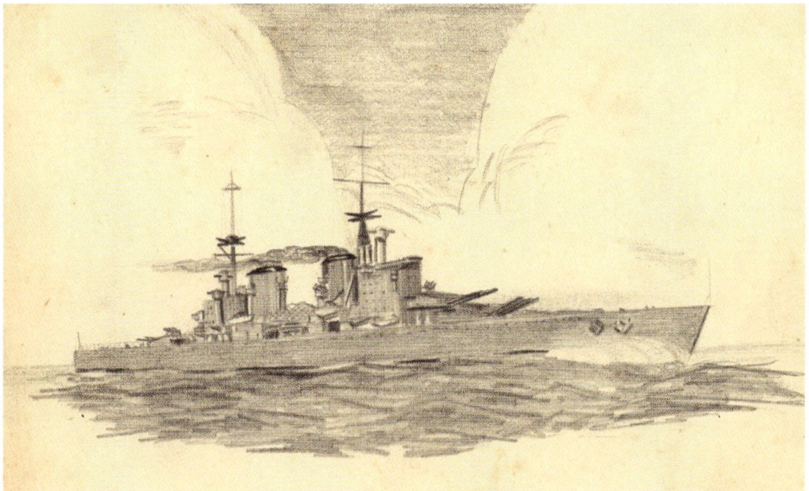

James' pencil drawing of HMS King George VI made when James was around 12 years old.

STUDENT DAYS

One day his boss surprised him at his sketching. Terrified he was going to get into trouble, as he had all his life for drawing, he tried to hide what he was doing under the desk. His boss asked to see, and amazed James by saying "If I give you half a day a week off work, will you go to art school?" James was sixteen, and this was the first encouragement he had ever received for his art. He started going to evening classes at the Central School of Arts & Crafts (later the Central School of Art & Design, and now part of Central Saint Martins College of Art & Design).

Unfortunately drawings from this period do not survive, but James retained this interest in images of buildings and some of his later pen and ink drawings testify to his skill as an observer and draughtsman.

As a teenager during the war James had dreamed of being a fighter pilot and longed to join the RAF. When he turned eighteen in May 1945, just after Victory in Europe, he was called up for Military Service and joined the RAF. He passed all the tests to be selected for training as a pilot, but now the war in Europe was over they were not just training pilots for the short term, and he would have had to sign up for 12 years with 10 years in the Reserve. This he did not want to do so he started and finished his four years Military Service as Aircraftman Chambury. He went first to India, where he felt more sympathy for the Indians demanding independence than he did for his role as upholder of Empire. In those days, people had far less access to images of different countries, and although he had grown up in poverty, he was shocked at the poverty he saw around him in India.

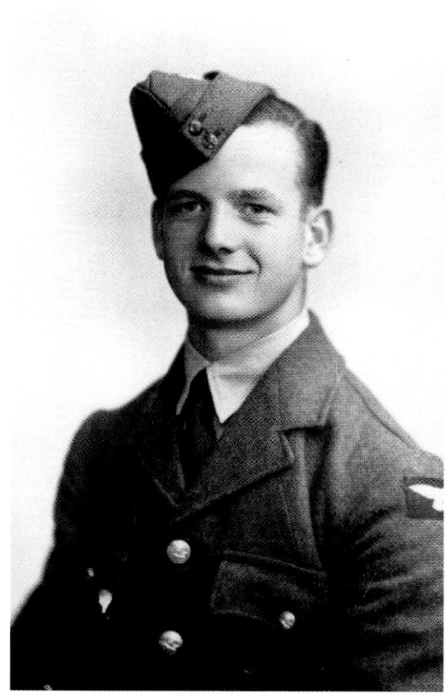

James in the RAF, 1945-1948.

After a few months James went to Nagasaki in Japan as part of the occupation forces. This was about eight months after the second atom bomb had been dropped on Nagasaki, killing between 60,000 and 80,000 people. James had read about Japanese art and culture and was looking forward to learning more, but instead, found devastation. Fraternizing between troops and the Japanese was forbidden. He found this intensely frustrating. His one escape was church parade. He was brought up a Catholic, so he and a couple of other airmen went to mass with an old Japanese priest, possible because the mass was still said in Latin.

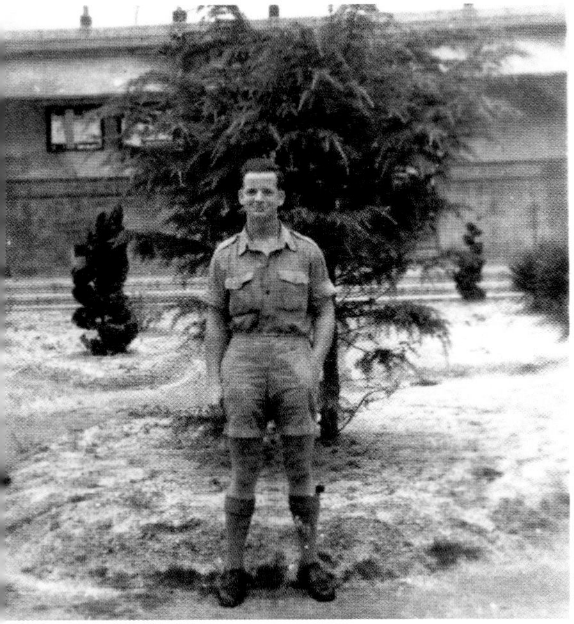

James in the Far East.

Attending church services gave them the opportunity to take their time on the way there and back, and see something of the country. James was deeply saddened at the devastation all around him and the low state of the people. They were frightened of the occupation forces, fearing they were going to abduct their daughters and kill the men. The terrible aftermath of war affected him deeply and he was anti-war for the rest of his life. He was moved to see how people sought out the plot of land where their house or shop had been before the bomb and started rebuilding in the same place. The Japanese were in desperate straits, and would barter anything they had for a bit of food or a couple of packets of cigarettes. James returned home with three silk paintings and some exquisite paper-thin porcelain.

After his RAF service James returned to London and continued art classes at the Sir John Cass College (later Sir John Cass School of Art, and now part of London Metropolitan University). In all, he attended art school part-time for about a decade, not including the time spent in the RAF. He used to say that when classes started in September, there would be twenty or so pupils, and by November there would be just two of them left.

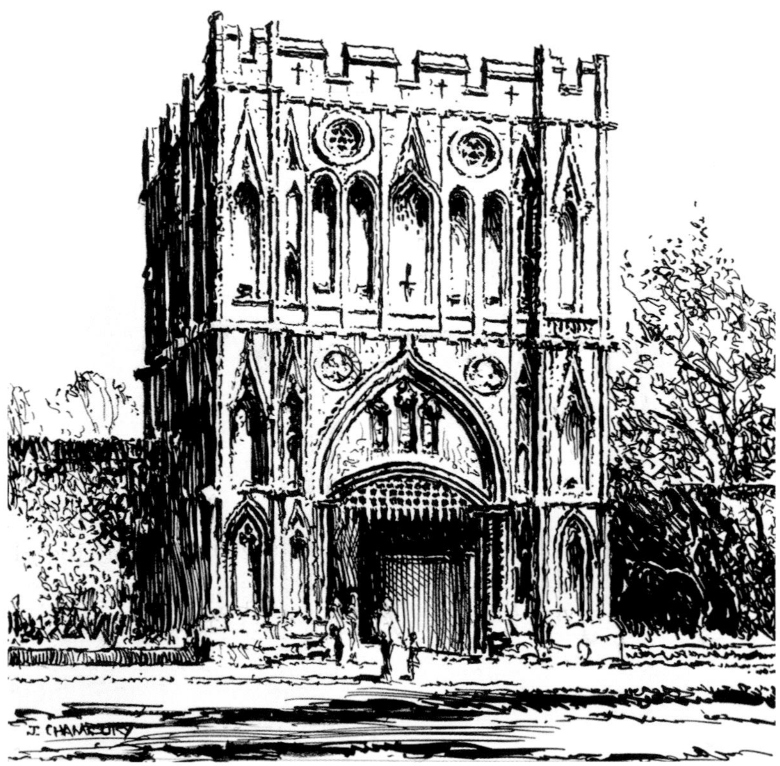

The Abbey Gate, Bury St Edmunds.
pen and ink 13x13cm

ILLUSTRATOR & COMMERCIAL ARTIST

By day James worked as a commercial artist. He was interested mainly in magazine design and illustration. His first job on leaving the RAF was creating artwork for an RAF magazine. This gave him the chance to indulge his teenage passion for drawing airplanes and to start his career as an artist.

James shared an office with George Thompson, who was also a musician and bandmaster of the Odhams Press Brass Band. Towards the end of one working day a young student opera singer arrived at the office. Josephine Petronzio had been sent by her singing teacher, Maestro di Veroli, for music theory lessons with George Thompson. James saw her arrive each week, and fell in love, but thought that she was out of his league.

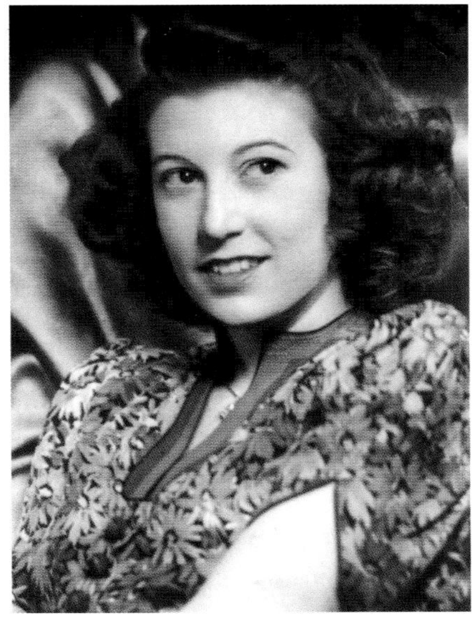

Josephine Petronzio.

It took him six months to ask her out. Their courtship was hard as Josephine was touring in the chorus of the Carl Rosa Opera Company and their families were opposed. Josephine's family was Italian. Her father's parents had come from near Naples at about the turn of the twentieth century to live in 'Little Italy', Clerkenwell in London. They came with small children, and had other children, including Josephine's father, once they had settled in England. The sons were all cabinet makers and they did well. The family moved out to Finchley when Josephine was a child.

Josephine's family did not want her to marry an impoverished artist and go backwards financially and socially, as they saw it. James' family thought he was marrying out of his class and objected out of inverse snobbery. James and Josephine were fed up with the arguing and in 1952 they married in Caxton Hall, London, and settled in Finchley.

Children soon followed, Louise in 1954 and Nicola in 1958. James and Josephine were determined to give their daughters the kind of family life they had not enjoyed themselves, and there was always a lot of lively discussion! Books and drawing materials, model kits and craft activities were encouraged. James was always very skilled in all kinds of manual work, and made many beautiful wooden toys for his daughters, such as a motor boat for Louise and a yacht for Nicola, which were sailed on the boating pond on Hampstead Heath.

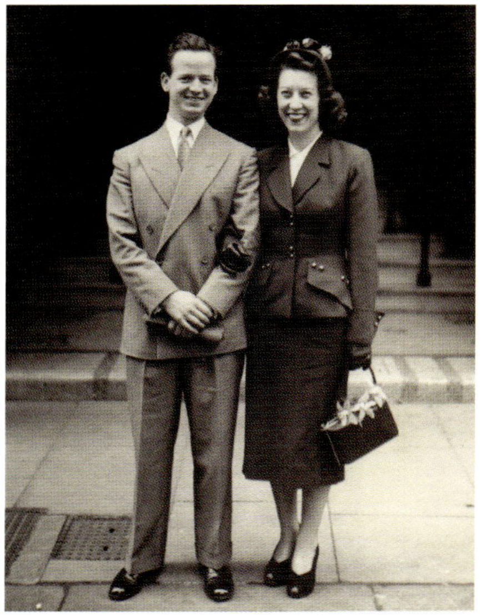

Wedding photo, 3 April 1952.

After he left *The People* James worked in commercial art studios and as a freelance designer, producing drawings and lettering for adverts and information leaflets. In those days most lettering had to be hand drawn, and James was highly skilled in producing fine lettering. His superb draughtsmanship was to prove a good training for his later career as an artist.

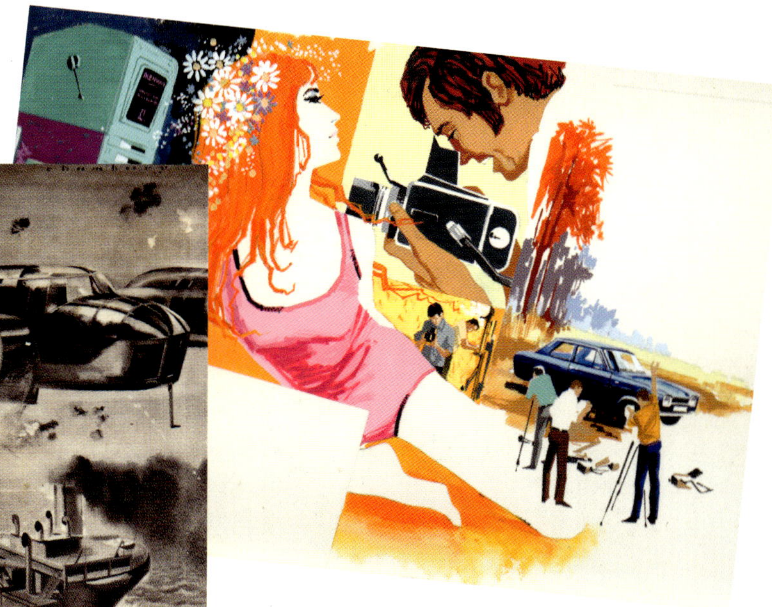

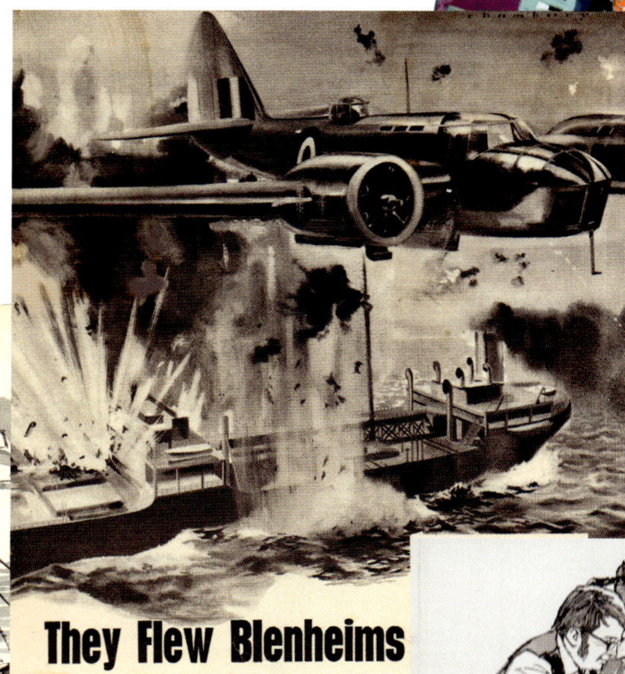

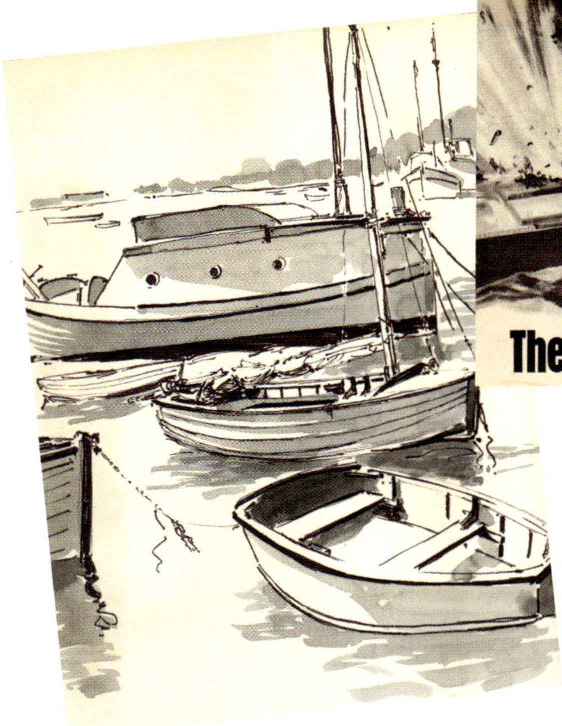

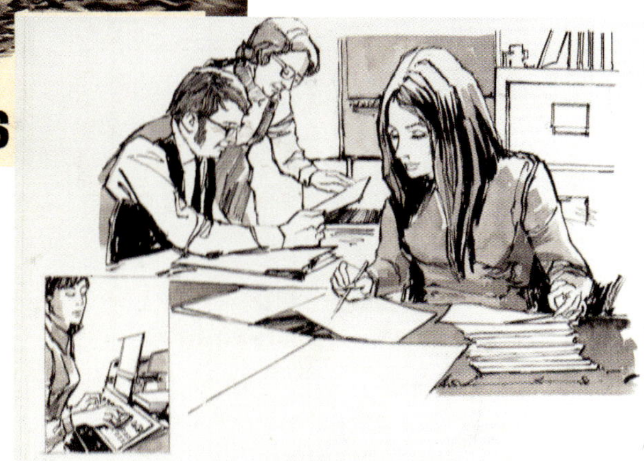

Commercial artwork from the 1950s and 60s.

ESCAPE TO THE COUNTRY

Being a professional artist is what James had been dreaming about. His love of painting was always at the forefront. After a period of depression and emotional turmoil his doctor advised him that he could not help him until he changed his way of life. So in 1967 James took the momentous decision to move out of London to Billericay in Essex, where Josephine had family connections. He was now able to concentrate on land, sea and skyscapes.

The early years were a struggle, as he had to find his voice as an artist as well as struggle with financial hardship and chronic pain from an old back injury. After years of excruciating pain, including two years spent mostly in bed, he had an operation on his spine. This reduced his suffering significantly, but for the rest of his life he had difficulty walking, bending and stretching and lived with discomfort and pain.

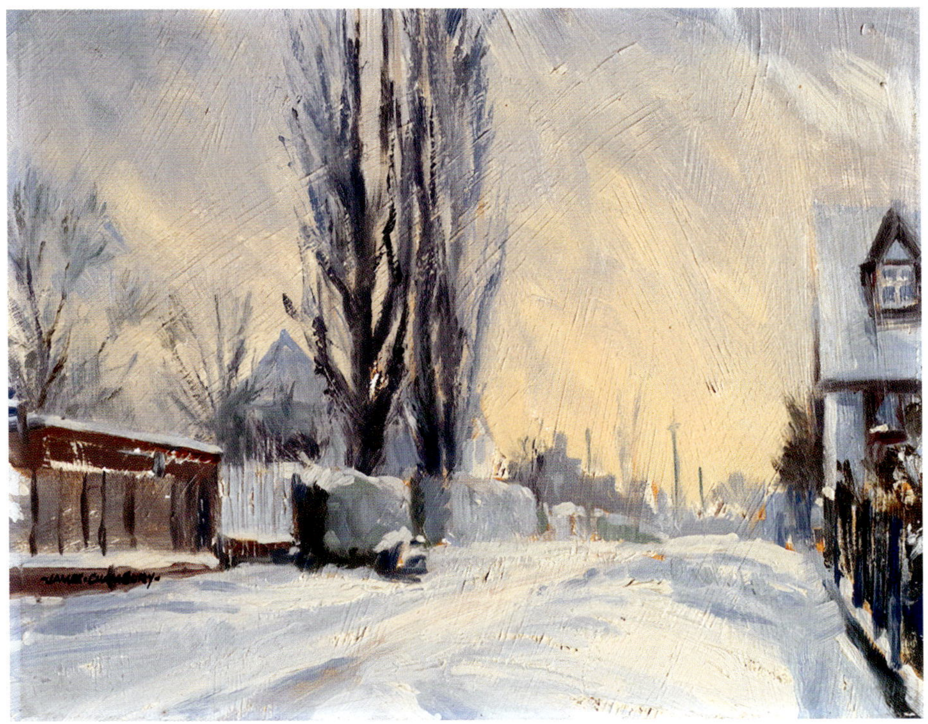

The road running up the side of the garden of the house James lived in at Shanklin Avenue, Billericay. Oil 28x21cm

In spite of this, he worked as hard as he could, outside in all weathers throughout the year sketching, always overdoing it and suffering later. Gradually he found his voice and his audience, drawing and painting all aspects of the Essex and later the Suffolk coastline as well as the inland scenery. All of his pictures show his concern with the effects of light on the landscape.

From the start of his career as an artist James liked to have a major exhibition every year or two. This was the spur to creating new work. He once said "Every exhibition is a fresh challenge and I feel nervous on the opening day. But I like living on the edge!" His first one man show was at Galleria in Maldon, Essex in 1971. This exhibition received good newspaper reviews, and Mr Hinderer started to collect James' work and he continued to buy paintings on a regular basis until James' death in 1994.

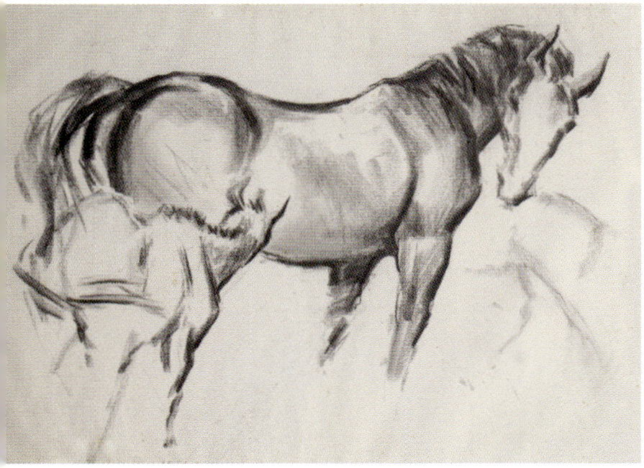

A horse and foal drawing that appeared in James' 1971 exhibition.

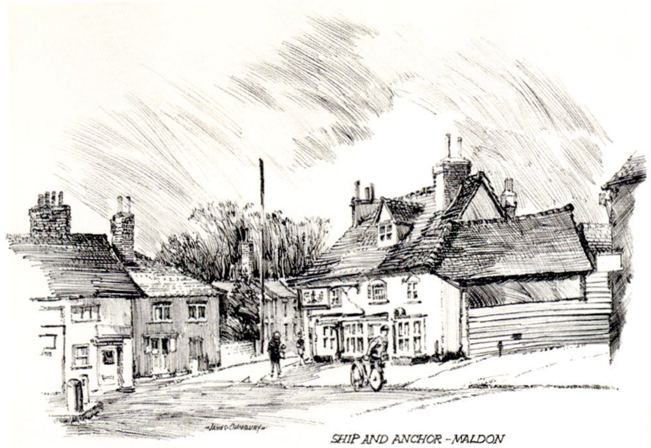

The Ship and Anchor Inn, Maldon.
Pen and ink sketch 19x15cm

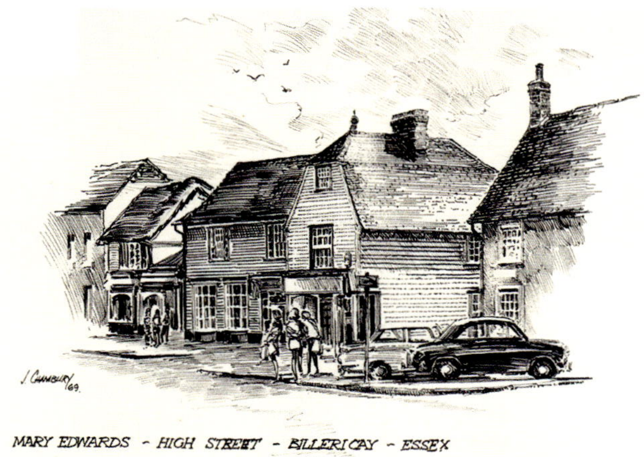

High Street, Billericay.
Pen and ink sketch 19x15cm

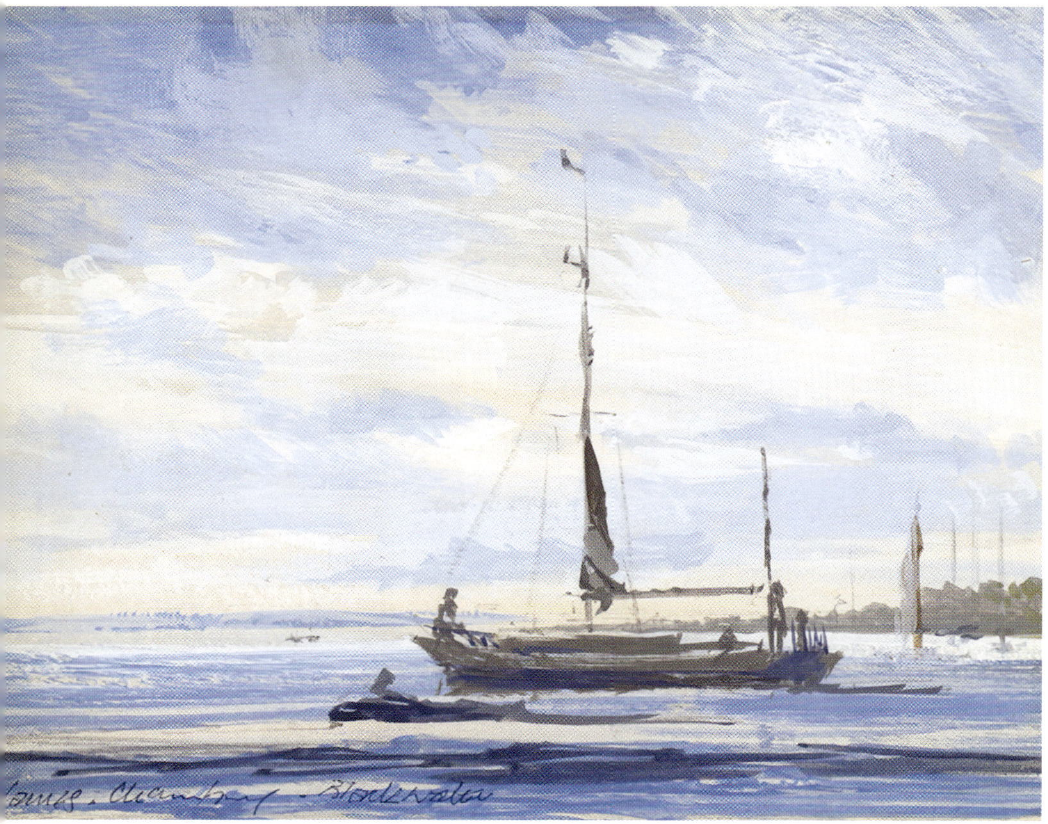

Blackwater, Essex
Watercolour 16x13cm

James always drew from nature, and when the light was right would not miss the opportunity to go out sketching, whatever the time of day. He would sketch in the unmade road outside the house or go to his nearest sketching ground at Buttsbury and Mountnessing, just outside Billericay. It became a family joke that if he was not to be found in the studio, or on hand to help with the washing up, then he must be 'down the Mountnessing Road'. This was the period of Dutch Elm Disease, and he was able to capture how the landscape looked before it was changed dramatically by the loss of these spectacular trees (see over). He had another successful exhibition two years later, in 1973, at the Templeman Galleries in Brentwood, Essex.

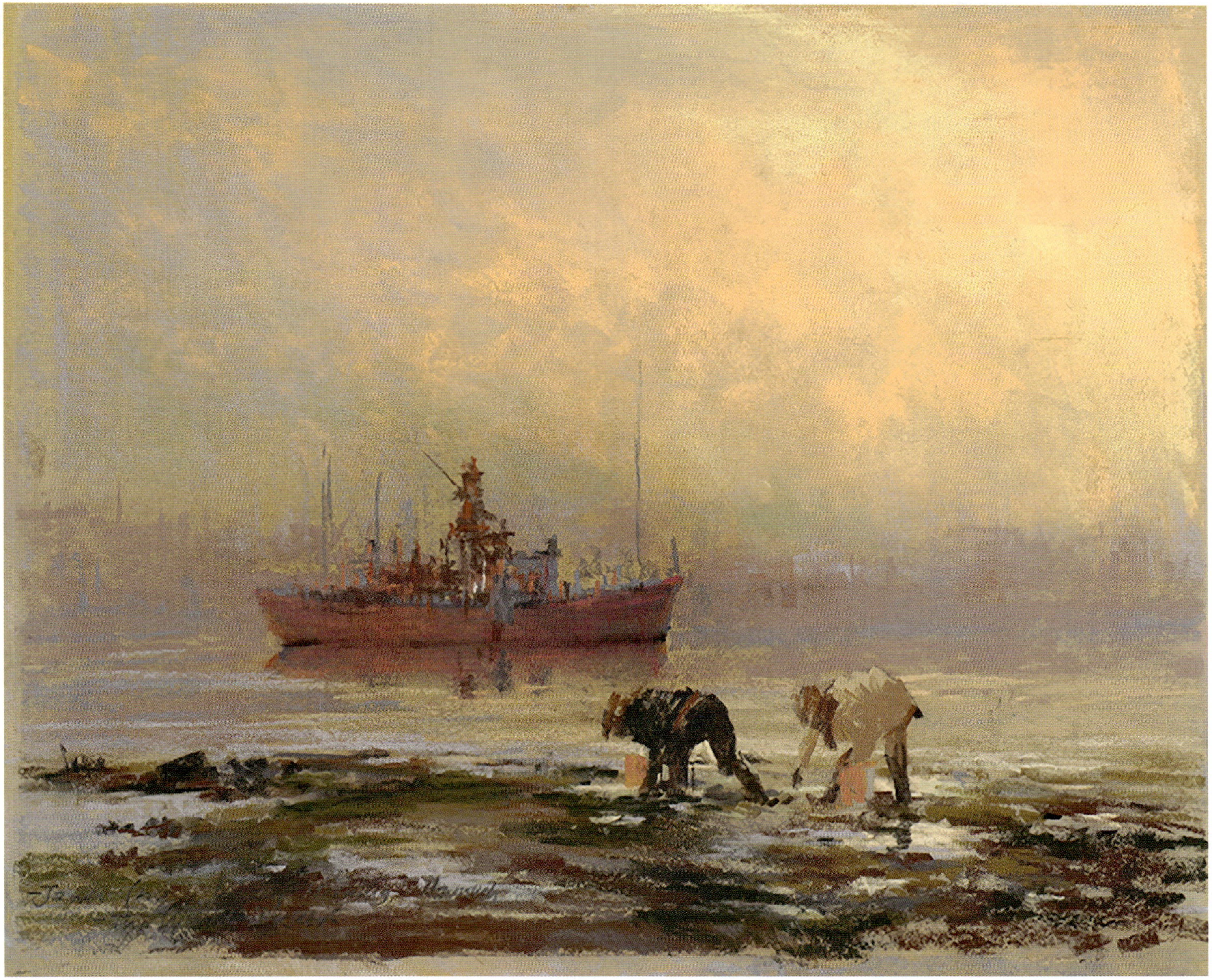

Cockle Pickers - Harwich.
Pastel

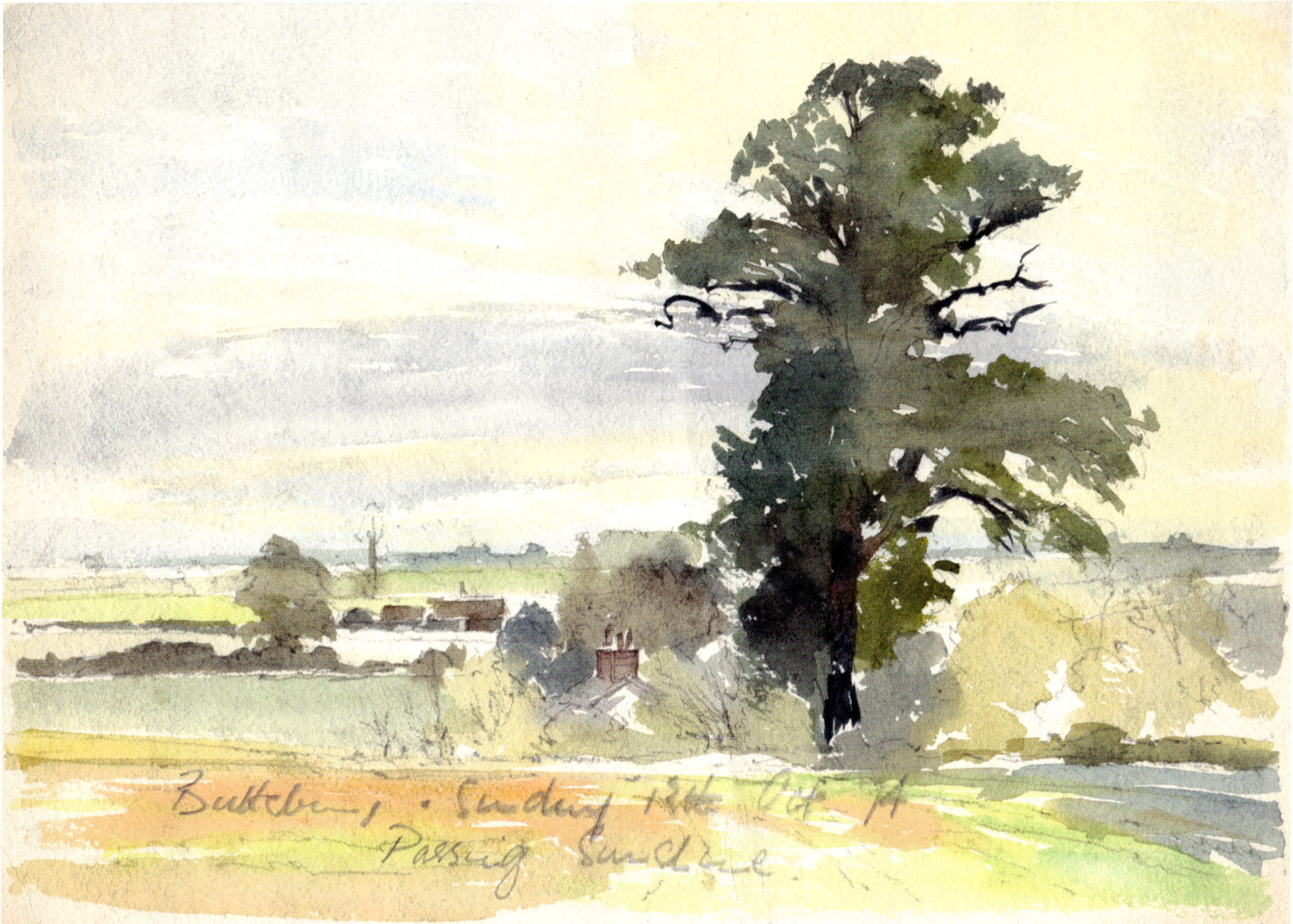

Buttsbury Ford and Big Elm, preliminary sketch.
Watercolour

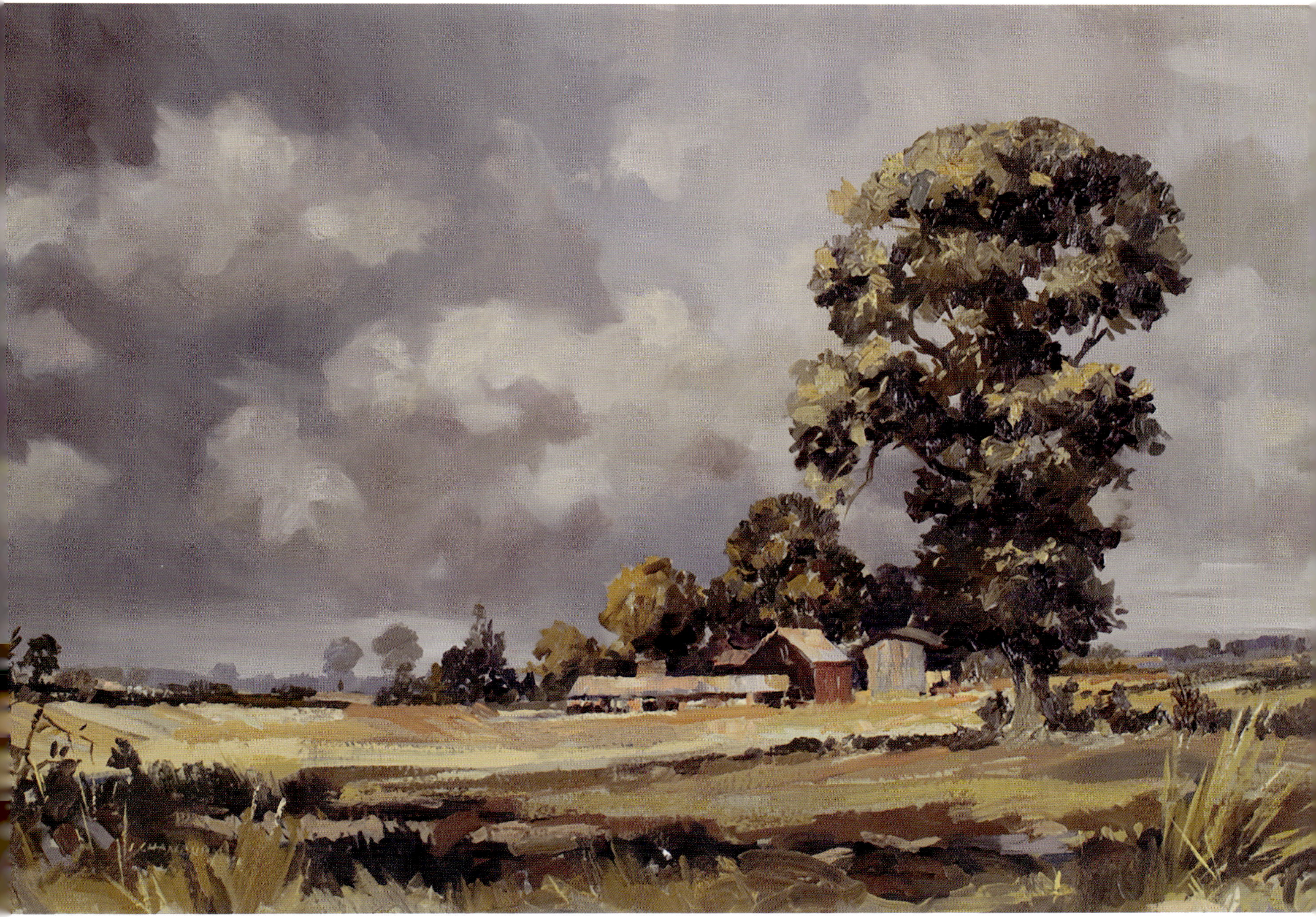

Buttsbury Ford and Big Elm.
Oil 74x50cm

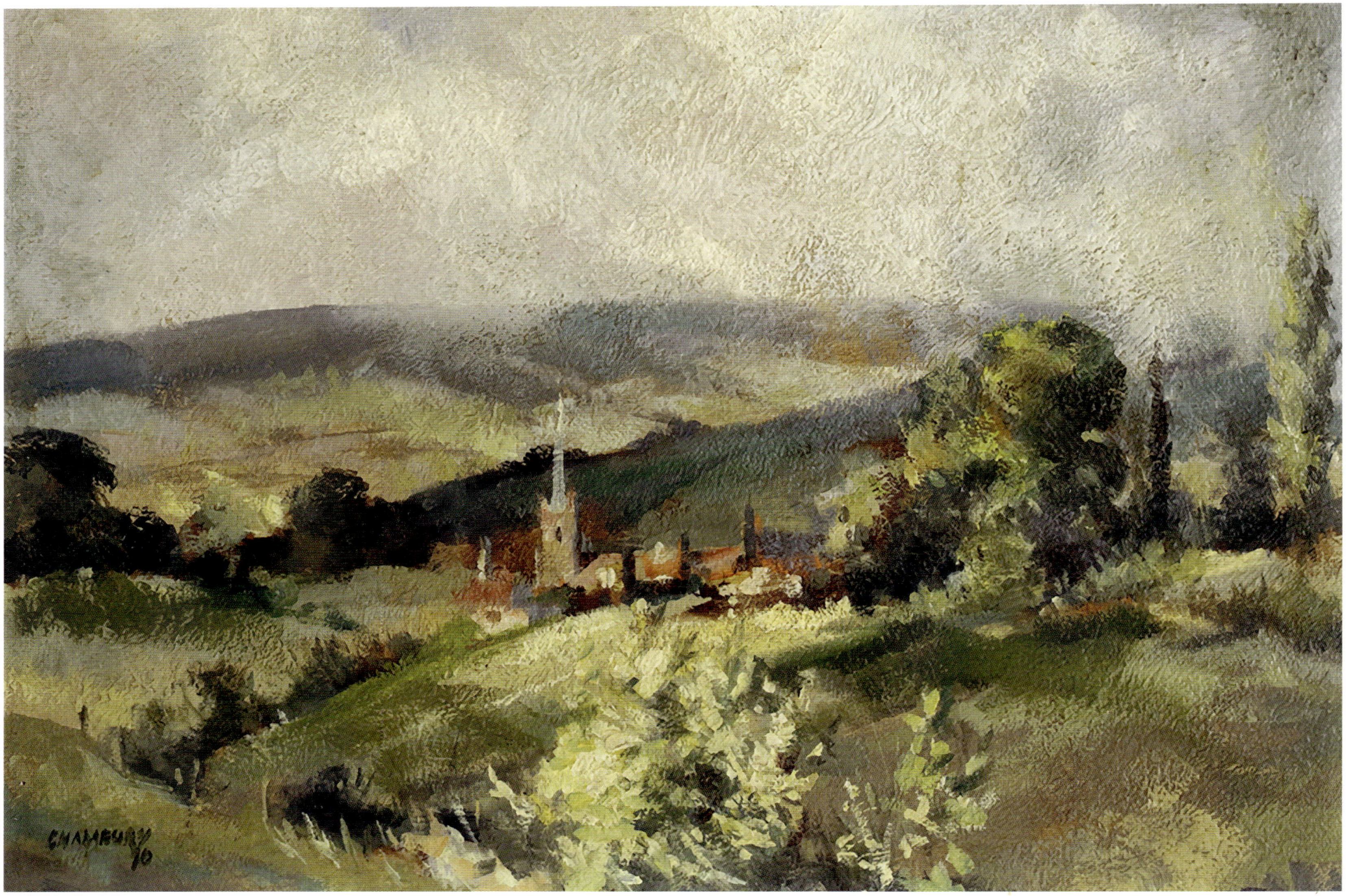

Cotswold Scene.
Oil 40x26cm

James made a few trips to the West Country, either on painting holidays or visiting relatives, and made one visit to Scotland in 1974, removing the passenger seat of the family Austin A40 and installing a camp bed. He spent two weeks travelling through the Lake District and up the West Coast of Scotland, returning through the Highlands. This was quite a trip, with roads in Scotland in particular much more difficult to travel on than today. He did some sketching and painted a few oils and watercolours back in his studio, but found the landscape, colours and light very different from Suffolk and would have liked to have spent much longer in Scotland.

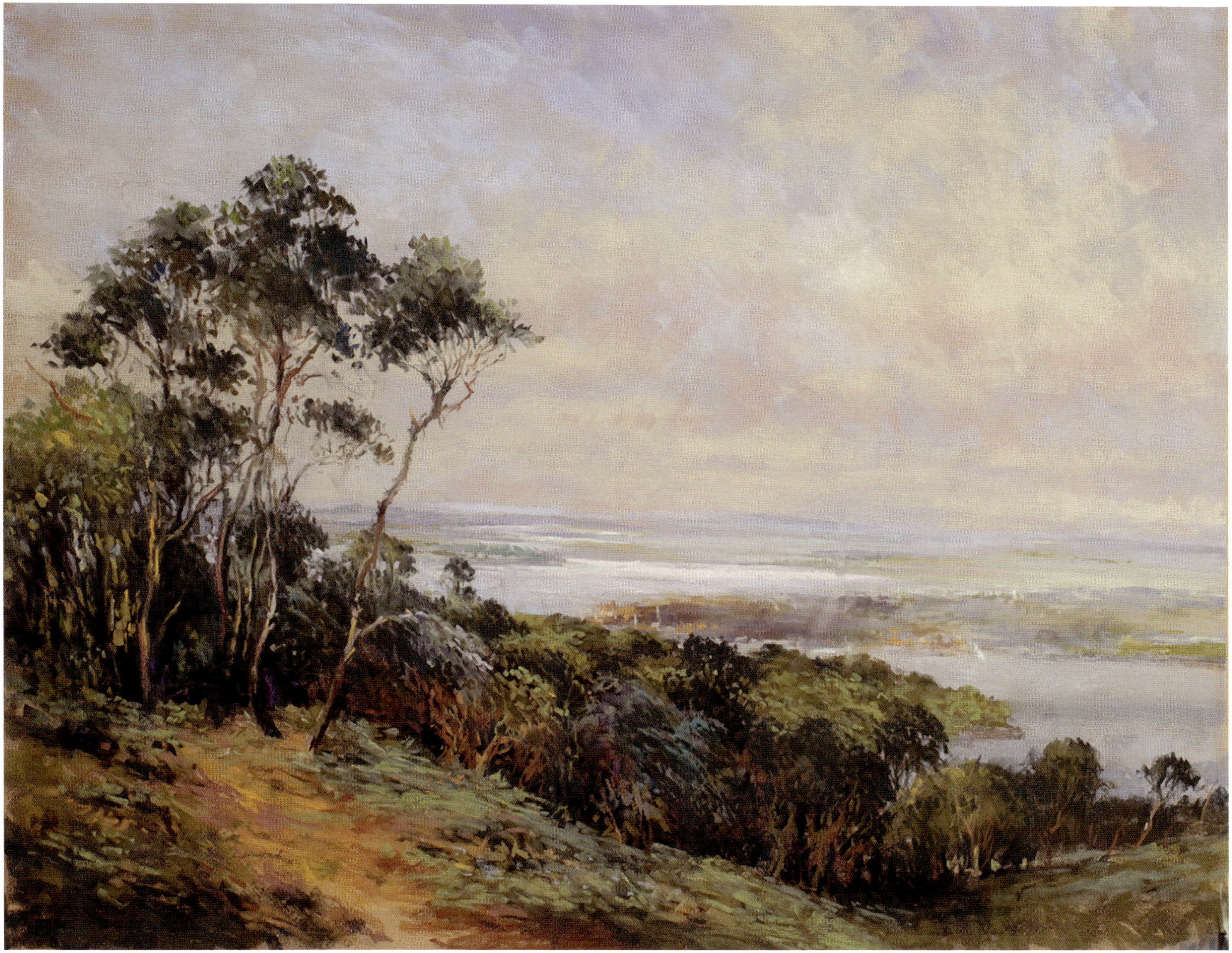

Mount Edgcumbe overlooking Plymouth, Devon.
Pastel 61x4cm

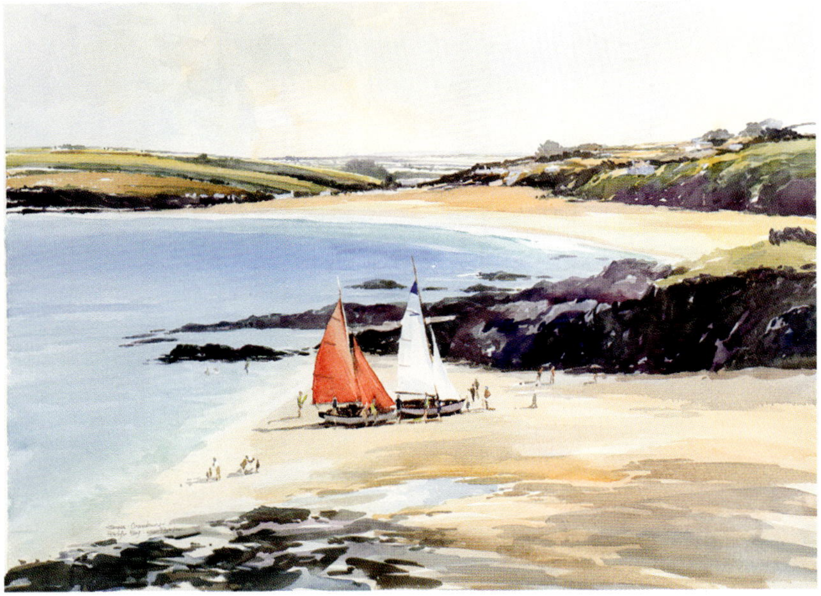

Harlyn Bay, Cornwall.
Watercolour

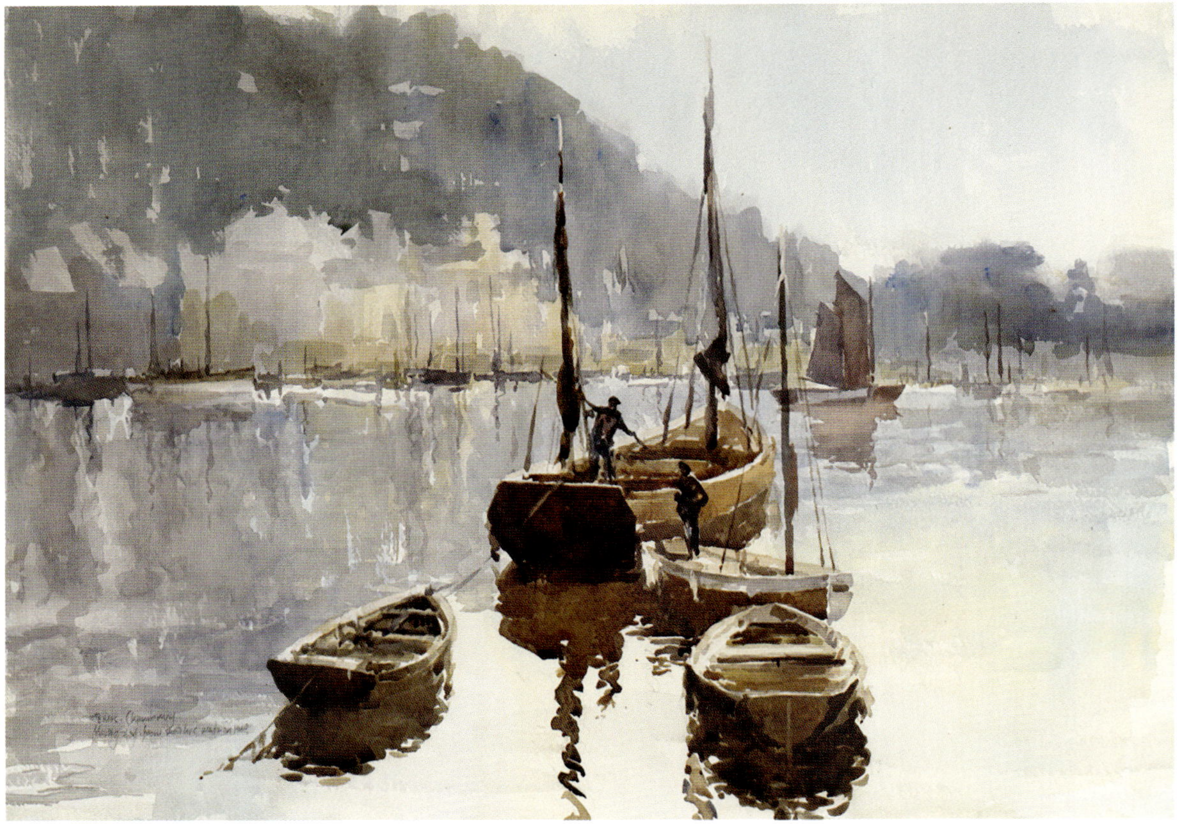

Mevagissey, Cornwall (from sketches made in 1948).
Watercolour 52x38cm

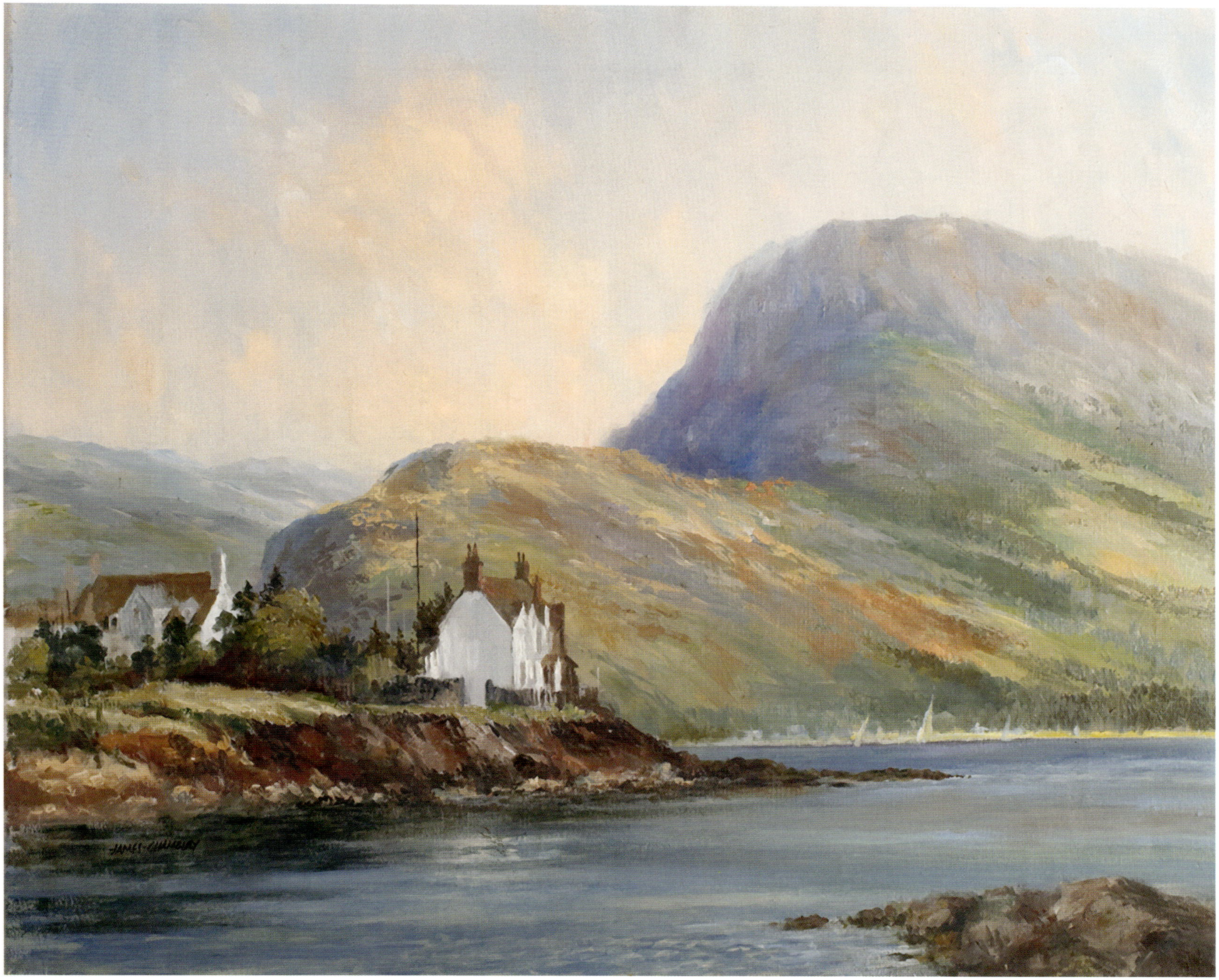

Gairloch, Scotland.
Oil 74x60cm

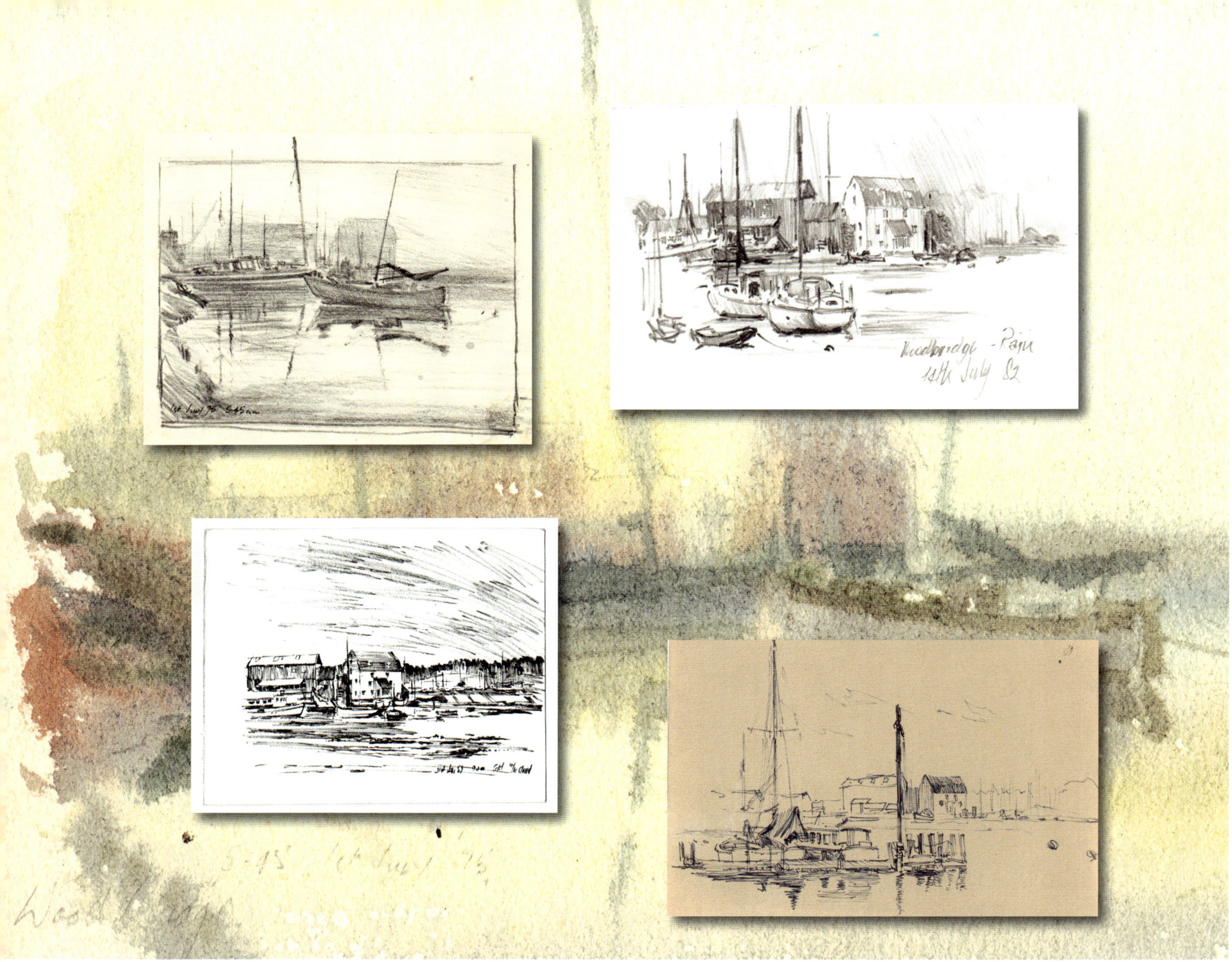

Various sketches of the same place (Woodbridge, Suffolk) made at different times.

For an artist like James, whose work springs from a strong sense of place, it is difficult to create meaningful work on casual acquaintance with somewhere new. James used to say "an artist cannot just sketch for the heck of it but should feel a certain bond with his subject which should border towards the spiritual. Only then will the feelings flow on to the paper."

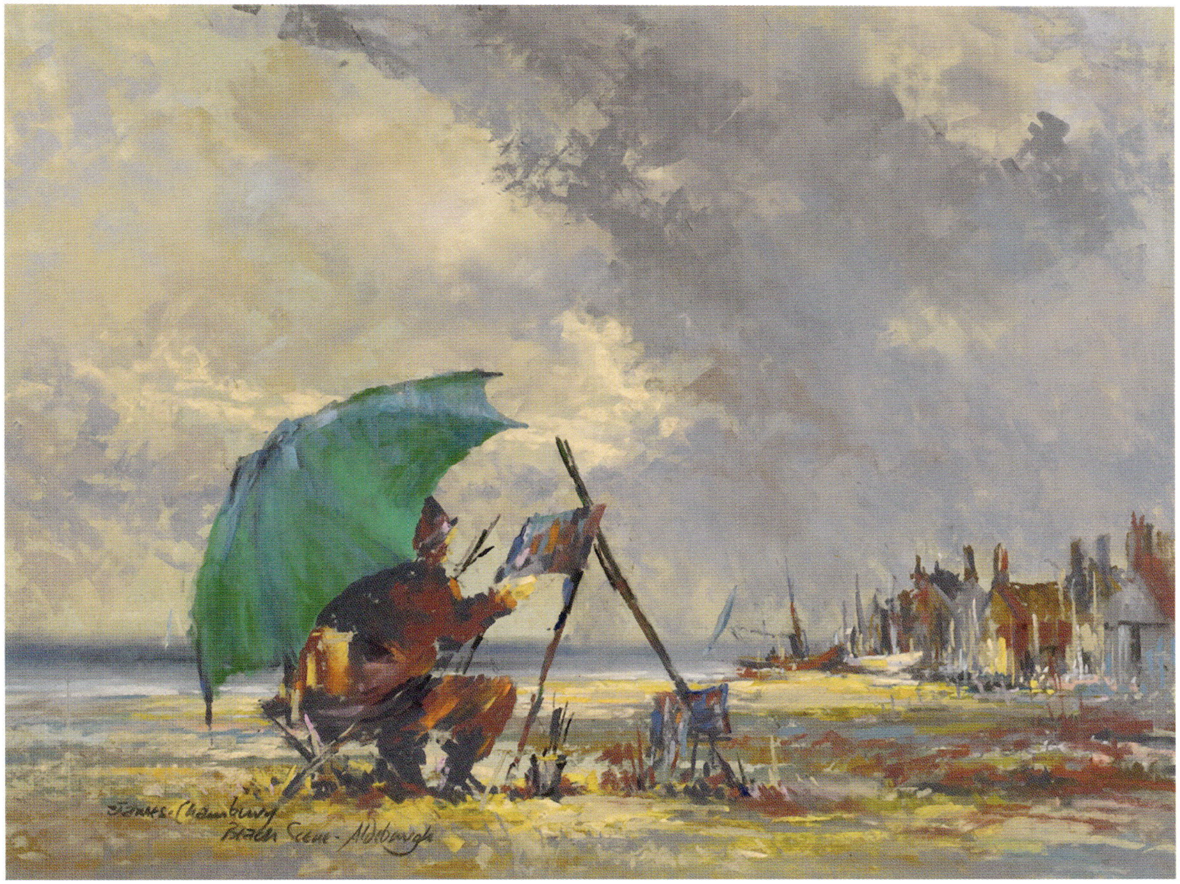

'The Man Who Has Everything', Aldeburgh, Suffolk.
Pastel 30x23cm

At this period James was sketching in pencil and pen for line and tone, and in watercolour for colour studies. His studio work was mainly in watercolour and oils. He was always a skilled woodworker and DIY-er and made his own sketching boxes. As he became increasingly unwell, these became ever lighter and smaller. He devised his own boxes partly for them to be able to contain whatever he felt necessary for a sketching trip and partly because he was left handed and commercially available boxes were often inconvenient. He went out sketching with the minimum of equipment, and was very amused once to see a fellow artist sketching on Aldeburgh beach. He called this painting 'The Man Who Has Everything"

He also enjoyed pottery very much, especially making clay models. He would have liked to pursue this path as well, but did not want to become jack-of-all-trades and master of none, so concentrated on painting and drawing. He liked drawing animals and made use of sculpture while doing so to help him feel the form of the subject and give him a three dimensional view.

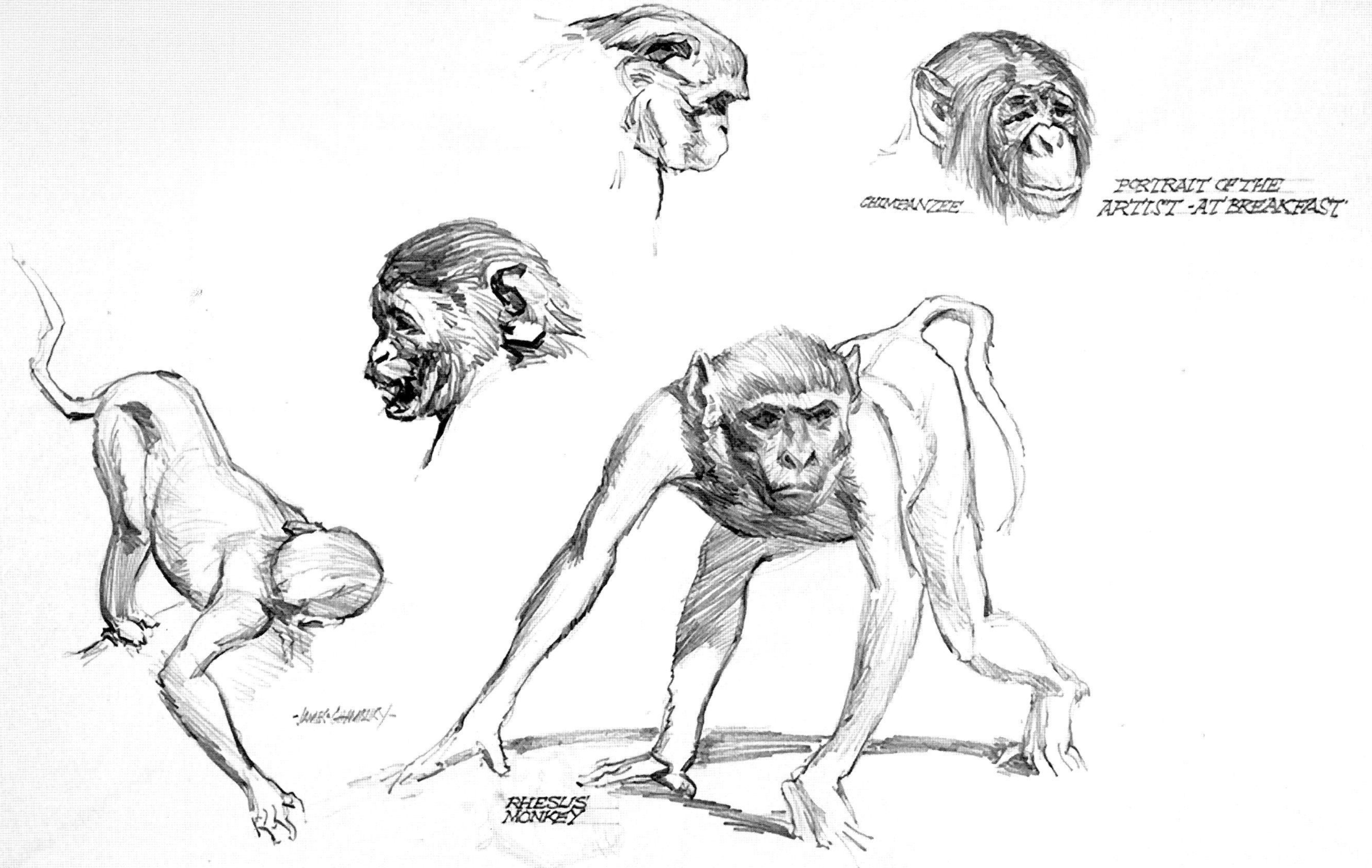

James' skill as a draftsman, and his sense of humor, is clear from these fine pencil drawings.

When he was well enough, his time was spent sketching and painting, and during this period he exhibited regularly in London at the Britain in Watercolour exhibition, the Medici Gallery, St Paul's Gallery, and with the Royal Society of Marine Artists at the Boat Show.

In 1975 he converted the air raid shelter in the garden into a studio and exhibition space. This was no Anderson shelter, but a very substantial masonry structure, with concrete walls a couple of feet thick. During the Blitz it would have offered some protection, but in the case of a direct hit things might have been worse than being in the house! A bay window had been put in after the war, and James spent a few months making the building into a studio and gallery space. The studio gallery was opened in 1975, but James only had the use of it for three years before he moved to Suffolk.

SUFFOLK, NORFOLK & BEYOND

James' great love for the Suffolk and Norfolk coast and landscape, and for the vast East Anglian skies, prompted his move to Hadleigh, Suffolk in 1978. He lived and worked here for the rest of his life, although his deteriorating health as he developed emphysema and asthma frustrated his desire to walk and explore the countryside as he wished.

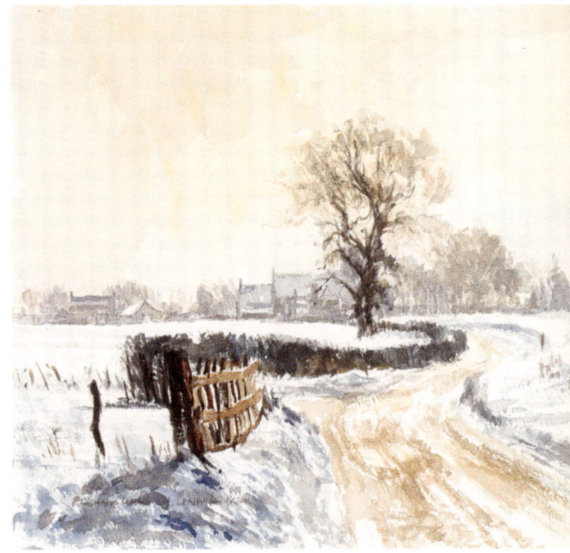

Snowy scene at Layham, a small village near Hadleigh in Suffolk.

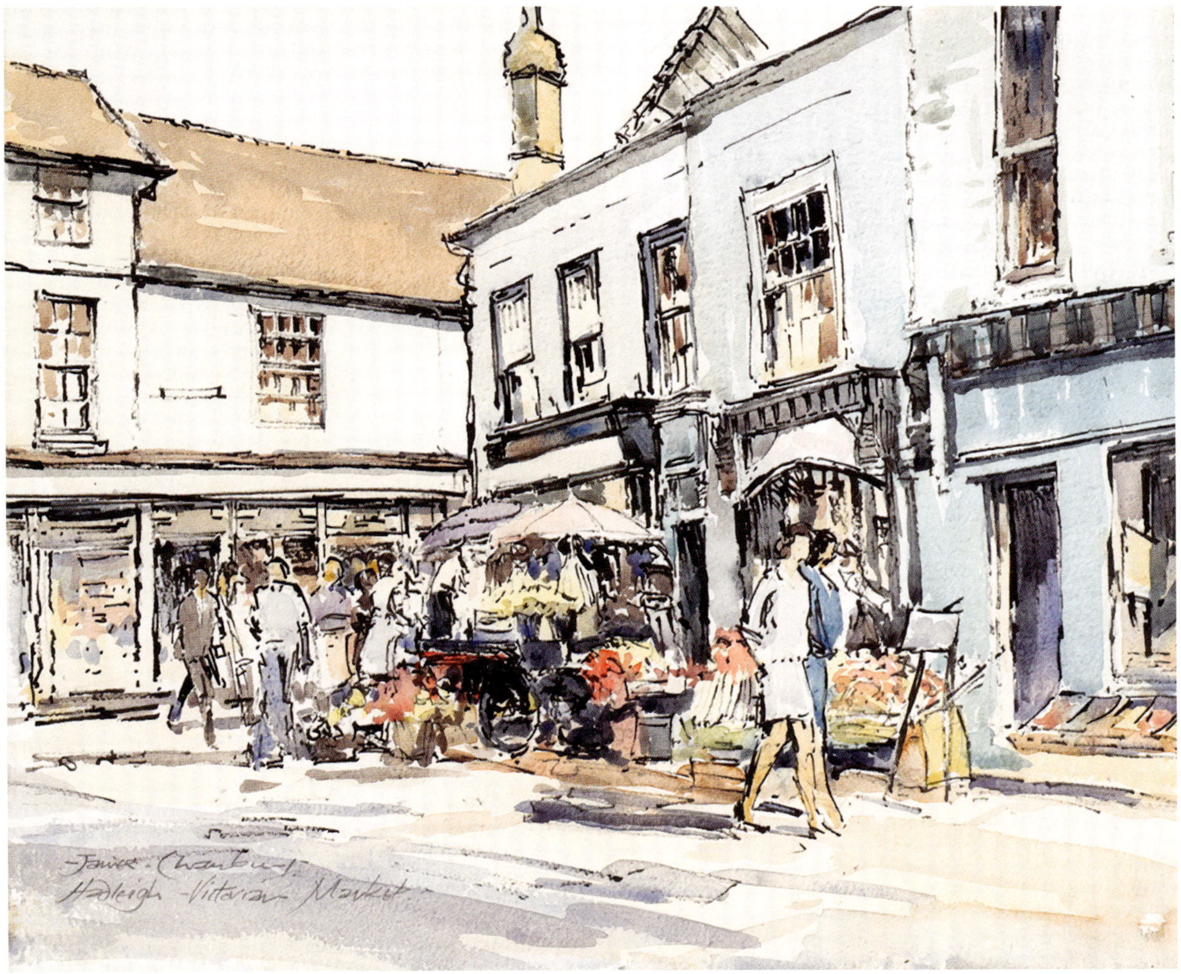

Hadleigh, Victorian Market, Suffolk. Line and wash 34x27cm

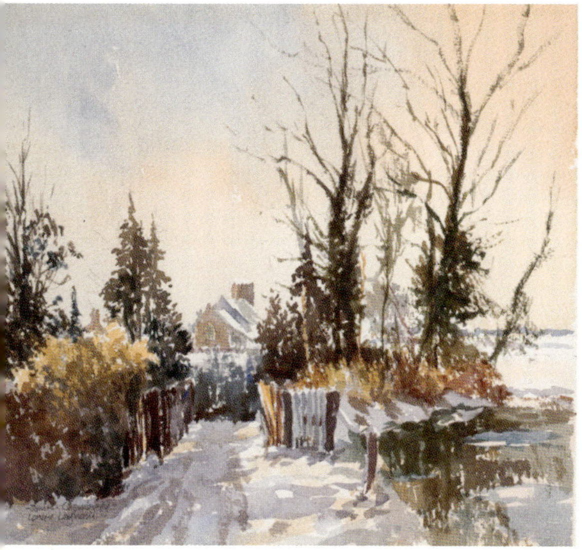

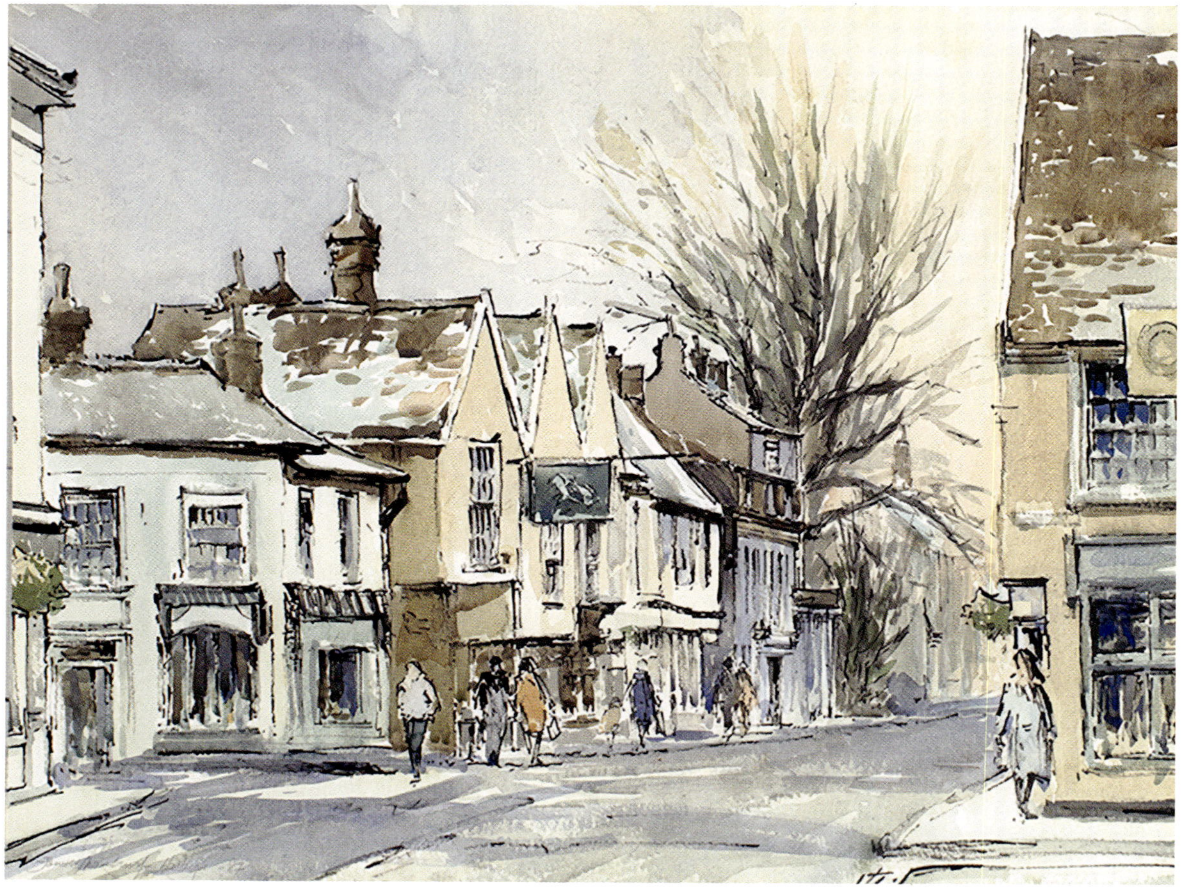

Above: Layham church, Suffolk.

Right: Hadleigh High Street, Suffolk Watercolour 47x38cm.

Below: James sketching at Hadleigh.

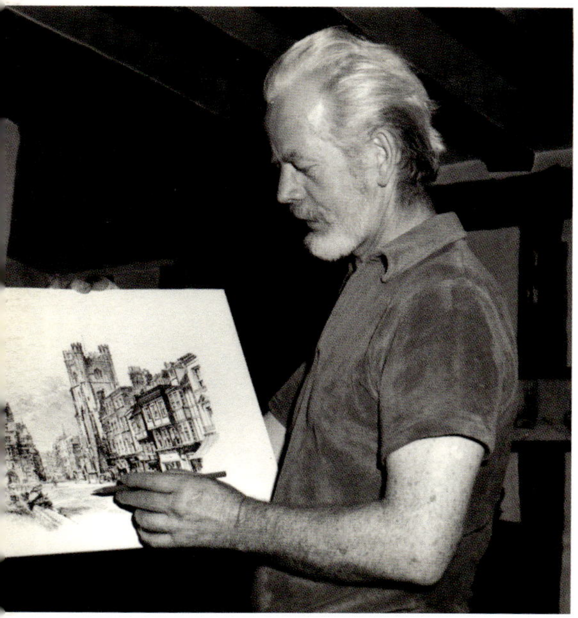

He was fortunate in living in Hadleigh which is an attractive medieval market town with beautiful villages and countryside close by. It was chance that brought James here. On a very rainy April day househunting in north Essex and south Suffolk, the last house to go and view was in Hadleigh. Tired and fed up with getting lost looking for houses, James was ready to go home but was persuaded to just go and see this last house on the way. As he stopped outside, the sun came out, and once through the front door, the family fell in love with the house at first sight.

James loved to walk down to the River Brett in the early morning, until it got too much for him, and often sketched by the mill pond and the medieval Toppesfield Bridge. The disadvantage with preferring the early morning is that it is usually cold, and James often had to wrap up in many layers of fleece and jumper to keep warm, and even so would return home frozen in most months of the year. But on misty or frosty mornings, there he was drawing, dedicated to his art.

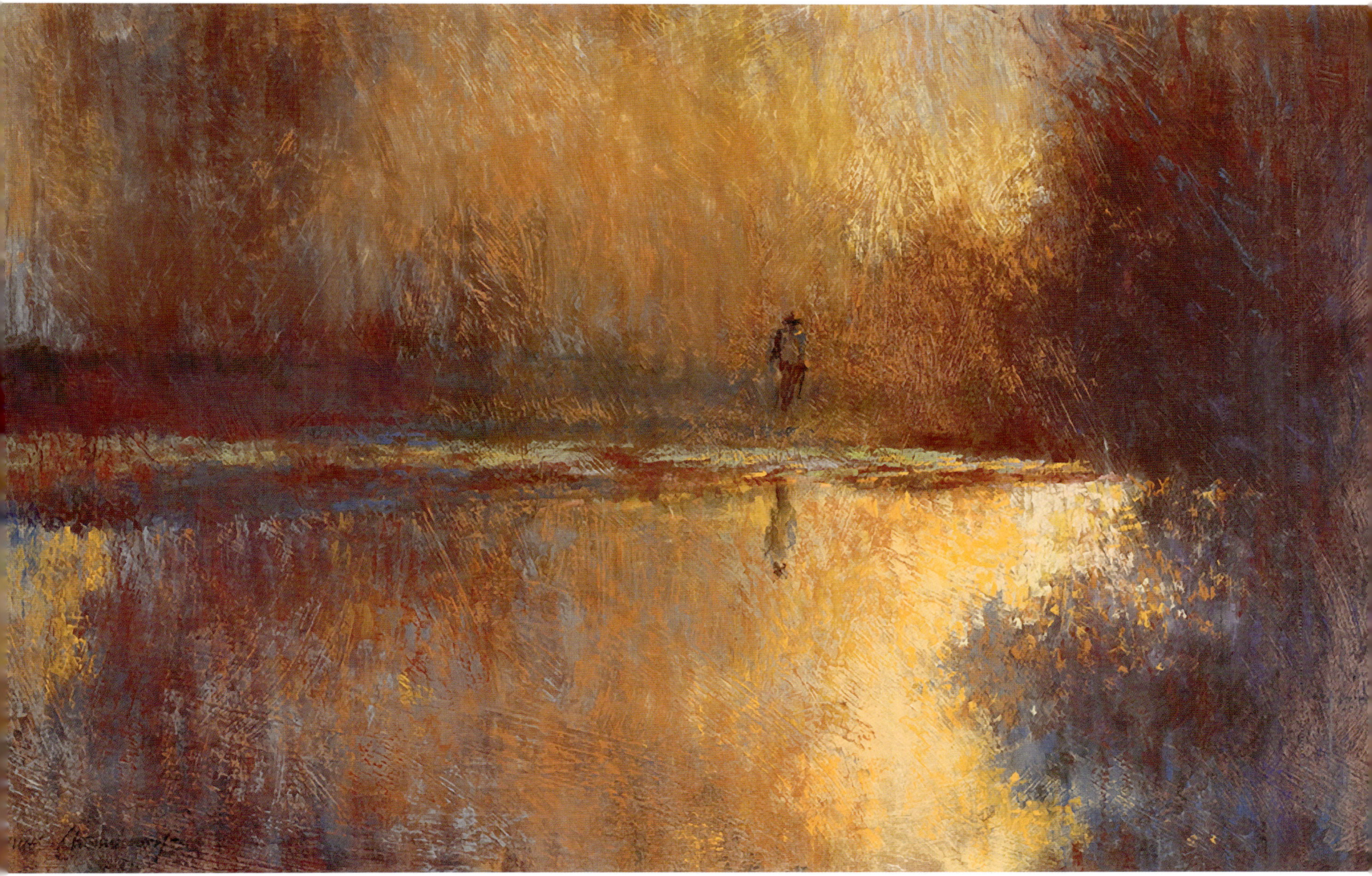

Autumn on the River Brett, Hadleigh, Suffolk.
Pastel 60x36cm

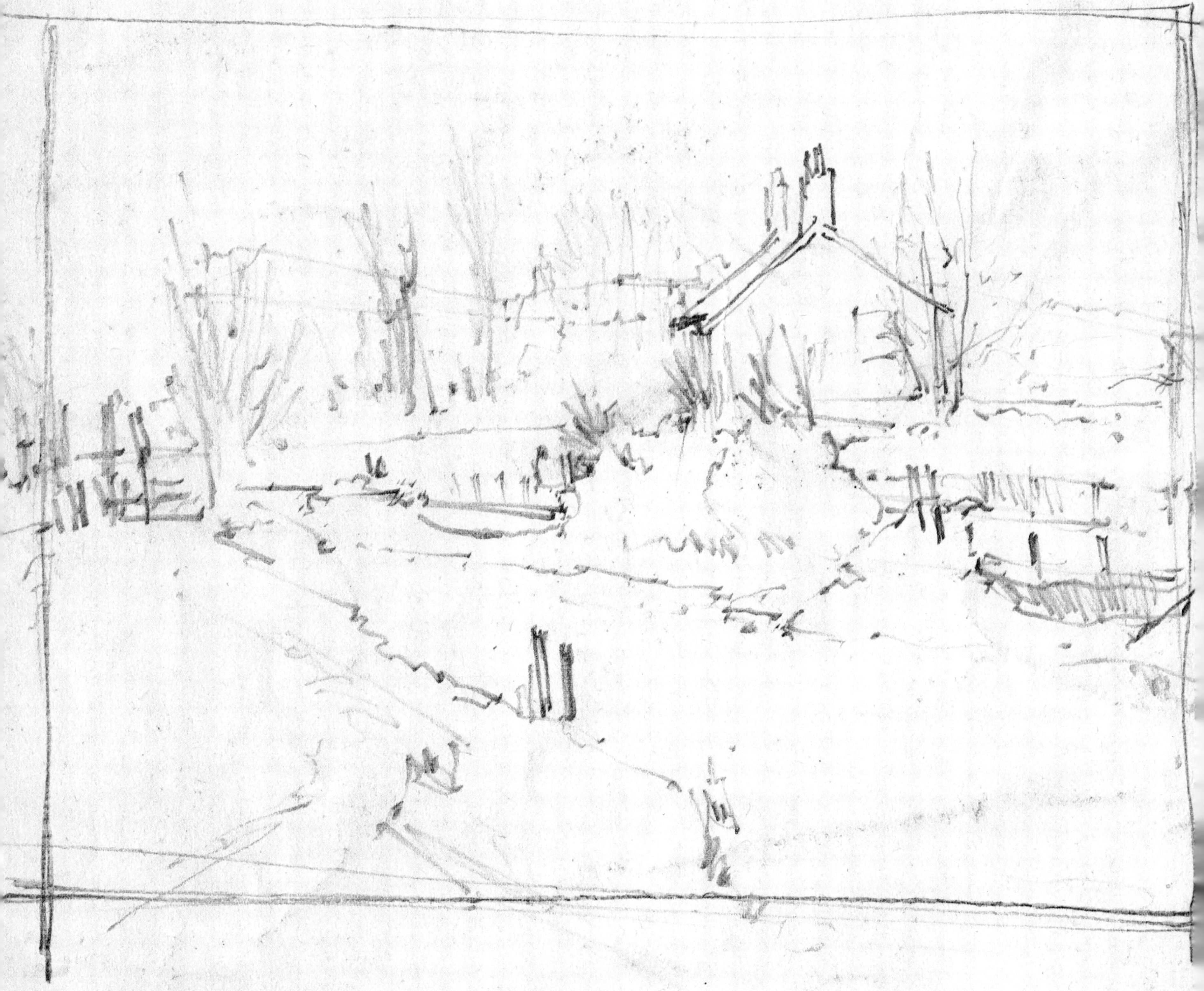

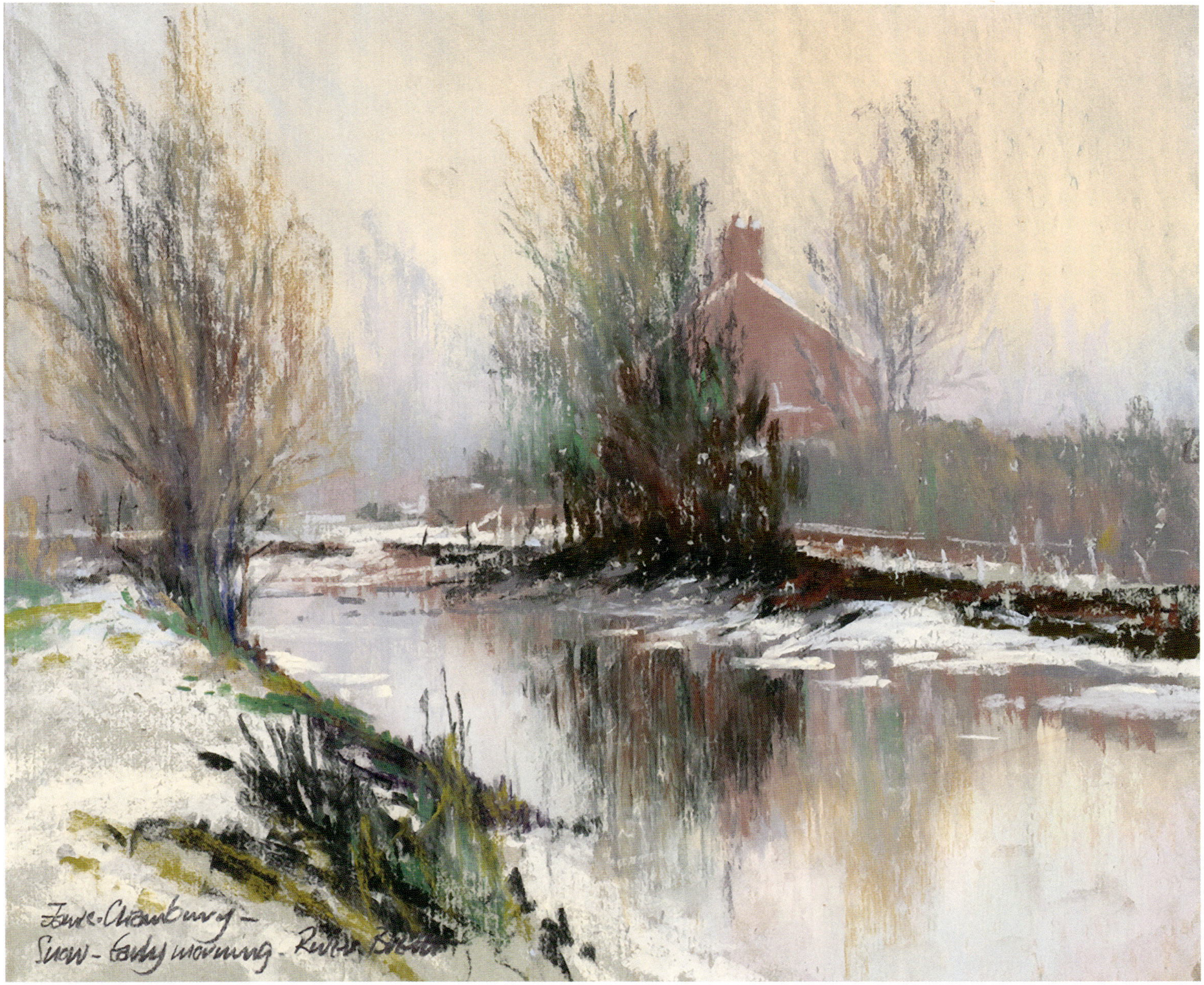

Opposite: preliminary sketch for Early Morning Snow.

Early Morning Snow, River Brett, Hadleigh, Suffolk.
Pastel 28x23cm

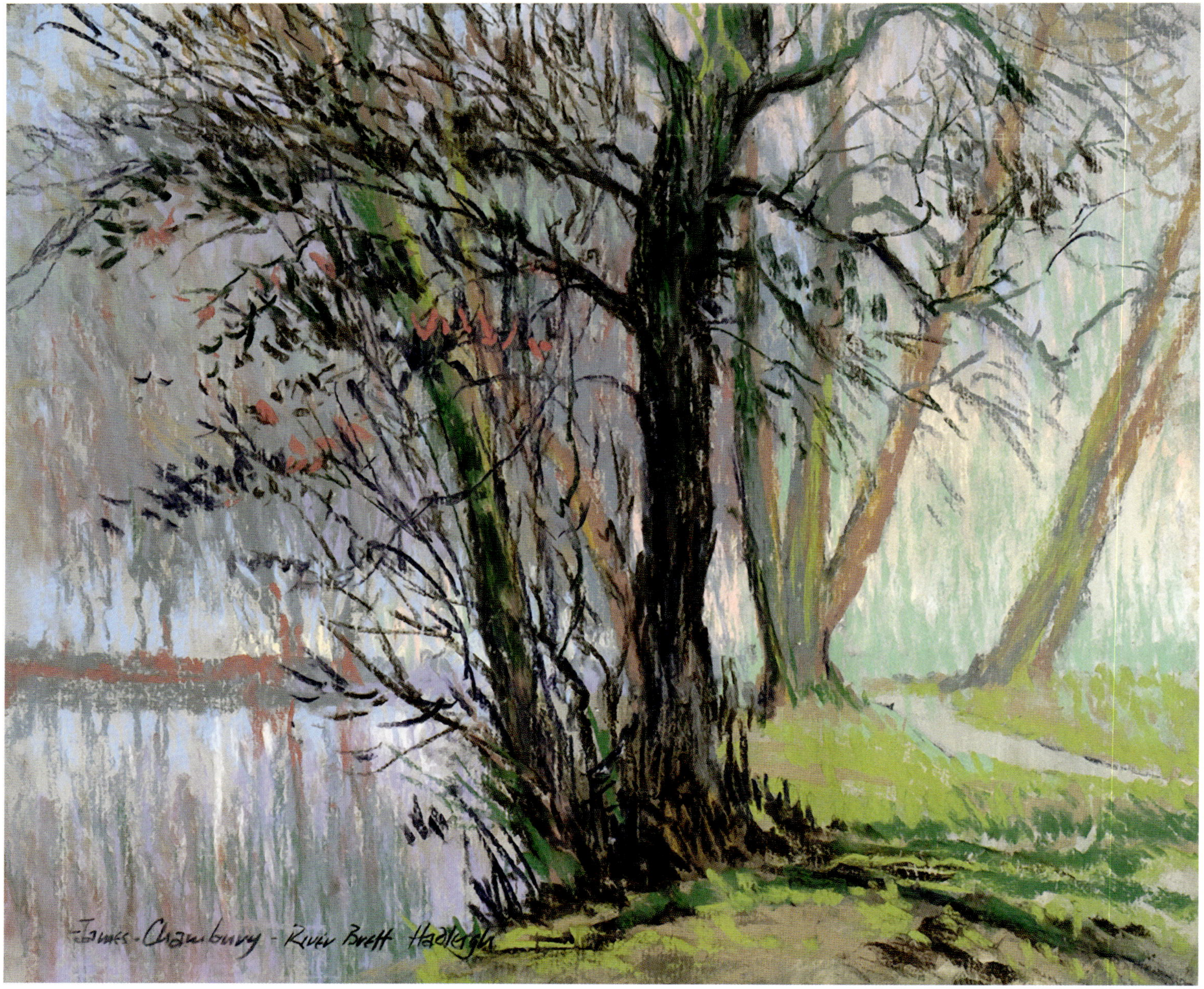

River Brett, Hadleigh, Suffolk.
Pastel 25x20cm

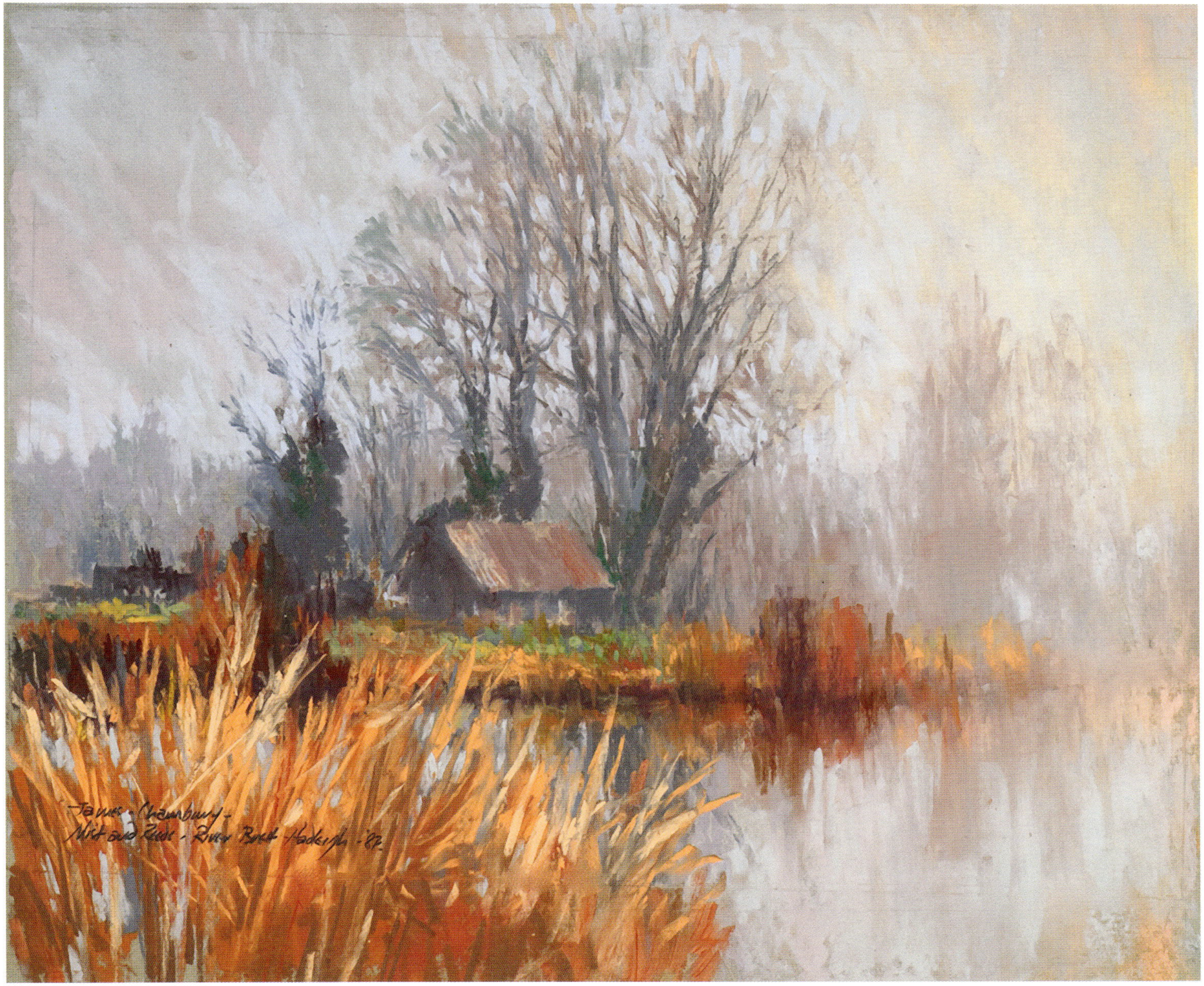

Mist and Reeds, River Brett, Hadleigh, Suffolk.
Pastel 33x23cm

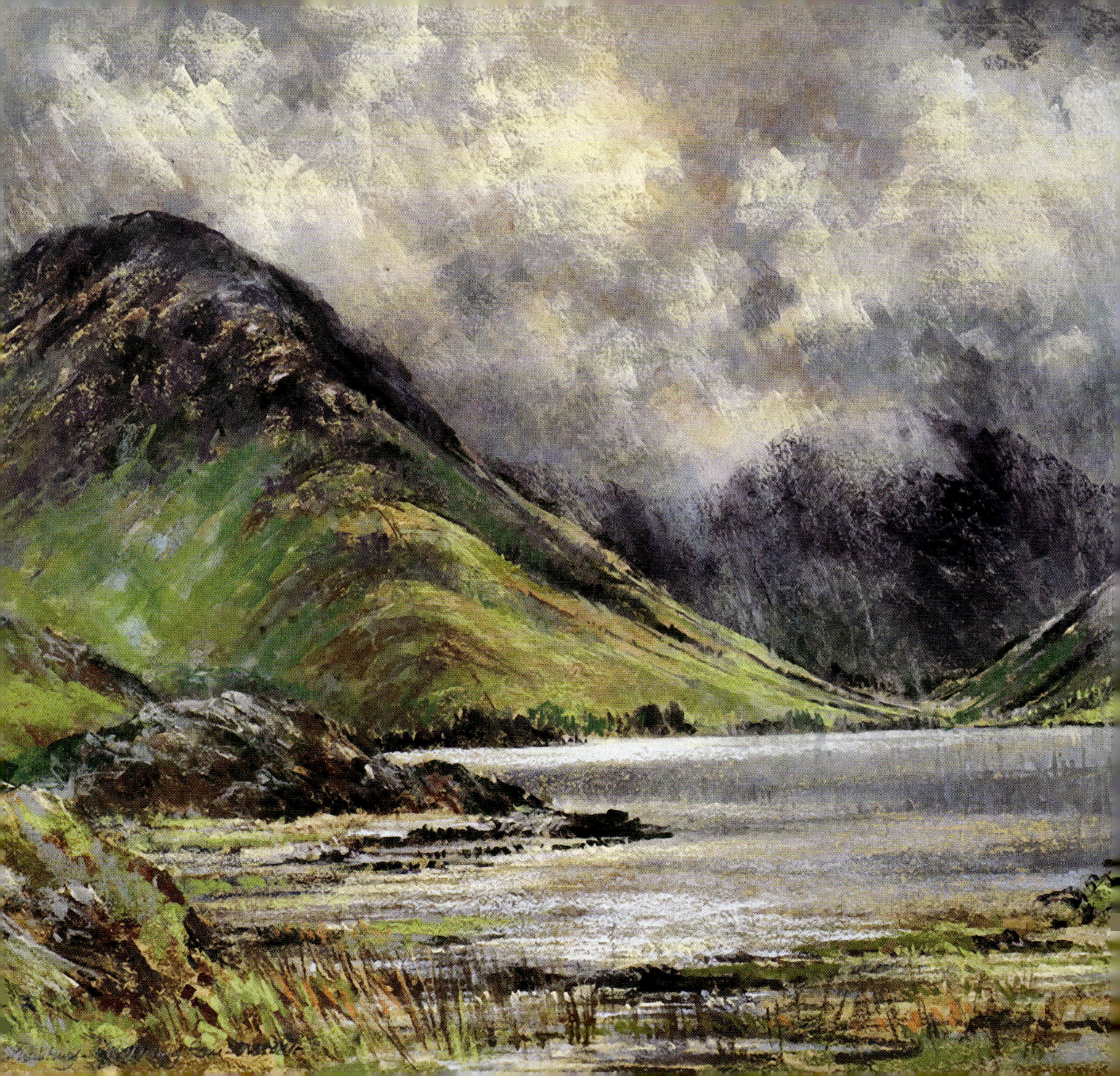

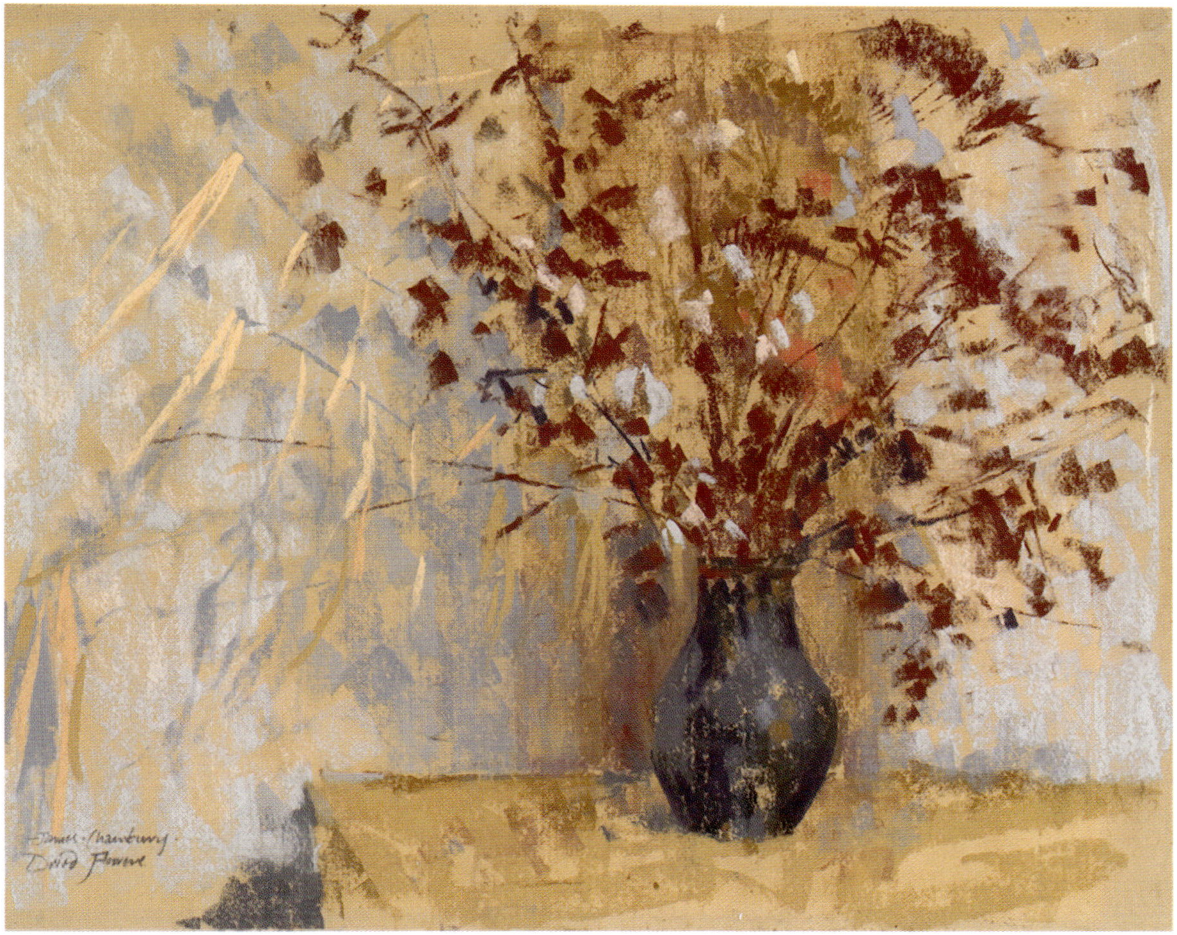

Dried Flowers.
Pastel36x29cm

In the 1980s James also sketched farther afield, enjoying several painting holidays in the Lake District, staying in Elterwater. The landscape is so different in topography, texture, colour and light from East Anglia but he found it inspiring also. Spending time in one place allowed him to get to know the area. To work well he always needed to do this.

He was an avid reader of the Wainwright guide books and would have loved to have gone hill-walking but his back and, later, breathing problems made this impossible. Nevertheless, he shows a great feeling for the landscape in the pictures he made there.

He also loved flowers, and often made impromptu watercolour or pastel paintings of blooms picked from the garden.

Opposite: Advancing Rain, Wasdale, Lake District.
Pastel 58x43cm

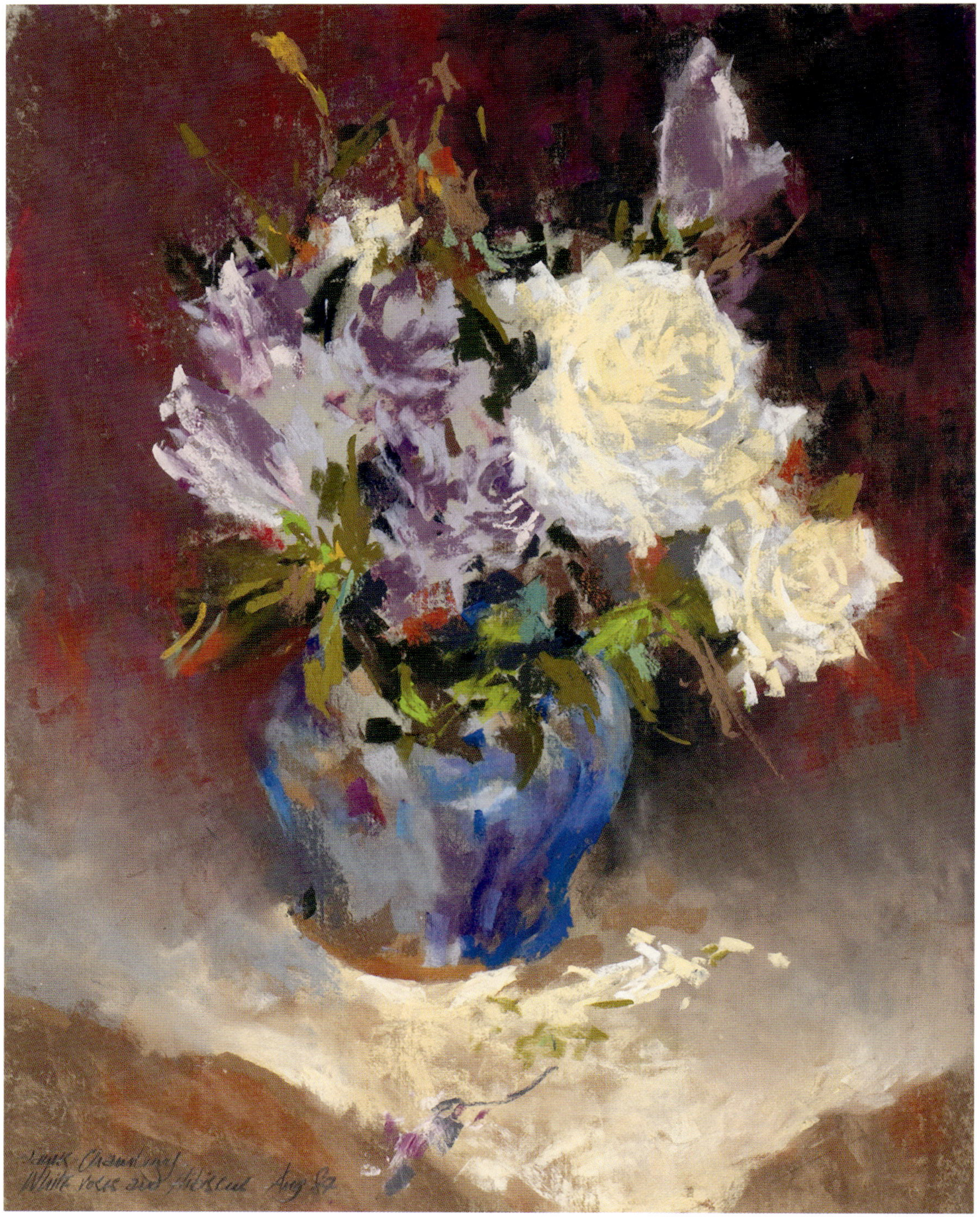

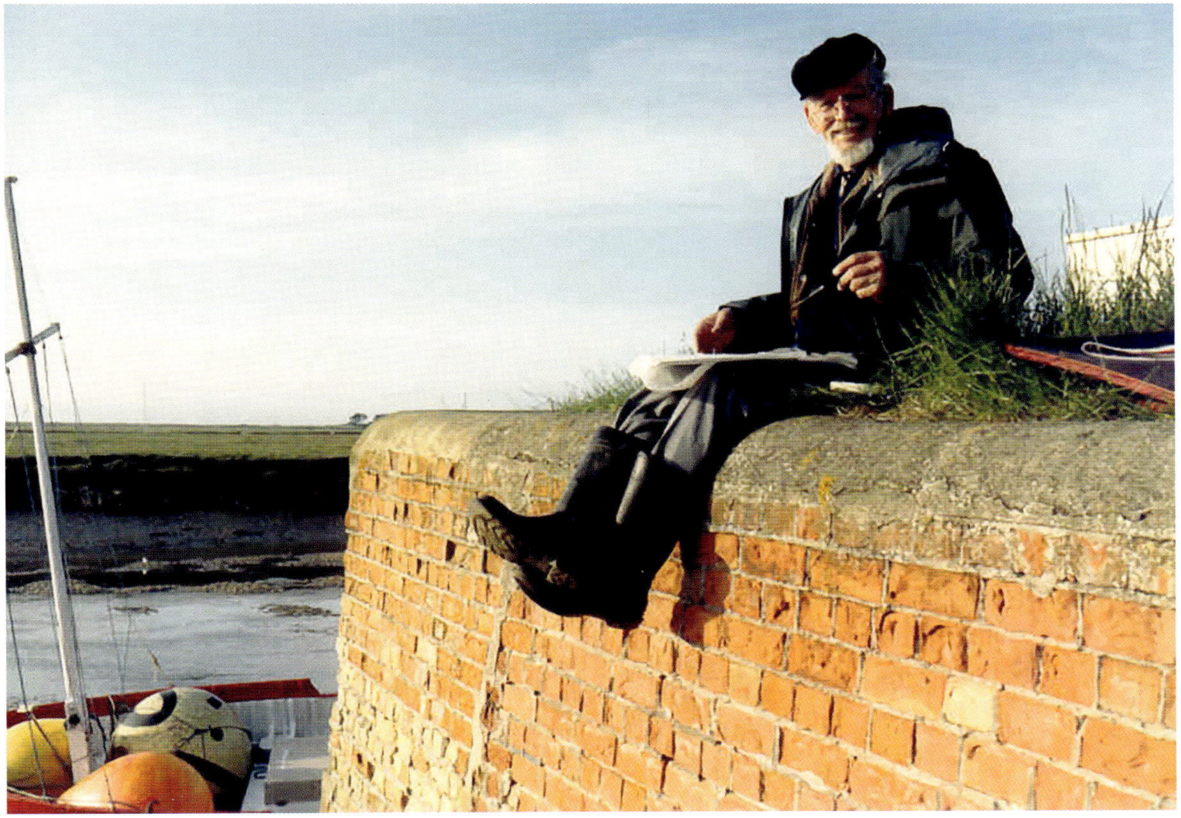

James sketching in Norfolk, 1985.

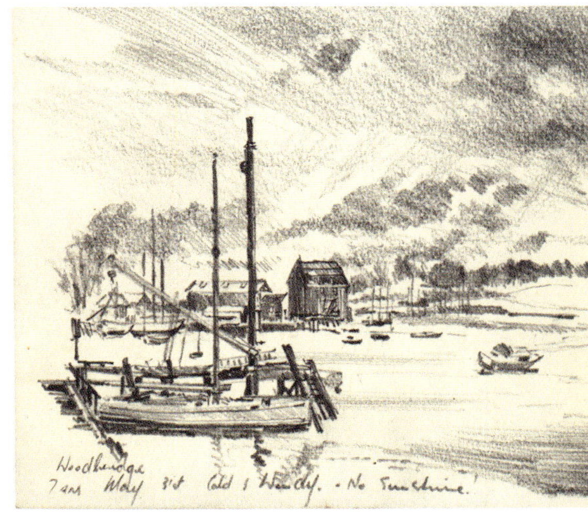

James' sketches became his 'shorthand notes'.

But the main focus of James' art remained East Anglia, especially the areas of Suffolk and Norfolk he knew and loved and revisited often. Woodbridge and the River Deben, and the coast around Aldeburgh, Walberswick and Southwold he especially loved.

As his health deteriorated, he devoted more and more time to the villages of the north Norfolk coast where he spent several happy sketching holidays, and places in and around Hadleigh.

James was always sketching, first in pencil and then in watercolour. He preferred to sketch early in the morning as he liked the clarity of the light and the colour tones.

Over the years he created thousand of exquisite sketches and quick studies, which he called "his shorthand notes". He said he could "take out sketches many years later, the memories would come rolling back and a full size painting would be all set".

Opposite: White Roses and Hibiscus. Pastel 26x33cm

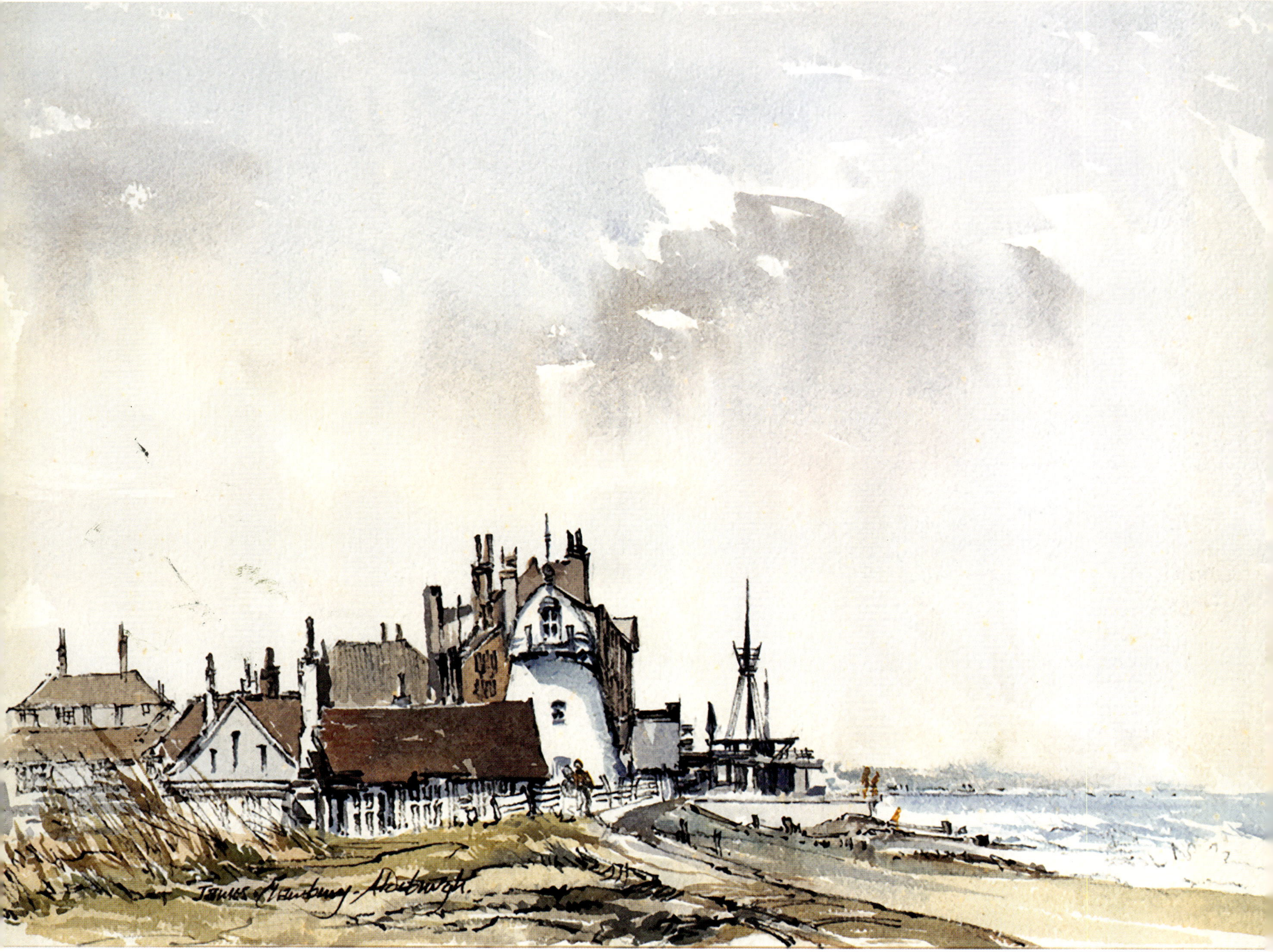
James Chambury - Aldeburgh.

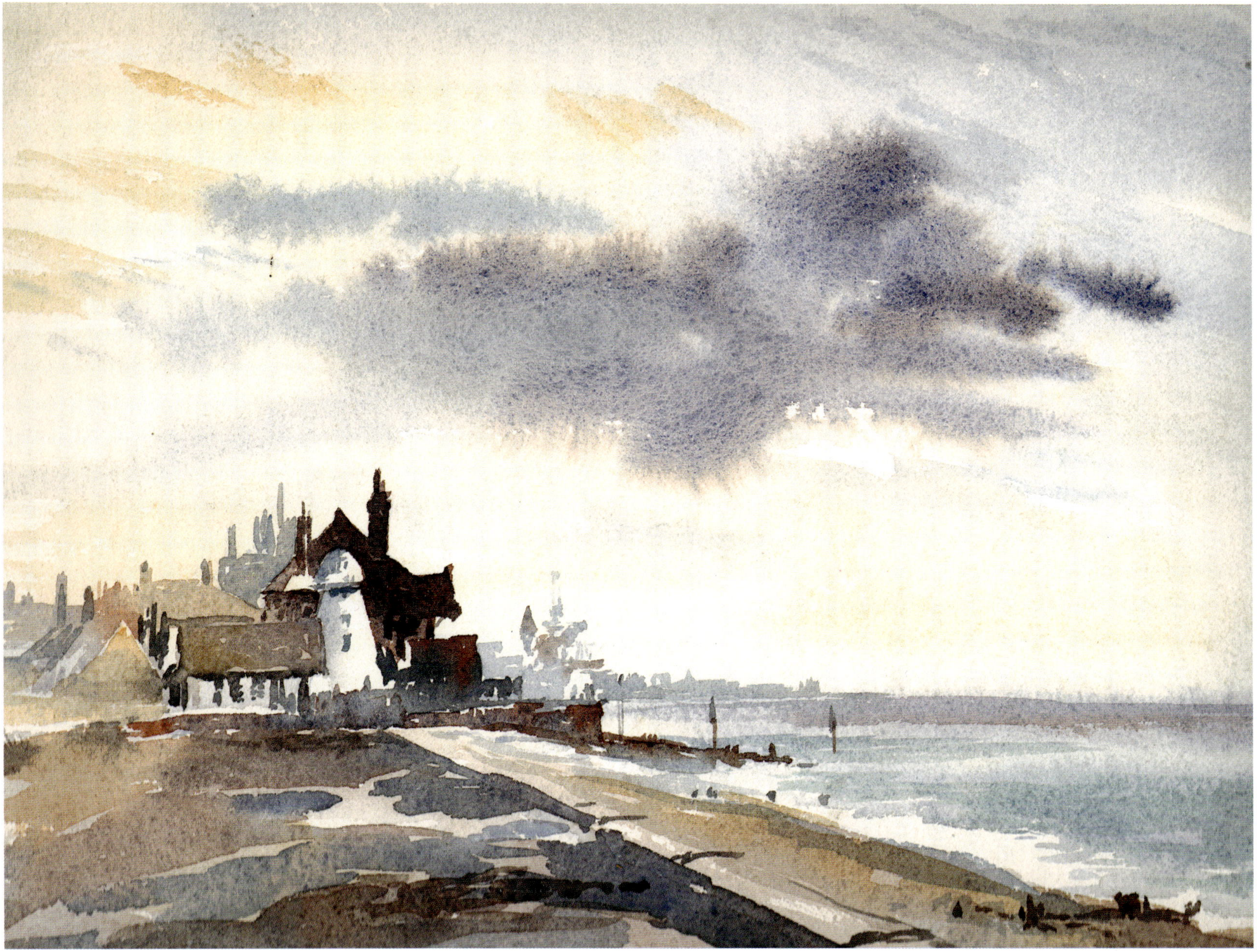

Opposite: Aldeburgh.
Line and wash 30x24cm

Preliminary watercolour sketch for Aldeburgh picture.

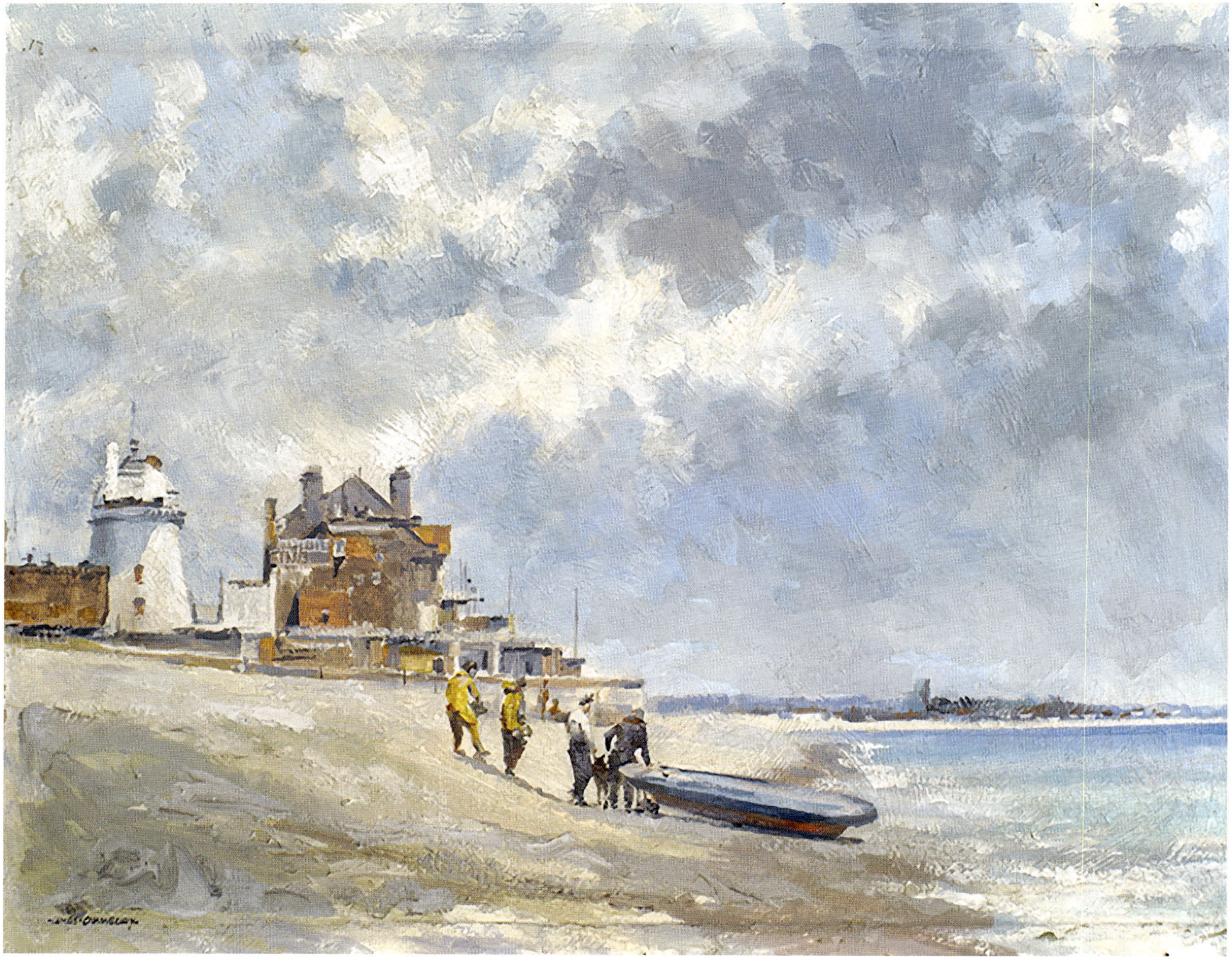

Boatmen on the Beach at Aldeburgh
Oil

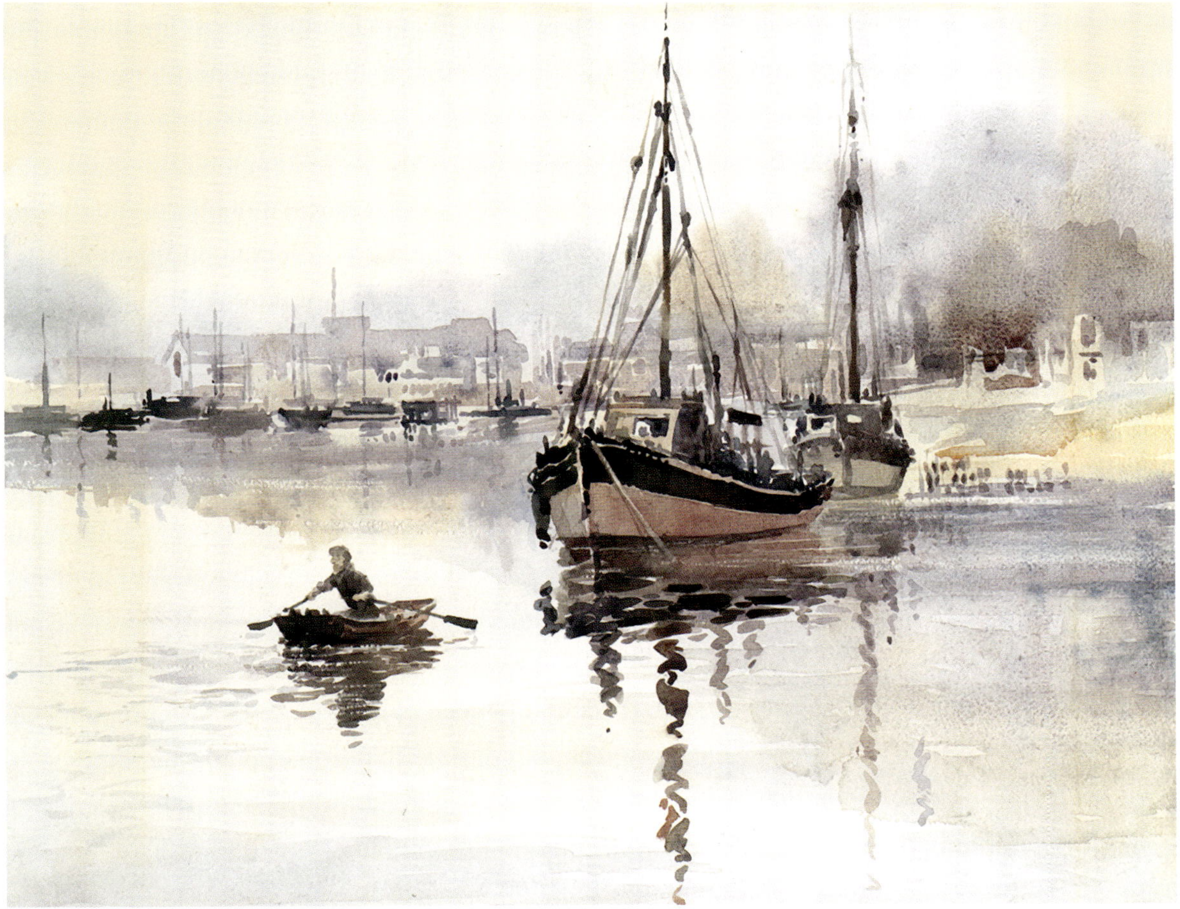

Rowing Boat on the River.
Watercolour 43x41cm

Although in increasingly poor health, James continued to work during the 1980s. He was a member of the East Anglian Group of Marine Artists, and the Suffolk Art Society, and was frequently invited to take part in mixed and solo shows. He often received letters of appreciation from people who bought his pictures, which he always treasured. Like many artists, he had huge doubts and lack of confidence with regard to his art. In May 1987, to commemorate a decade of Hadleigh being twinned with Rousies, Frances, a delegation from Hadleigh took one of James' paintings to Rousies as a gift, where it is on show in the Town Hall.

His daughter Nicola lived in the Netherlands in the 1980s. James sketched the dandelion field at the back of the house, the Dutch farmhouses and small lifting bridges on the canals, familiar to us from Van Gogh's early works. He did not find the landscape inspired him to paint, but he enjoyed visiting the great Dutch art galleries such as the Van Gogh Museum and the

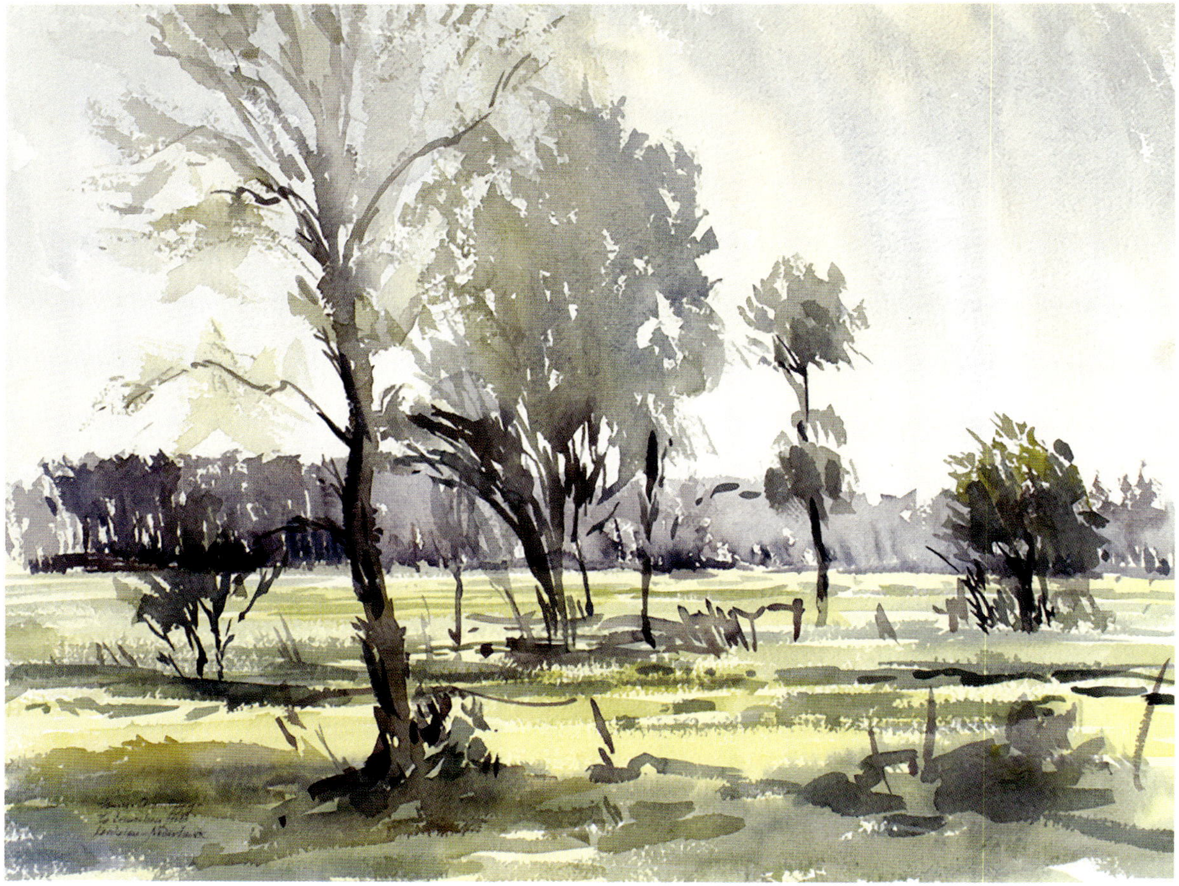

Dandelion Fields, Holland.
Watercolour

Rijksmuseum in Amsterdam, and the exquisite Kröller Müller Museum in Otterlo, where he became a regular visitor. James always had a excellent memory; he read widely, but especially art books. He was a walking reference book and could always tell you which museum or gallery held which paintings.

James sketched sky studies in watercolour and pastel all his life. Often he would do a series, sketched rapidly as the sky changed, until he had ten or twelve small paintings. Usually these were quick watercolour sketches, but when staying in Holland he produced some in pastel.

He was also a frequent exhibitor with the Royal Society of Marine Artists, the Pastel Society and the British Watercolour Society and took part in shows farther afield. His work was hung at the Barbican in 1982, in 'Five East Anglian Artists: Paintings and Prints', at Colchester in 1988 and at the British Watercolour Society exhibition at the Mall Galleries in 1989. In 1990

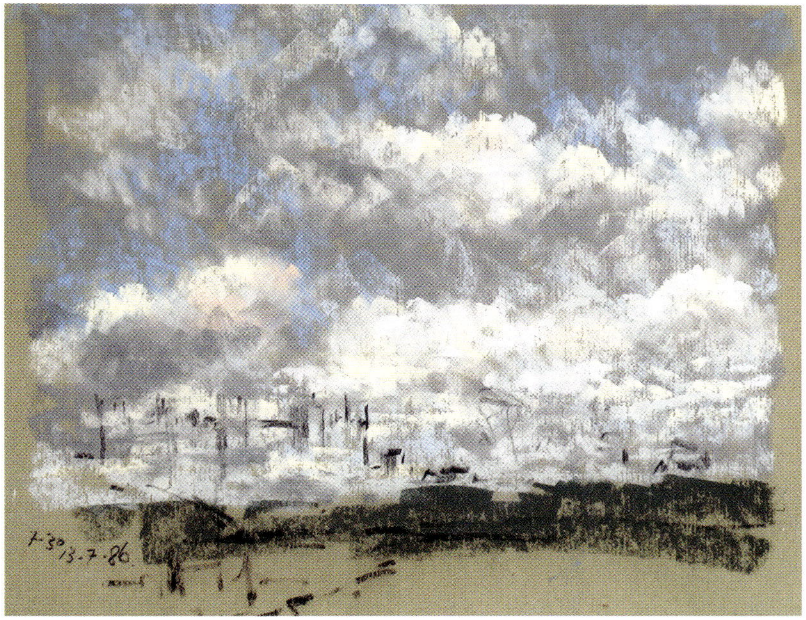

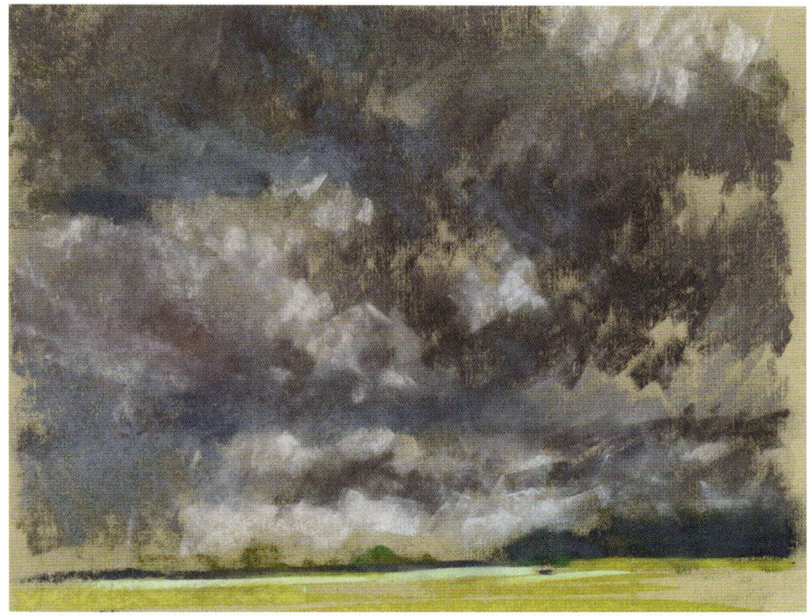

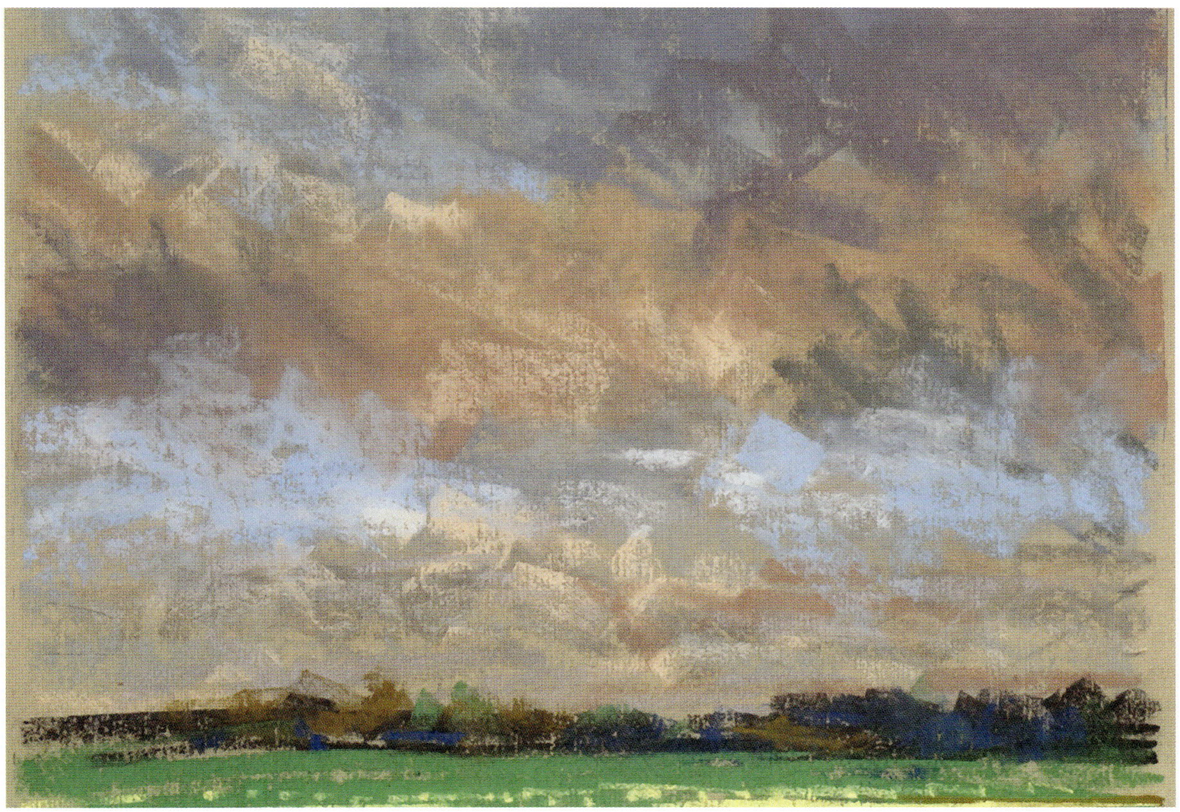

Sky Studies - made while at Wateren in the Netherlands.
Pastel

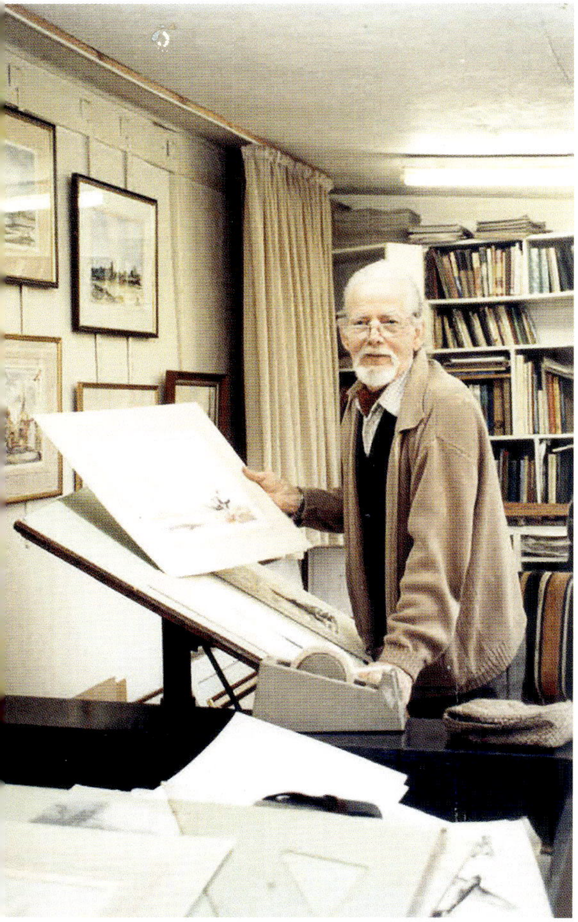

The artist in his studio.

James was one of the invited artists at the inaugural exhibition of the new art gallery in Halstead, Chipping Hill House. He exhibited regularly at the Haste Gallery in Ipswich, in mixed and solo shows and the annual exhibition of the East Anglian Group of Marine Artists. His work formed part of the 'Work of the Pastel Painter' show at the Haste Gallery in 1990 and was featured in a solo exhibition 'Recent Watercolours and Pastels' in 1991. In 1992 he was one of four artists exhibiting at the Haste Gallery and Wherry Quay, Ipswich, as part of the celebrations for the 150th anniversary of Ipswich Docks.

During the 1980s he was becoming increasingly admired for the beauty and deftness of his watercolours. He mastered this most difficult of mediums and created water that looked wet and light than was luminescent. He became widely know and his paintings were bought for private collections all over Britain and in North America, South Africa, New Zealand, France, the Netherlands, Germany and Oman.

He started drawing and painting with pastels during this time and became more and more well known for his work in pastel. He used very fine glass paper, as this has a much better tooth than any pastel paper available, but it was tough on his fingers! The pastel dust also caused

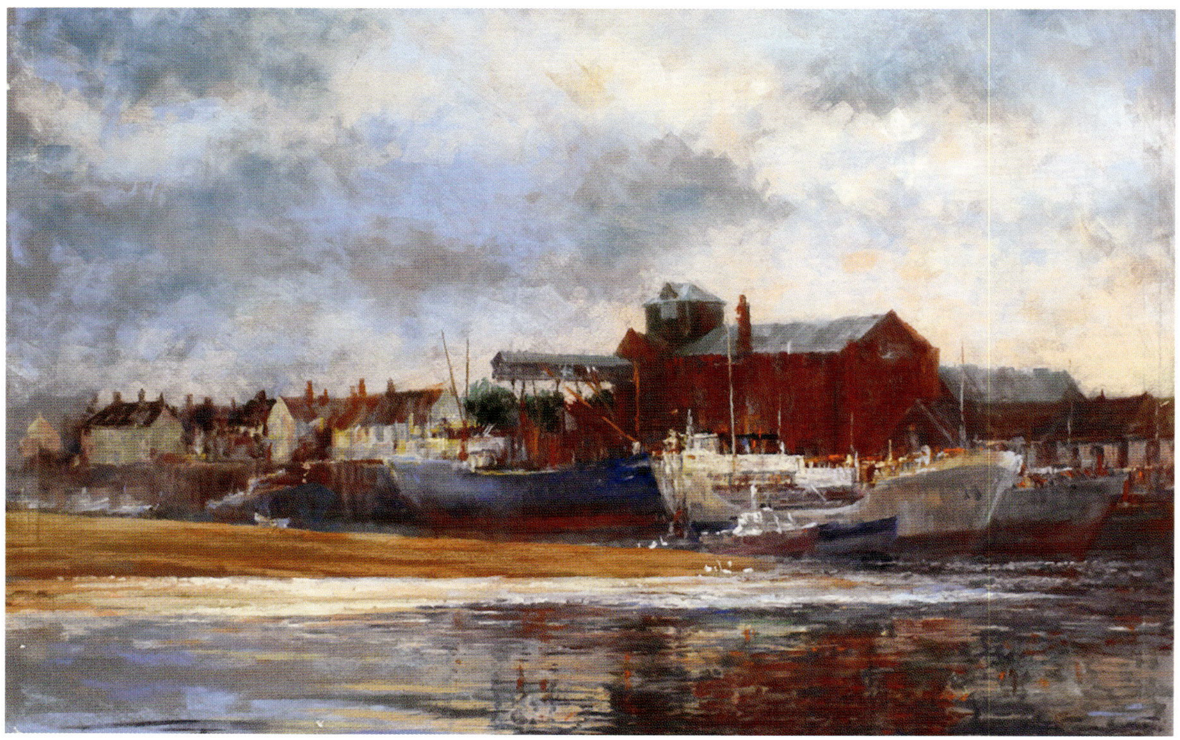

Evening – Wells-next-the-Sea.
Pastel 63x45cm

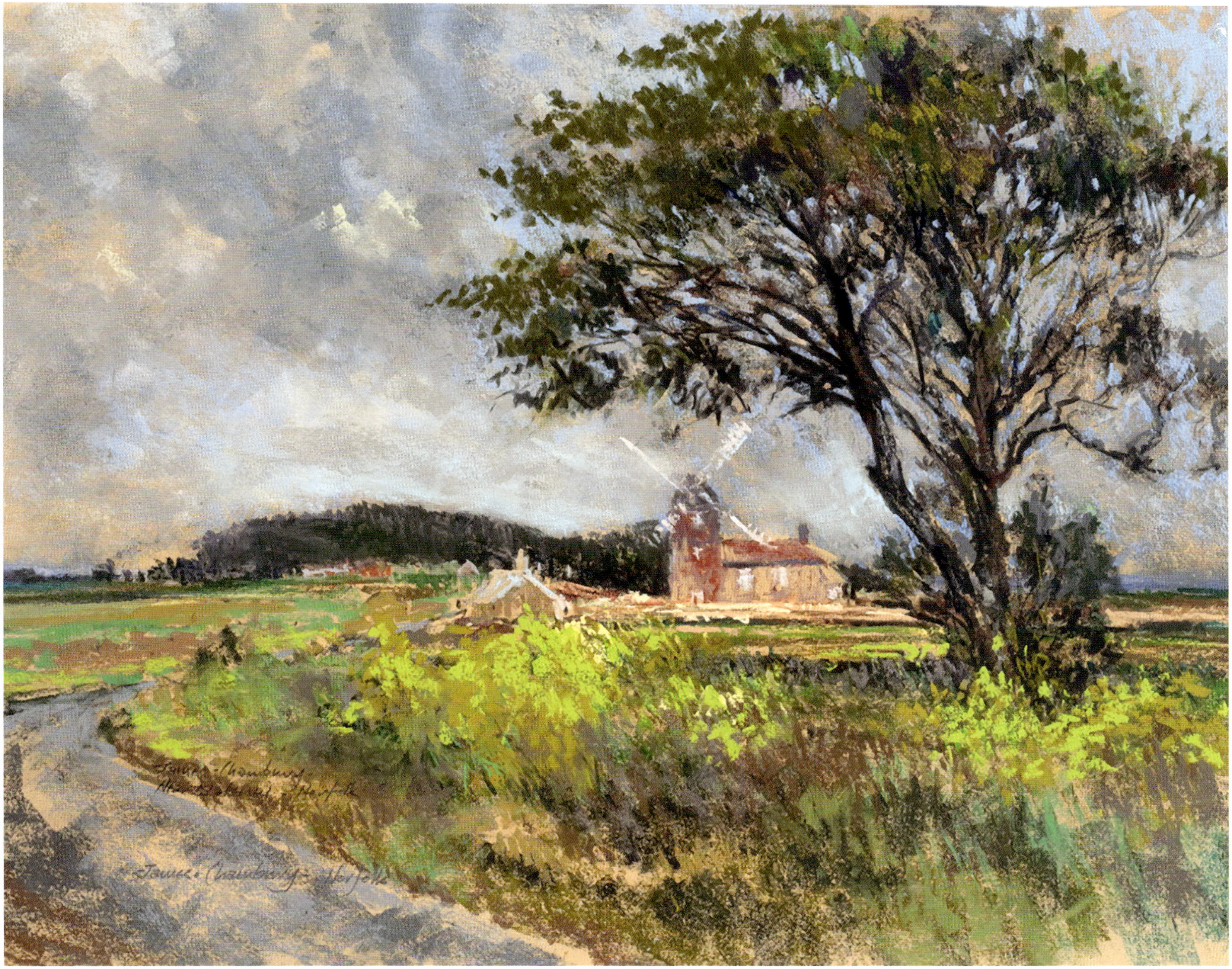

Near Blakeney, Norfolk.
Pastel 33x25cm

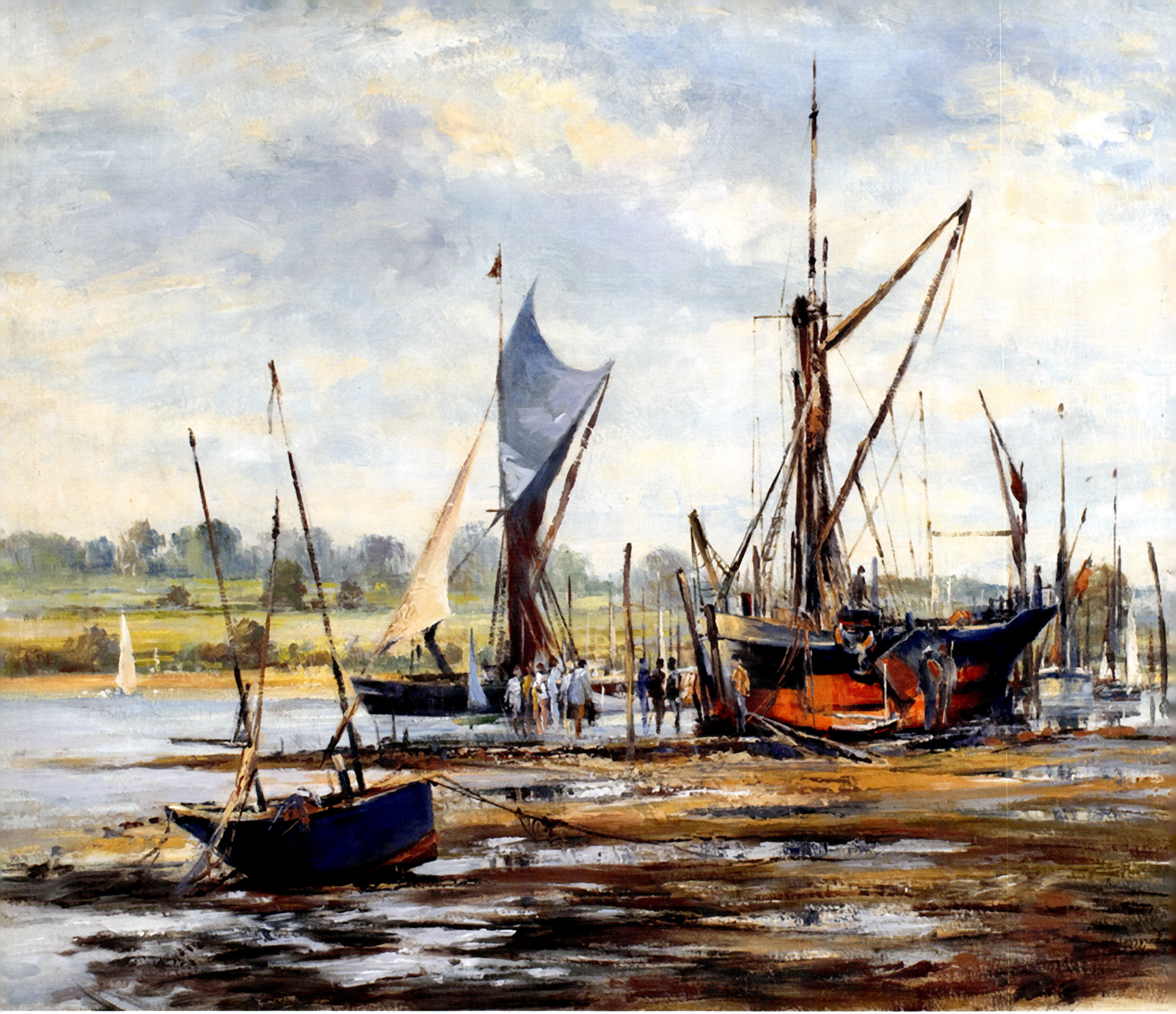

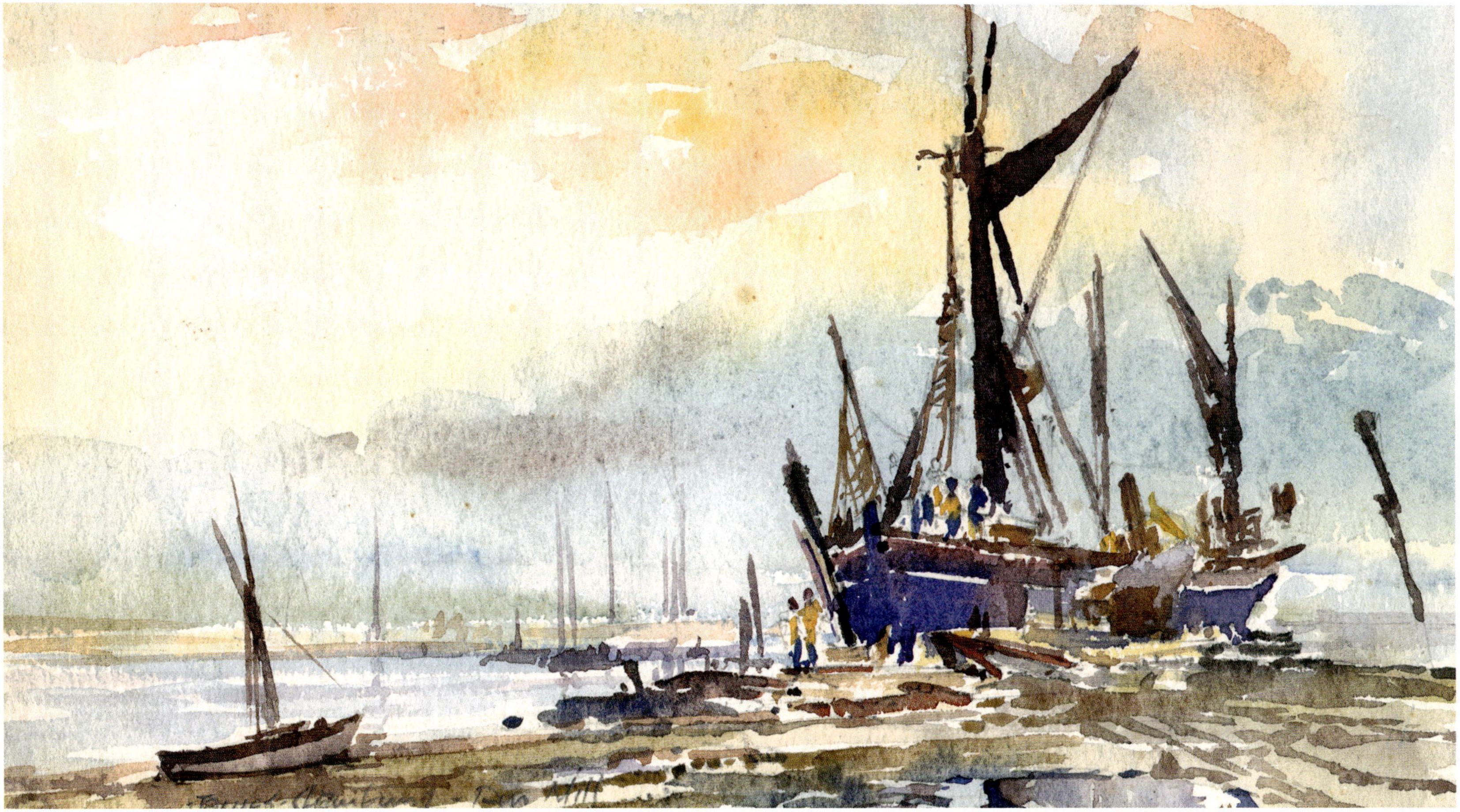

problems for his chest, and he tried working with a mask but found this was a barrier between him and the work. He did not fix his pastels as he believed this altered the colours, texture and appearance. He created works with great depth of colour and tone as the glass paper made it possible to build up many layers without the colours becoming flat or muddied. The *East Anglian Daily Times* correspondent, reporting on 'The Work of the Pastel Painter' exhibition remarked "For me, James Chambury is one of the most vital pastel painters seen locally. He uses colour dramatically and seductively."

James was always fascinated by boats and sailing, although he only ever went to sea a few times. Sailors felt he really captured the movement of the sea, and his skills as a draughtsman enabled him to capture the changing perspectives of a boat tossed by the waves. In the 1980s he was able to sail on Thames Barges at the annual Barge Match at Pinmill on the River Orwell.

Preliminary watercolour sketch for the pastel Fitting Out Barges at Low Water, Pin Mill.

Opposite: Fitting Out Barges at Low Water – Pin Mill.
Pastel 60x51cm

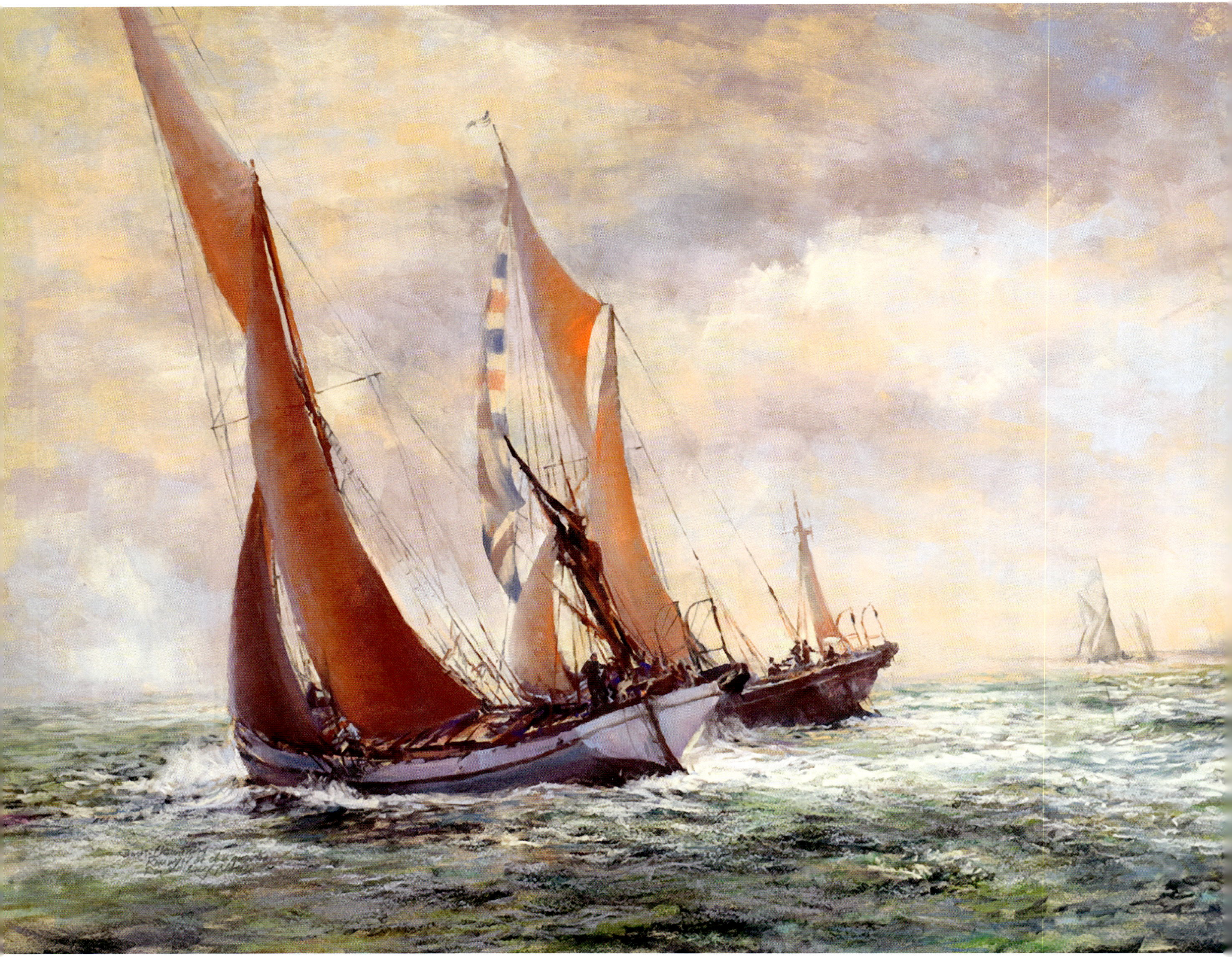

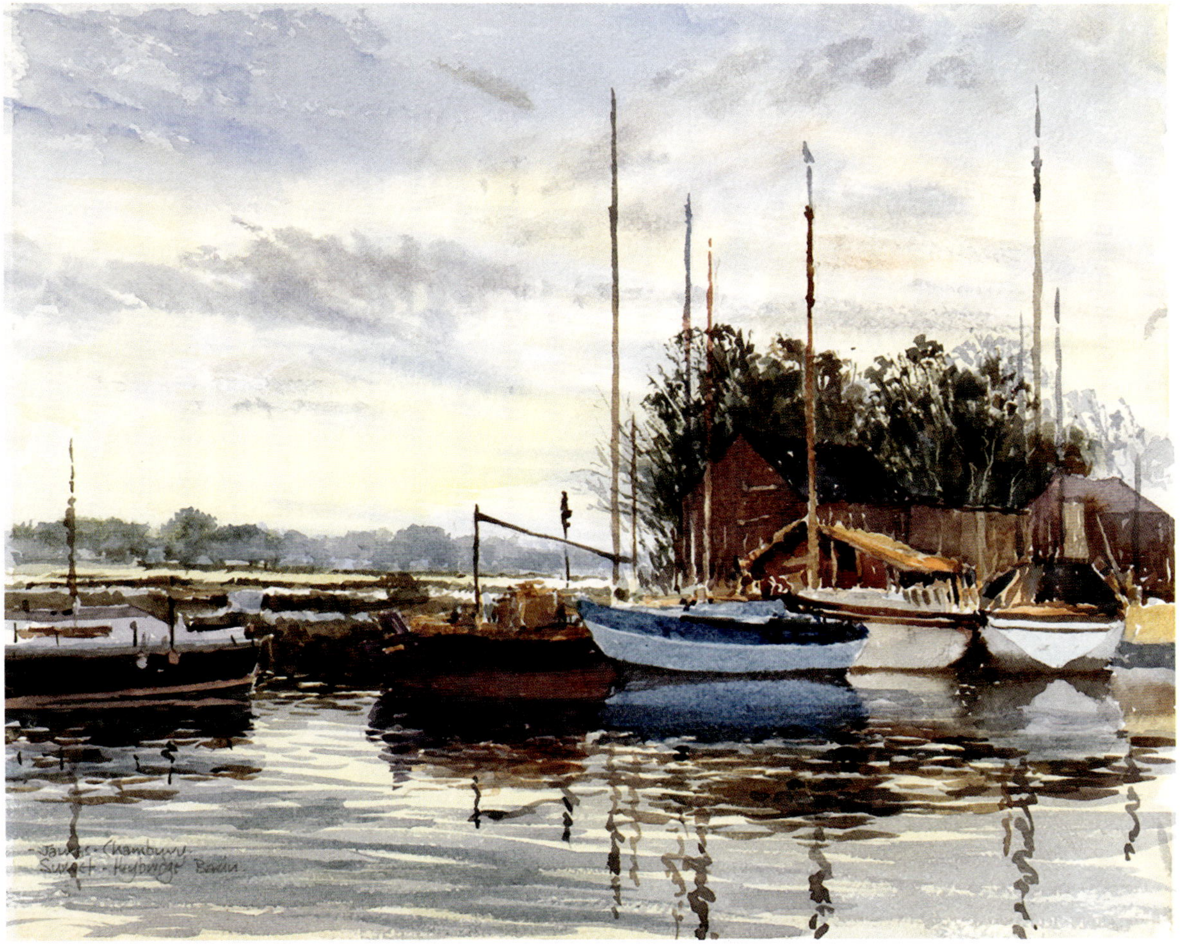

Sunset Heybridge Basin - Essex.
Watercolour 34x27cm

James was always happiest drawing the ever-changing East Anglian coastline. In the mid 1980s he had several sketching holidays on the north Norfolk coast. Staying in a cottage in Holt, he got to know the coast between Weybourne and Brancaster. He loved the Norfolk skies and the way the landscape and seascape are transformed twice a day by the movement of the tides, with the creeks and mudflats, rivers and sandbanks constantly changing with the ebb and flow. Often there is a confusion of mud and water and sky reflecting each other, with no certainty where the one begins and another ends. And larger scale changes occur too, with shifts in sand and mud after every winter storm.

During 1992 James was increasingly unwell but worked with his characteristic determination preparing for his solo show at Picturecraft in Holt. The successful exhibition in October that year proved to be his last show. Full of light and increasingly abstract and ethereal, these late

Opposite: Remainder *at close quarter*
Pin Mill Barge Race.
Pastel 60x46cm

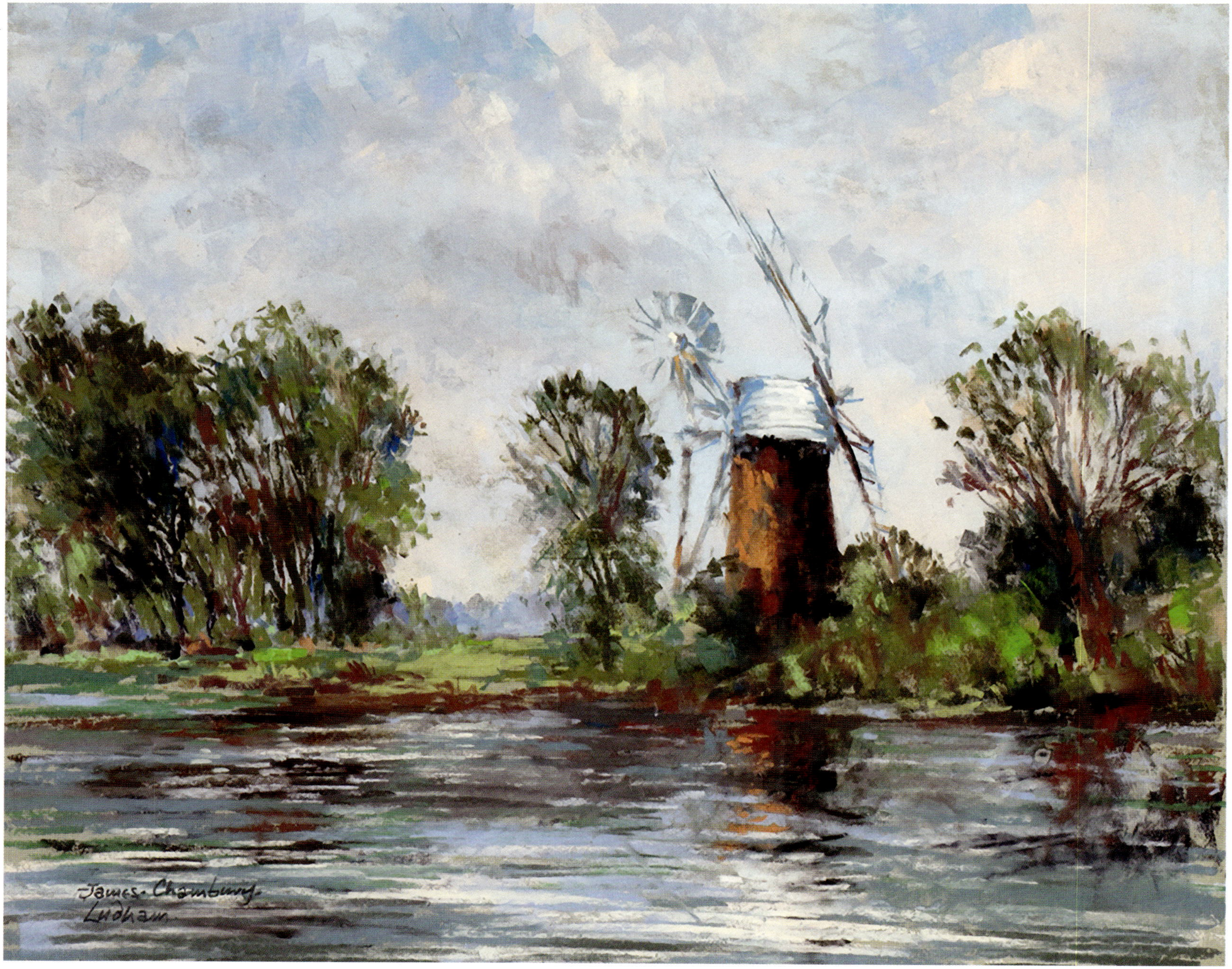

Ludham Windmill, Norfolk.
Pastel 35x27cm

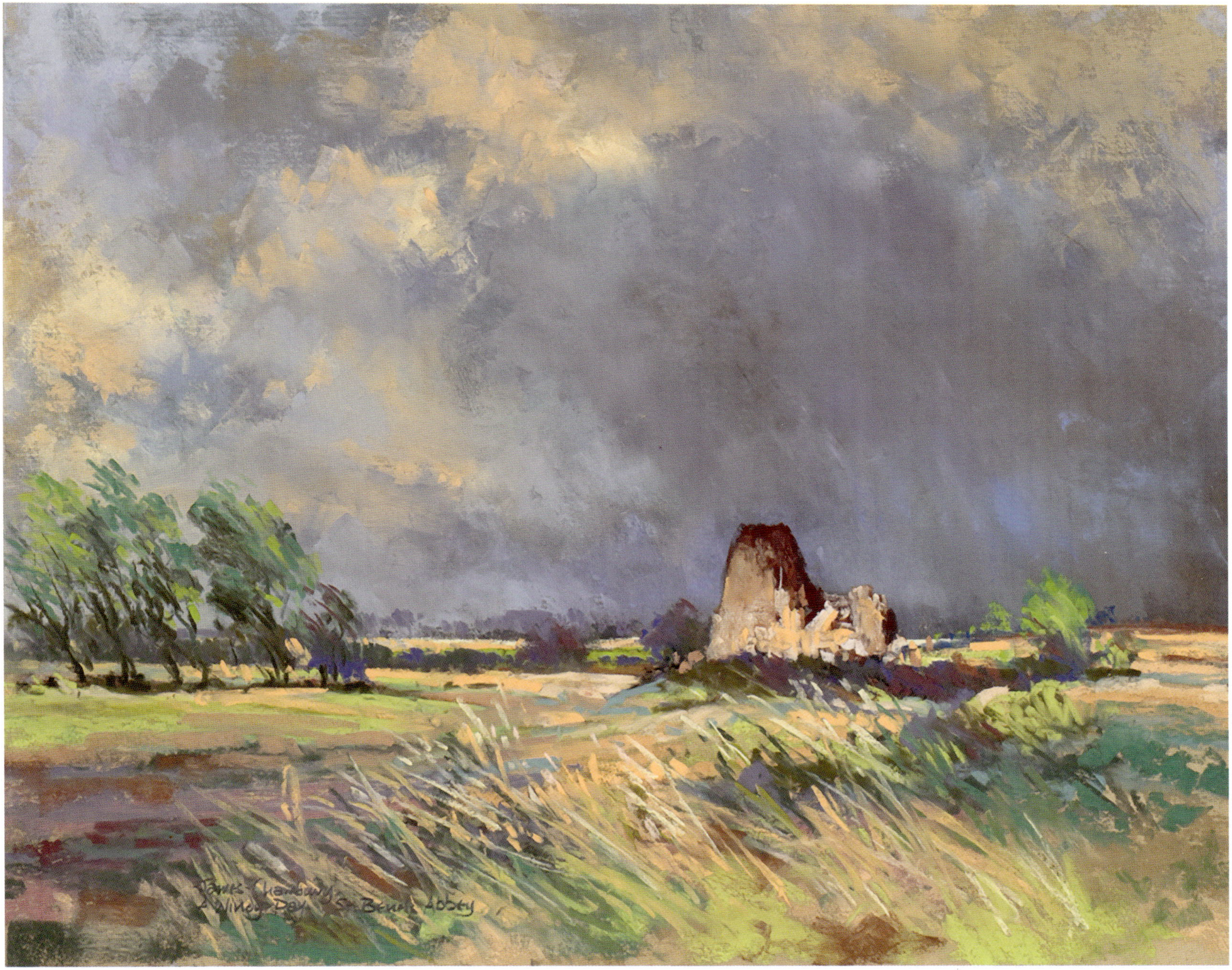

Windy Day, St Benet's Abbey, Norfolk.
Pastel 34x25cm

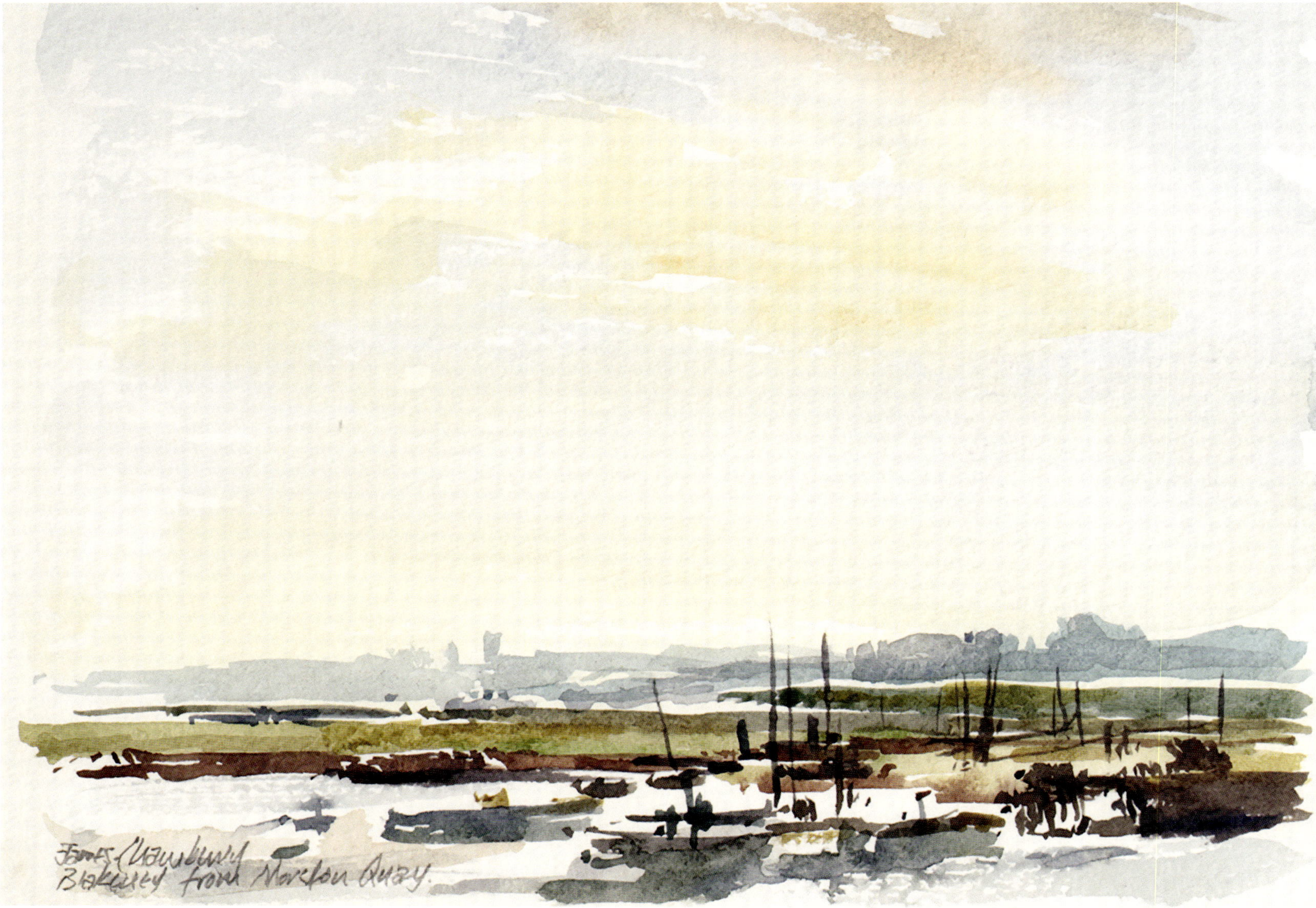

View of Blakeney from Morston Quay, Norfolk.
Watercolour 17x12cm

works hint at what he might have gone on to produce had he had longer to live. The gallery owners wrote to him after the show "Thank you for providing such a stunning exhibition in the gallery last week. The views expressed in the visitors' book reveal the impact that you so obviously made in presenting your paintings and we are continuing to hear favourable comments." A second exhibition was planned for the following October, but sadly he was too ill to take up this offer and in fact had only six months left to live.

OMAN & THE END

Towards the end of his life James' career took an unexpected turn. In 1988, he visited his daughter in the Sultanate of Oman, and this proved to be a huge source of inspiration. This varied and beautiful country opened his eyes to new colours, textures and light. He had to change his palette completely to cope with the intensity of the sun and alter his technique to cope with the extreme heat. This influenced the work he made back home in Suffolk as well as images he created of Oman. He returned to Oman in December 1991, and had an exhibition at the Yiti Gallery. The show was bought in its entirety by the wife of one of the top government ministers. He was also commissioned to produce dozens of paintings for their new villa, whatever size, medium and subject he liked.

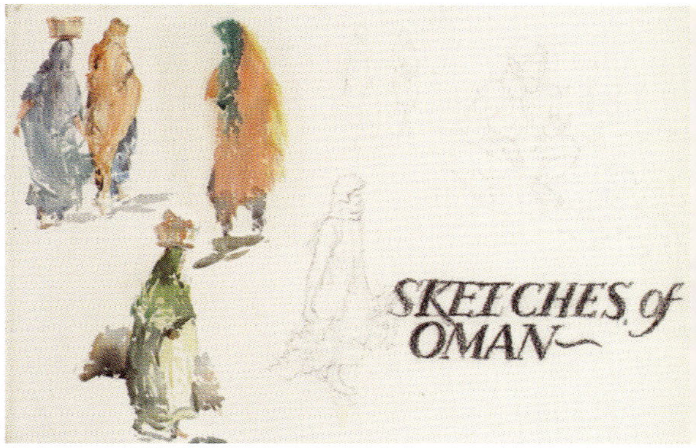

Oman exhibition poster.

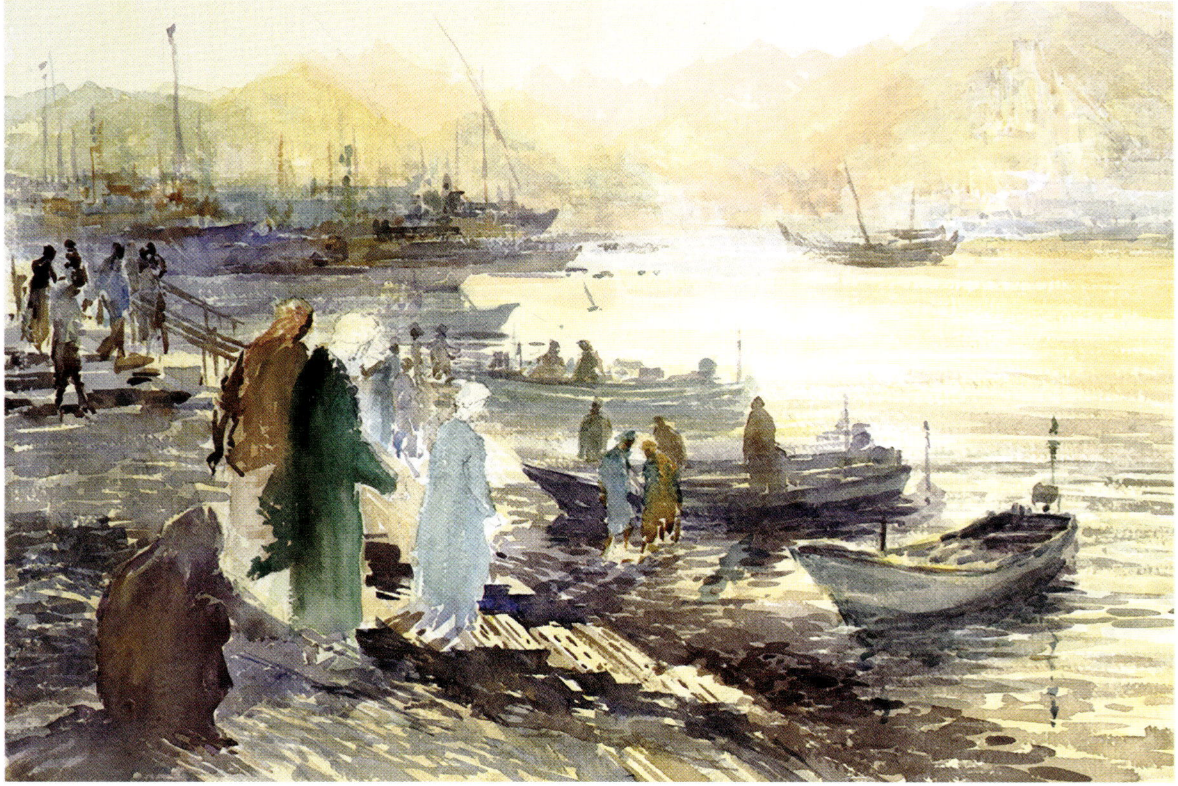

Mutrah Harbour, Oman.
Watercolour 52x35cm

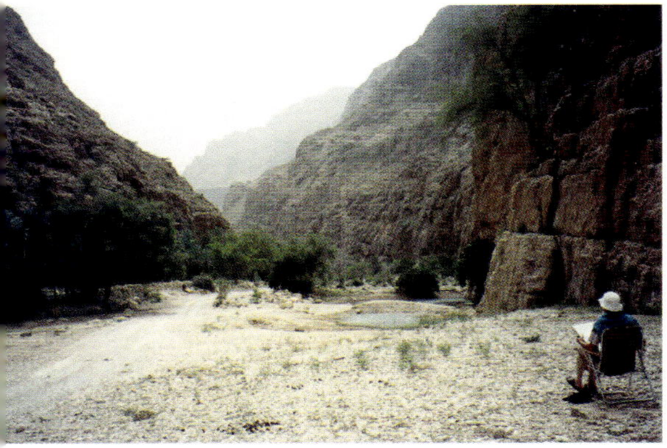

The artist at Wadi Tiwi, Oman.

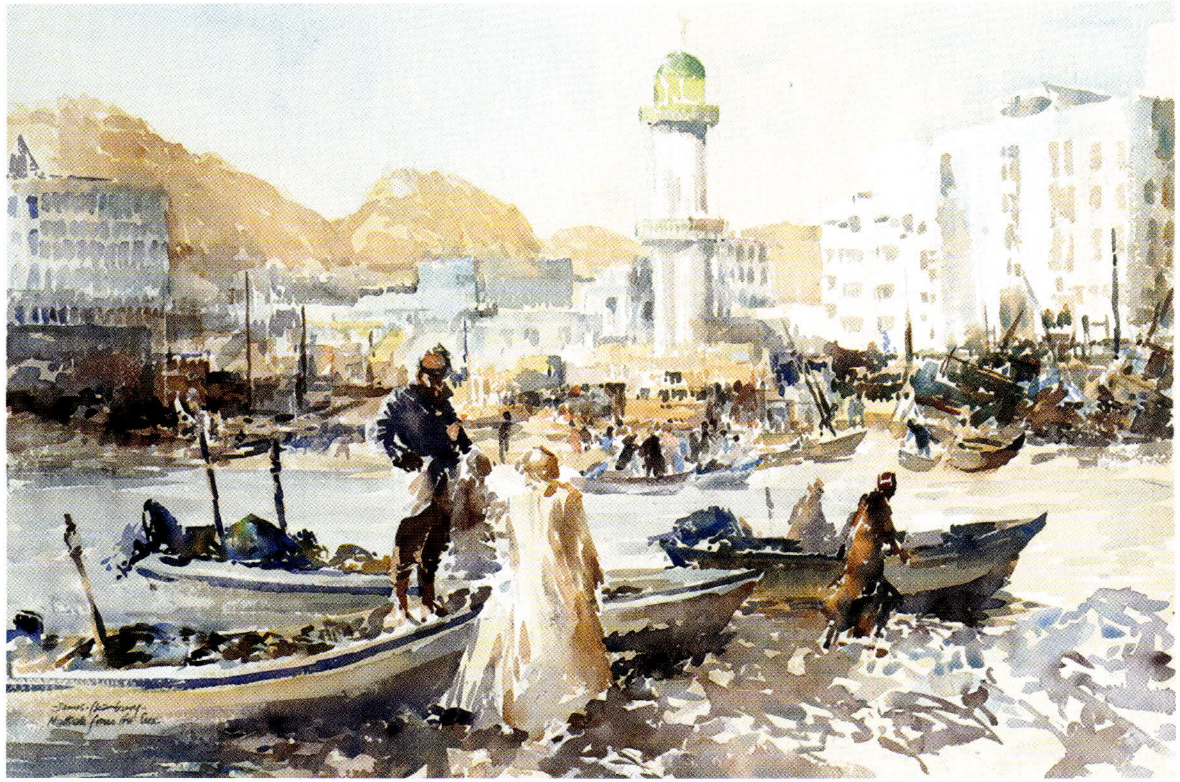

Muttrah from the Sea, Oman.
Watercolour 53x39cm

This was an artist's dream come true, and he was overwhelmed, full of excitement and enthusiasm. He flew out to Oman for a third visit early in 1992, and was provided with a driver three days a week to take him out drawing. The other days he went on longer trips with his daughter. James enjoyed a wonderful three weeks sketching. He returned home on the understanding that he would not start his Omani paintings until after the exhibition at Picturecraft in Holt in October that year.

After this exhibition he was only able to paint four large watercolours and ship them out to Oman. He was very ill over Christmas 1992 and was diagnosed with sideroblastic anaemia. For the next fifteen months he had to have a monthly transfusion of six pints of blood. He felt better, but not well enough to do much work. Most of the time he felt very ill because he was either needing the transfusion or recovering from it. After a year, this developed into acute blast cell leukaemia, and three months after this diagnosis, he died.

James' life was one of struggle against upbringing, ill health and pain, but also one of determination, inspiration and dedication to his art. His later works give us a tantalizing glimpse of what might have been had he lived longer, but we have been left with a body of work that shows his love, knowledge and observation of landscape which is amongst the finest of his generation. Over three decades he created art which explores the meaning we find in landscape as well as the transience of colour and light, and this grew from his first explorations of the mud flats and tides of Leigh-on-Sea. After his death, his family scattered his ashes in the tidal mudflats and rivers of Suffolk so he could become part of the landscape he loved so much.

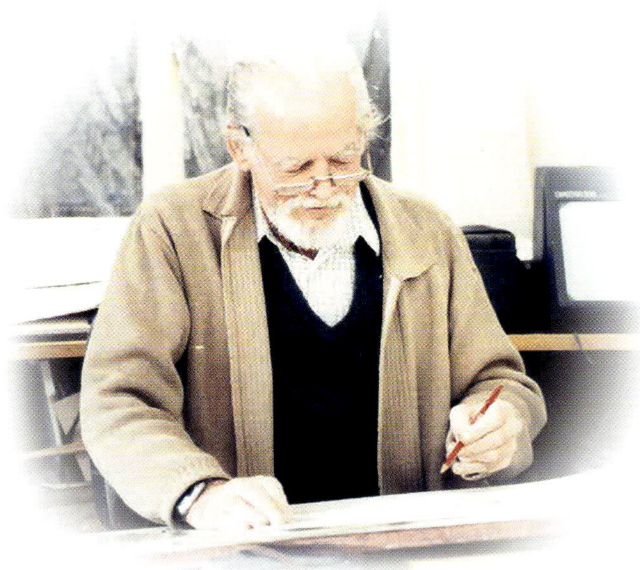

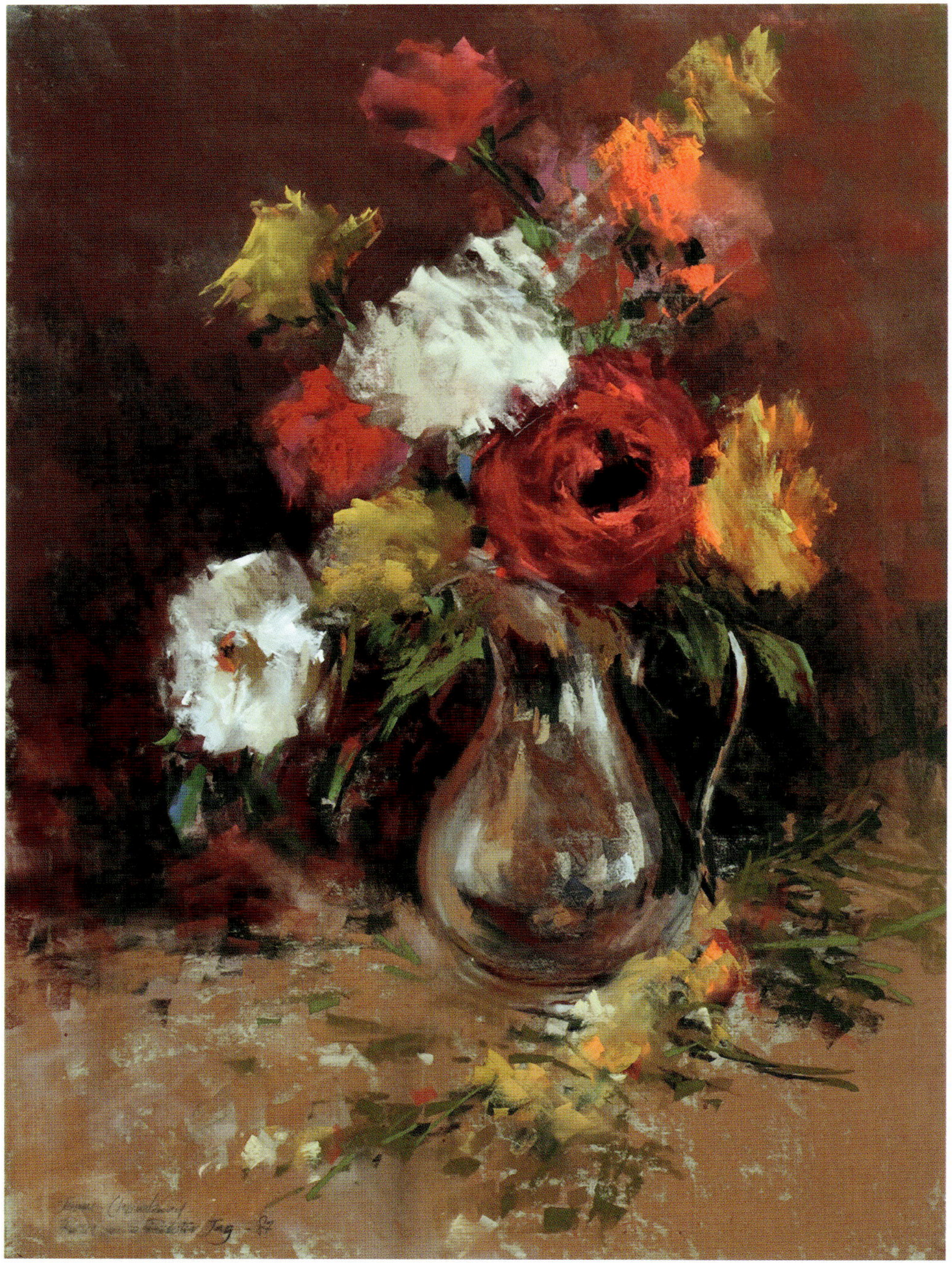

Roses in a Pewter Jug.
Pastel 37x53cm

Opposite: Near Wells-next-the-Sea, Norfolk.
Pastel 34x26cm

JAMES CHAMBURY
THE PAINTINGS

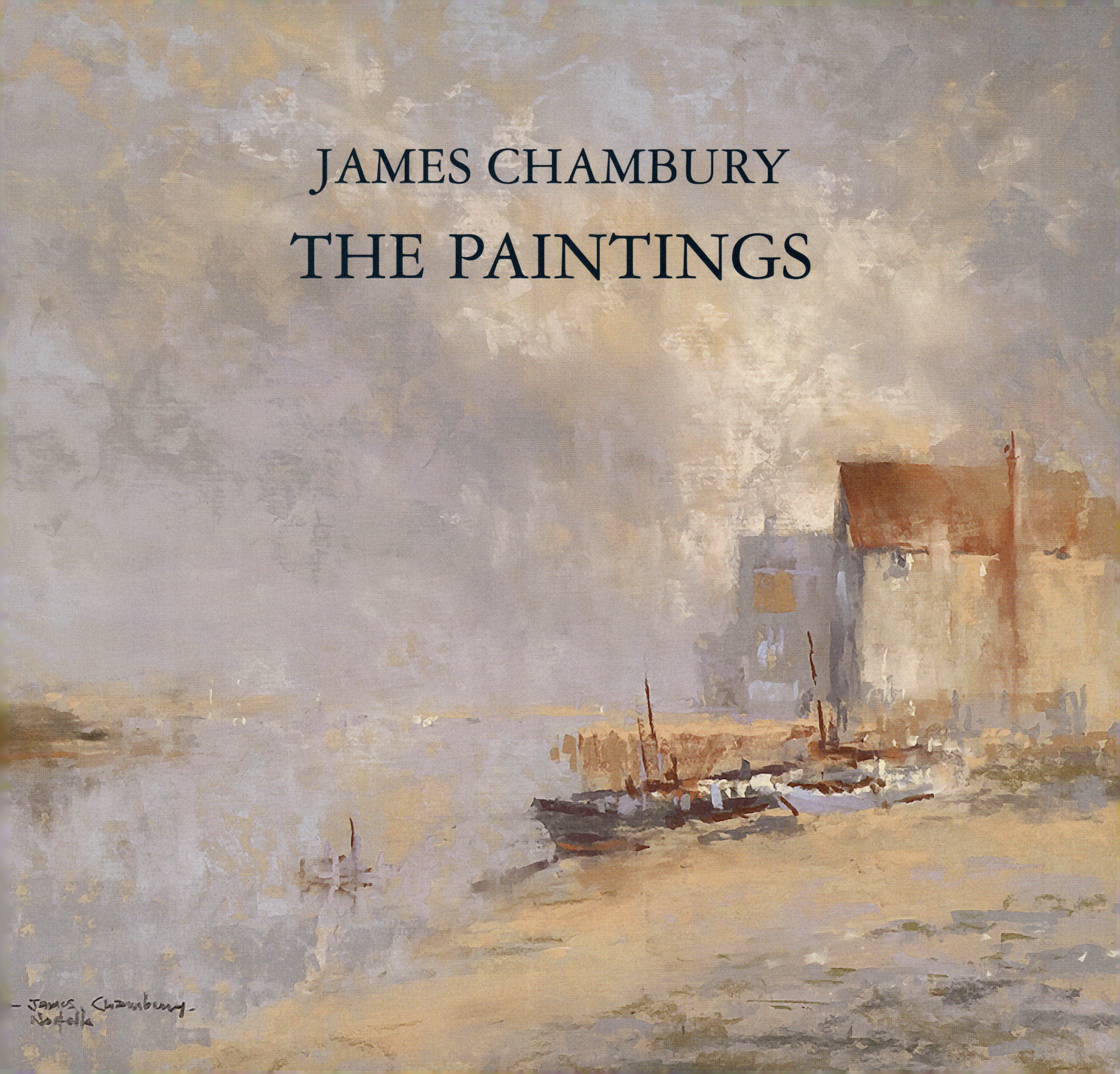

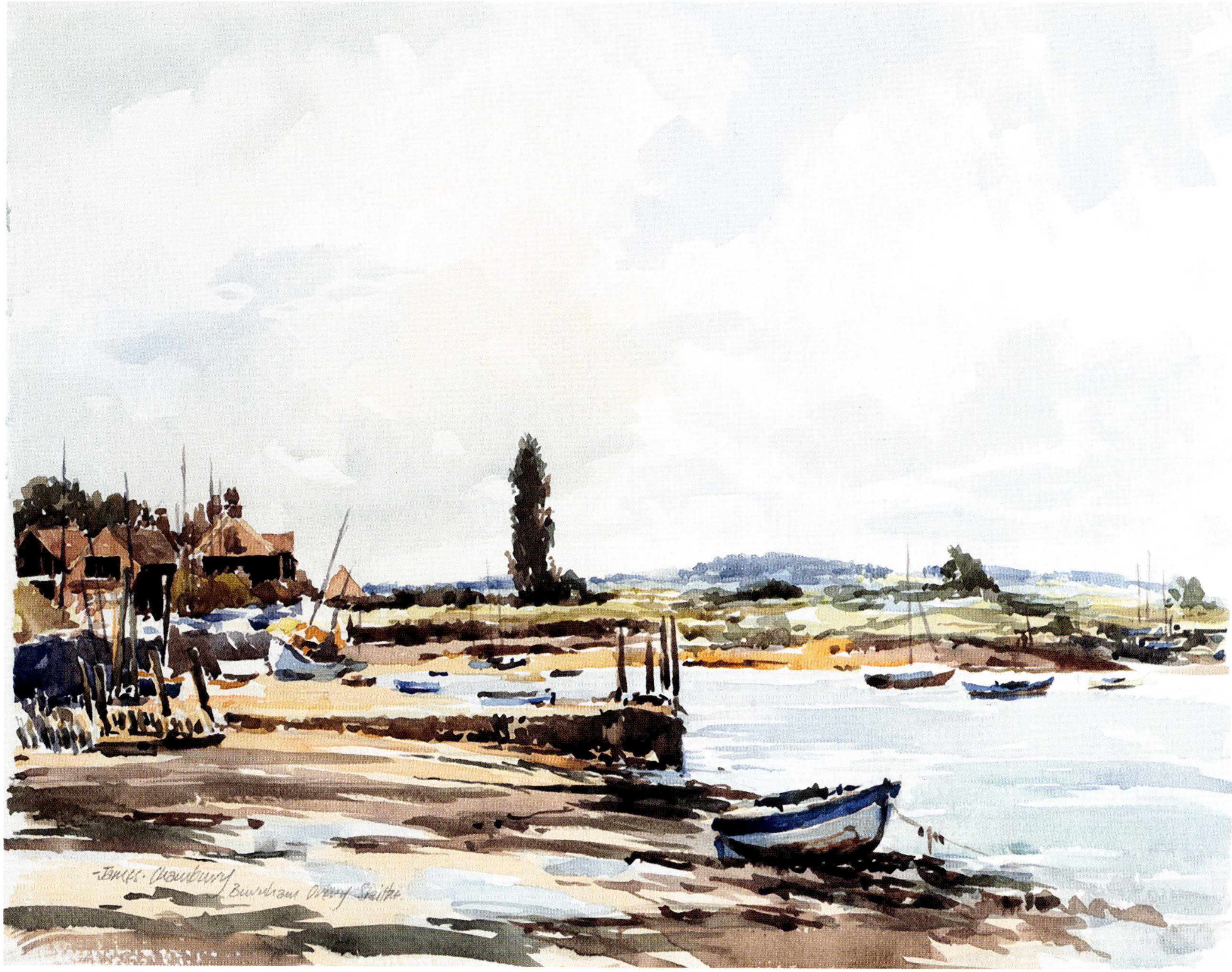

Burnham Overy Staithe, Norfolk.
Watercolour 34x27cm

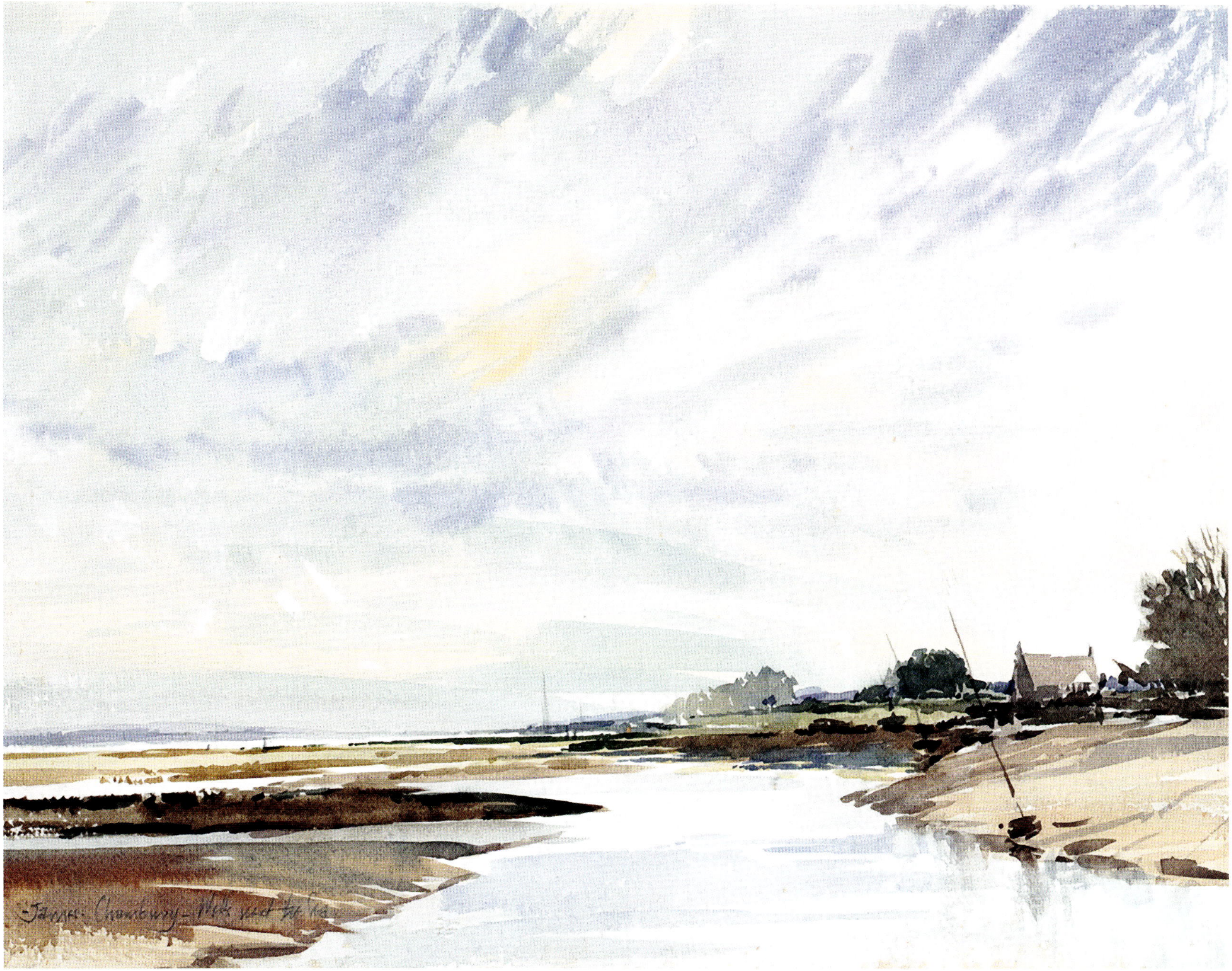

Wells-next-the-Sea, Norfolk.
Watercolour

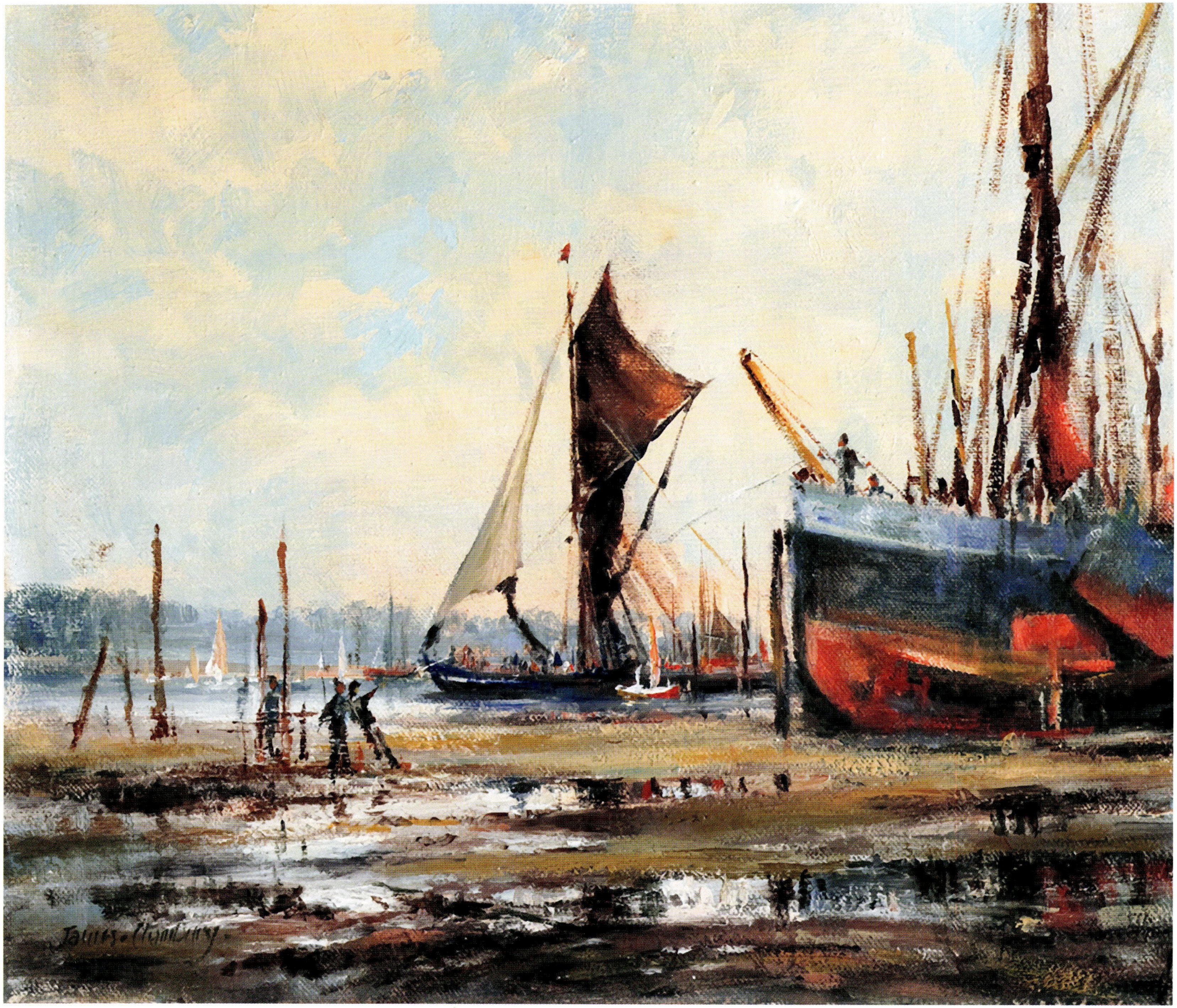

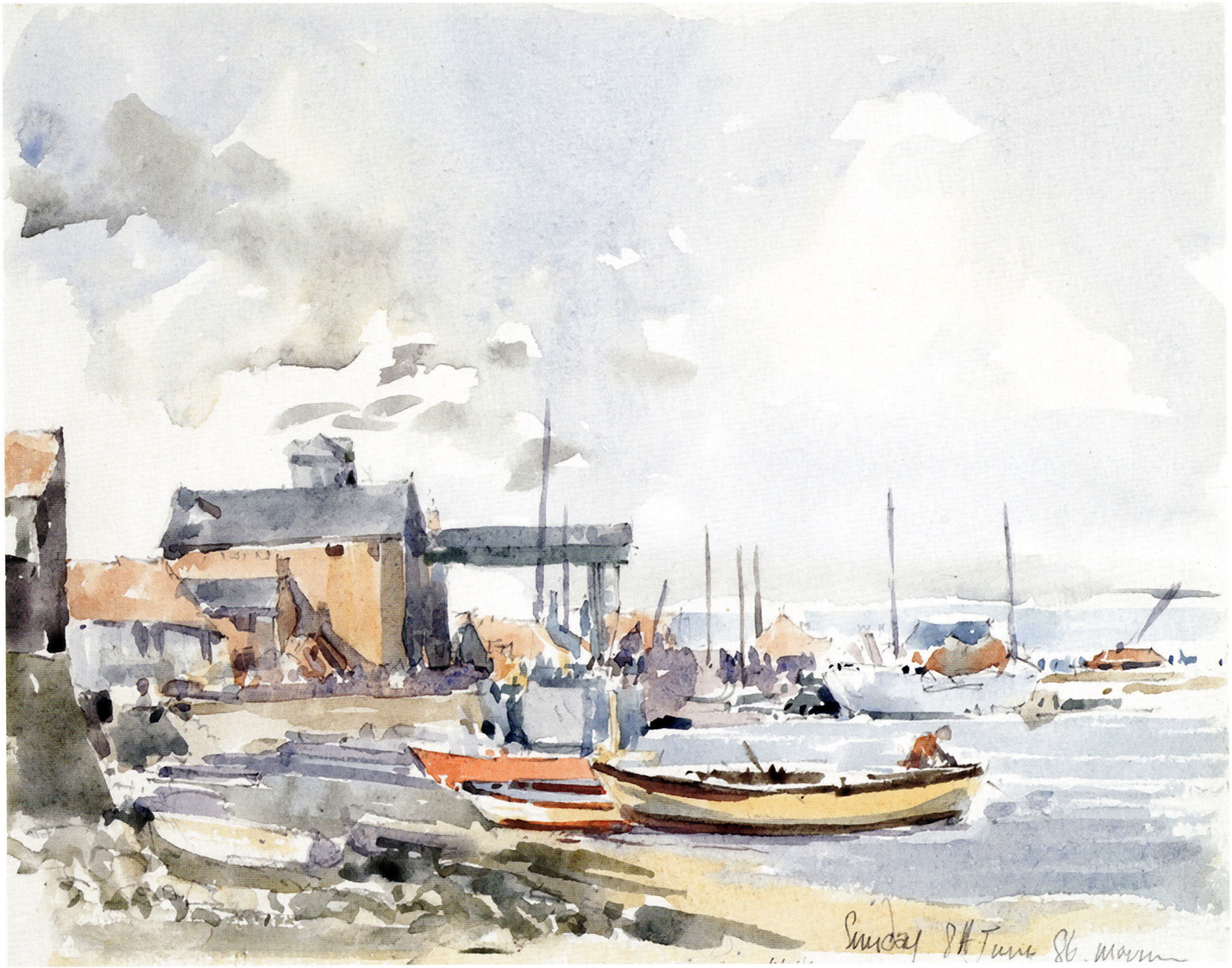

Opposite: Sunday Morning: Pin Mill on the Hard, Suffolk.
Oil 34x29cm

Wells-next-the-Sea, Norfolk.
Watercolour 21x18cm

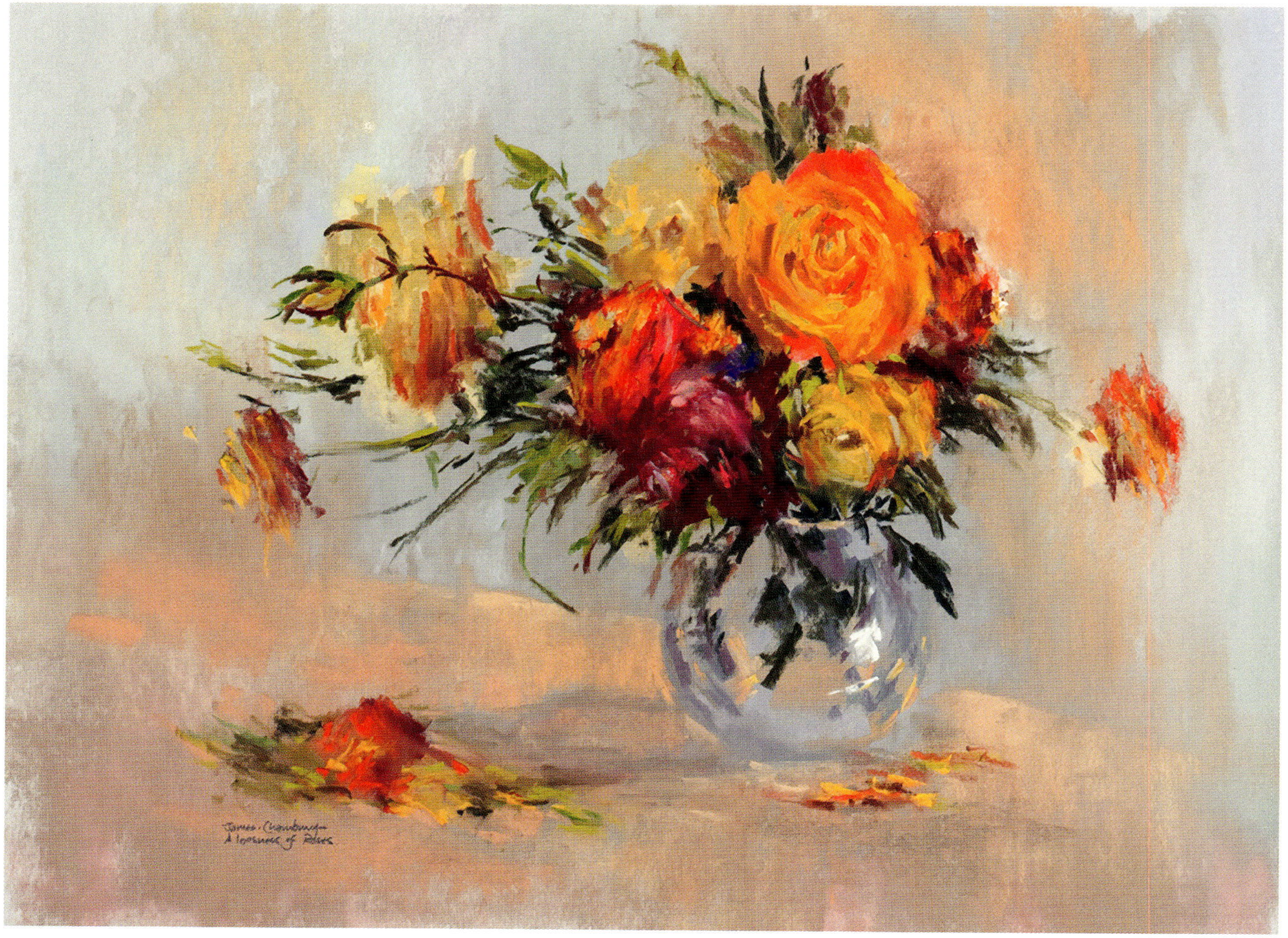

A Looseness of Roses.
Pastel 53x39cm

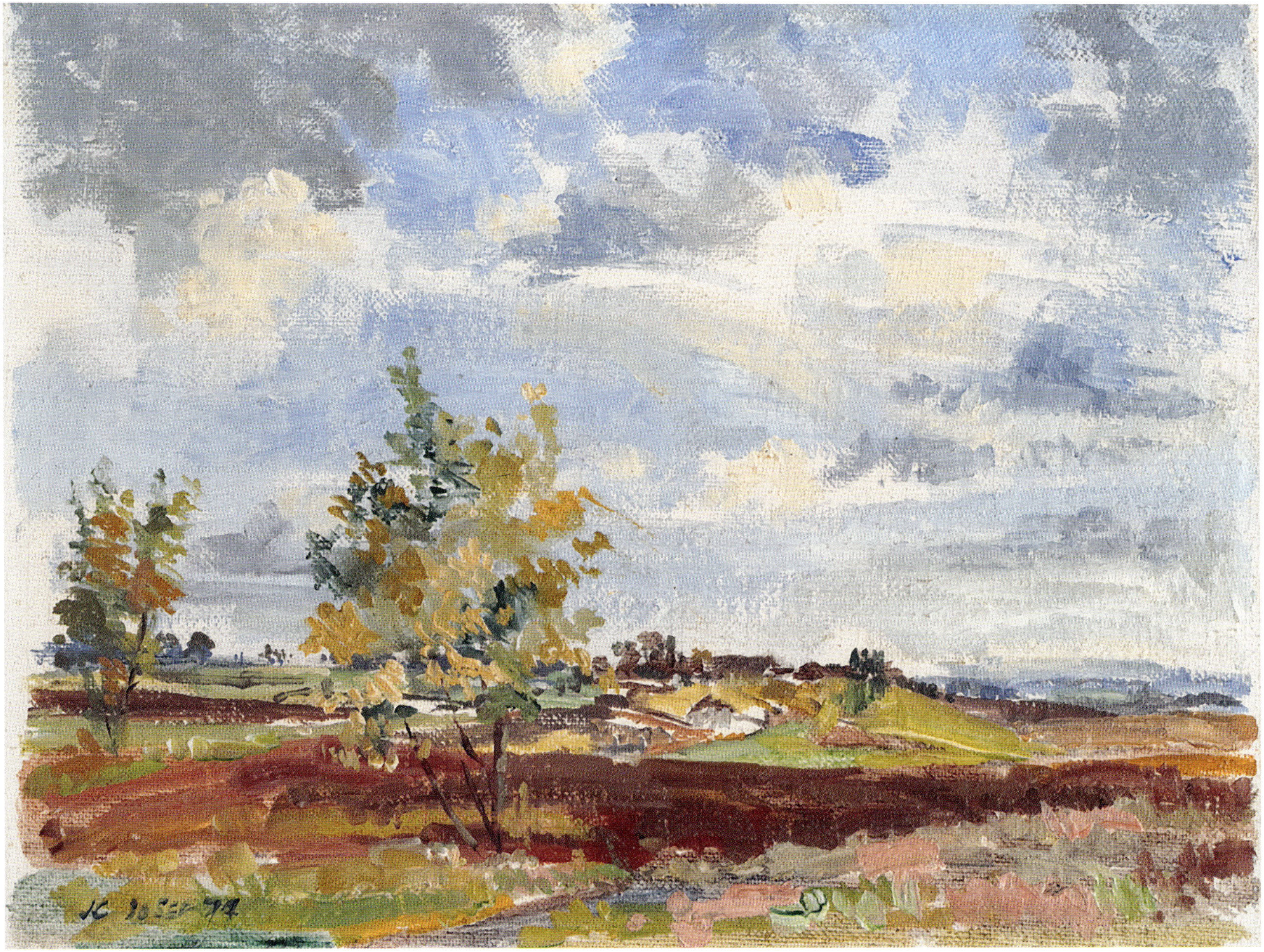

Sunlit landscape.
Oil 29x21cm

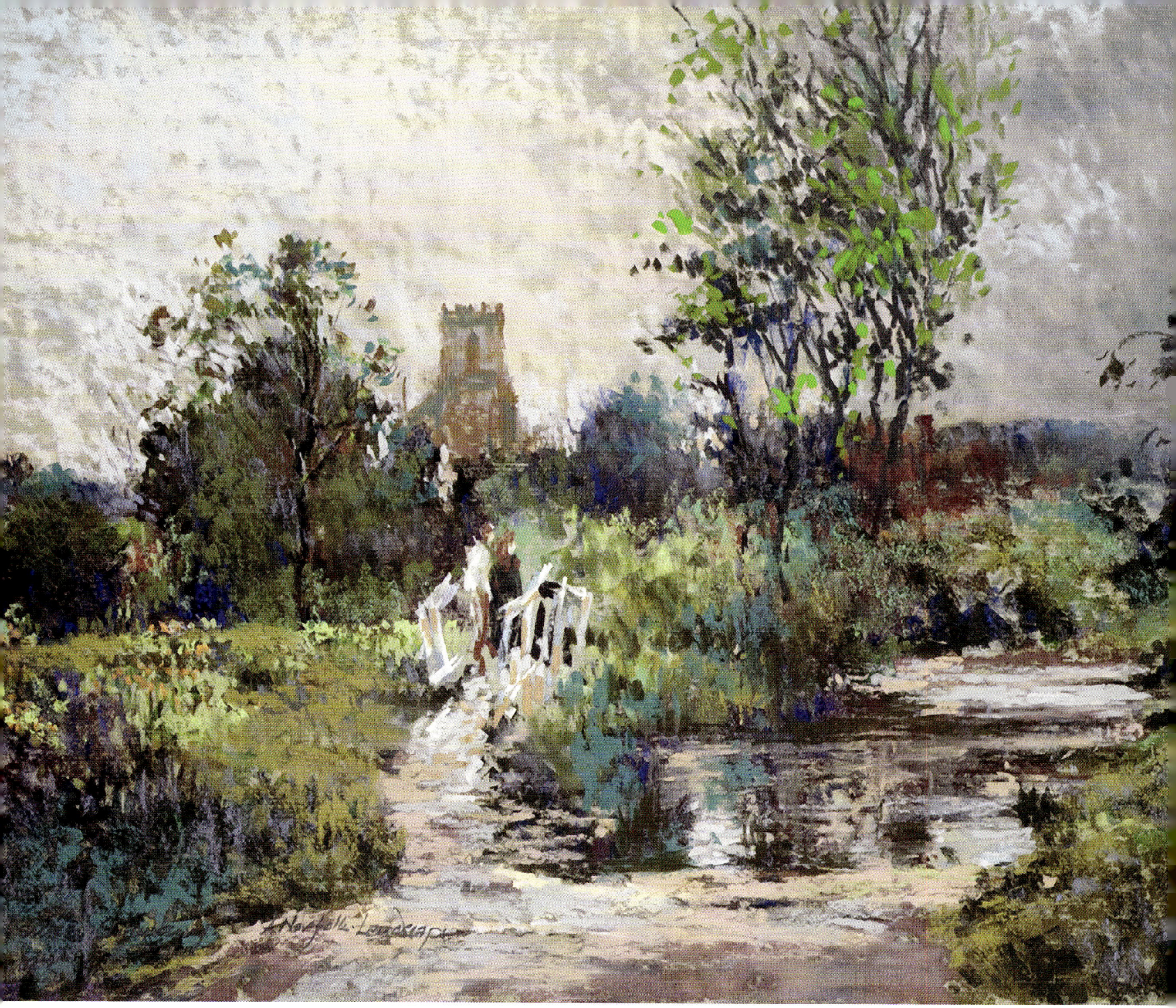
A Norfolk Landscape

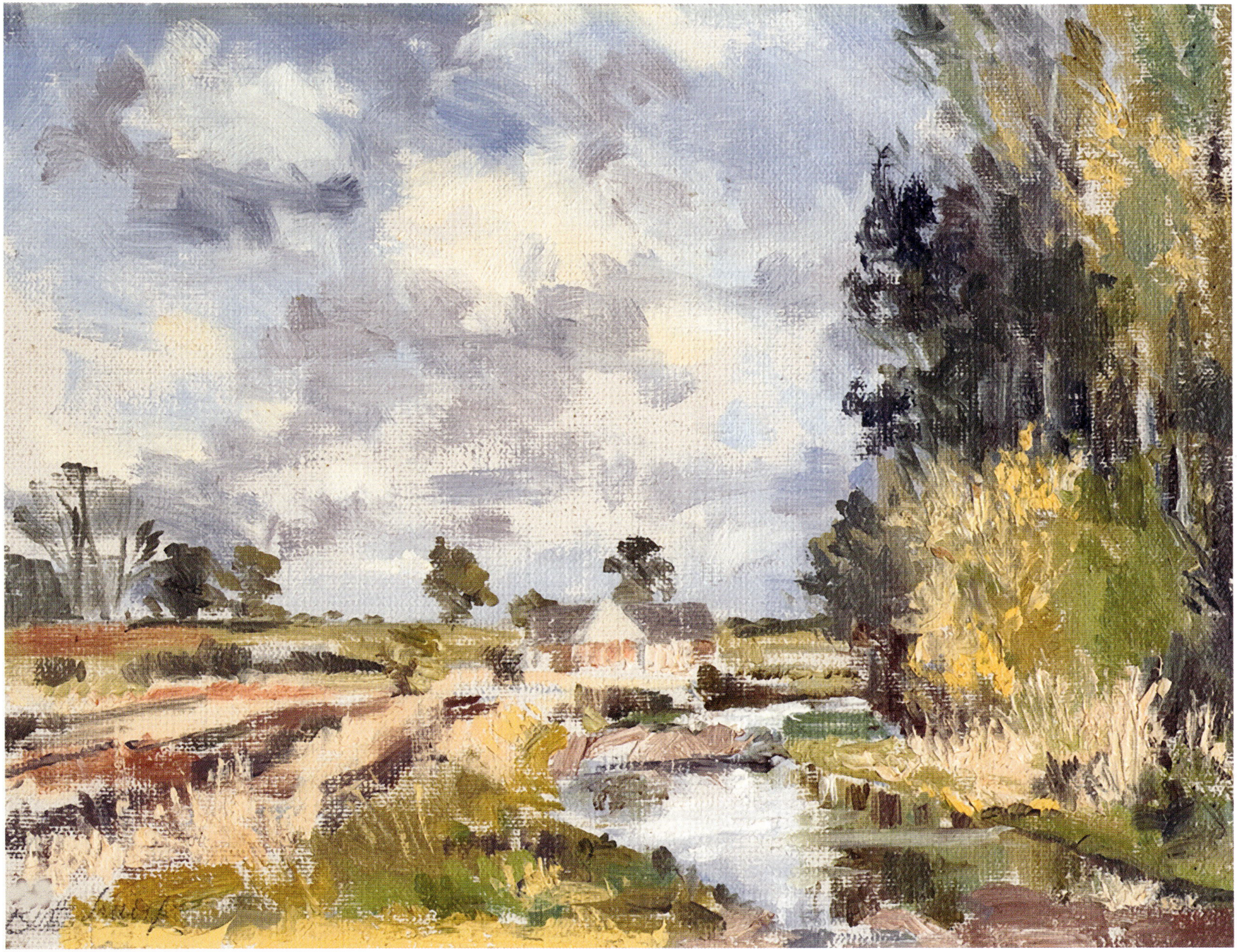

Opposite: A Norfolk Landscape.
Oil 34x26cm

Buttsbury, Essex.
Oil 28x21cm

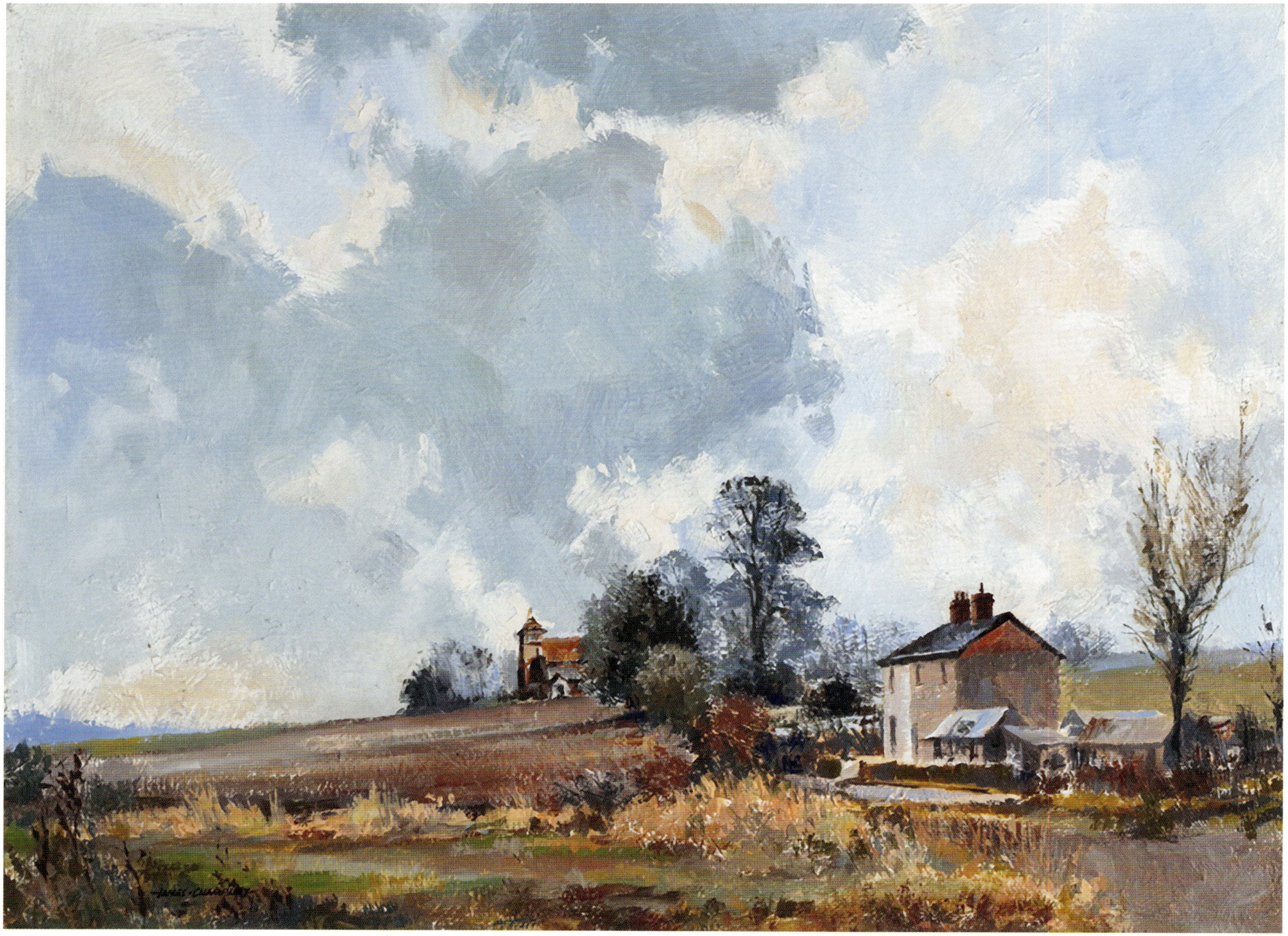

Buttsbury Church, Essex.
Oil 58x43cm

Opposite: Morning Snow on the Deben, Suffolk.
Oil 60x50cm

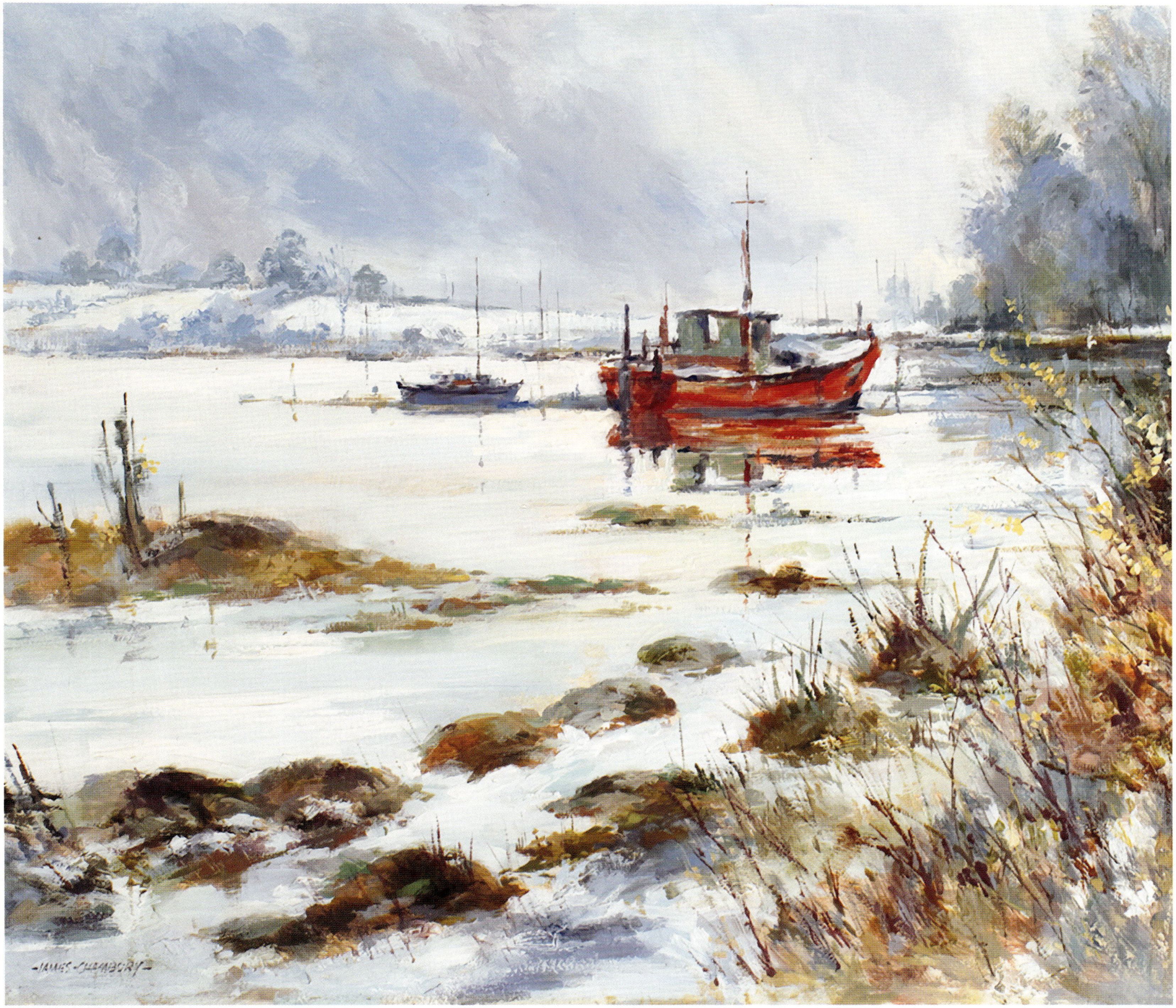
JAMES CHAMBURY

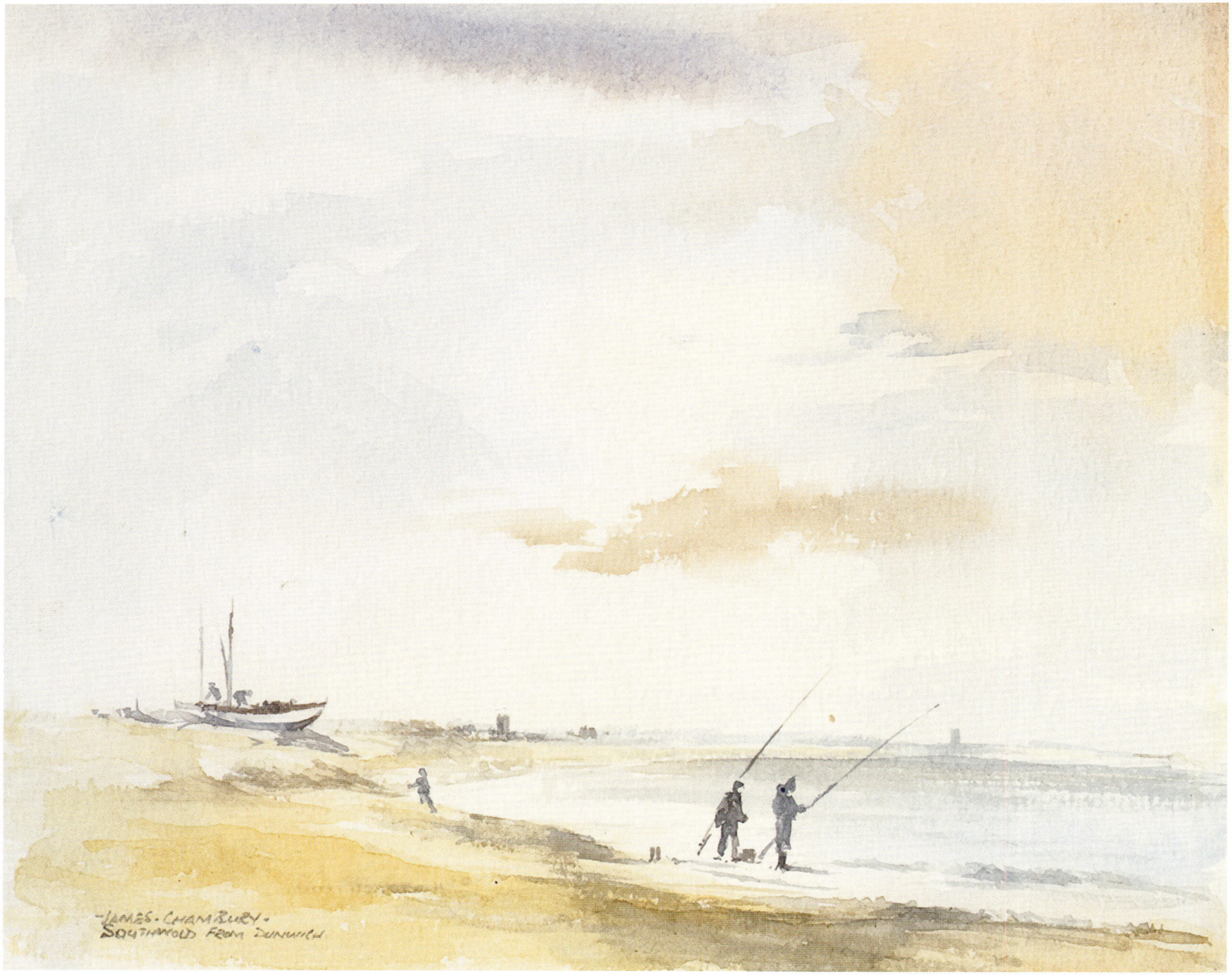

Southwold from Dunwich, Suffolk.
Watercolour

Opposite: The Sluice Gate Brancaster Staithe, Norfolk.
Pastel 37x28cm

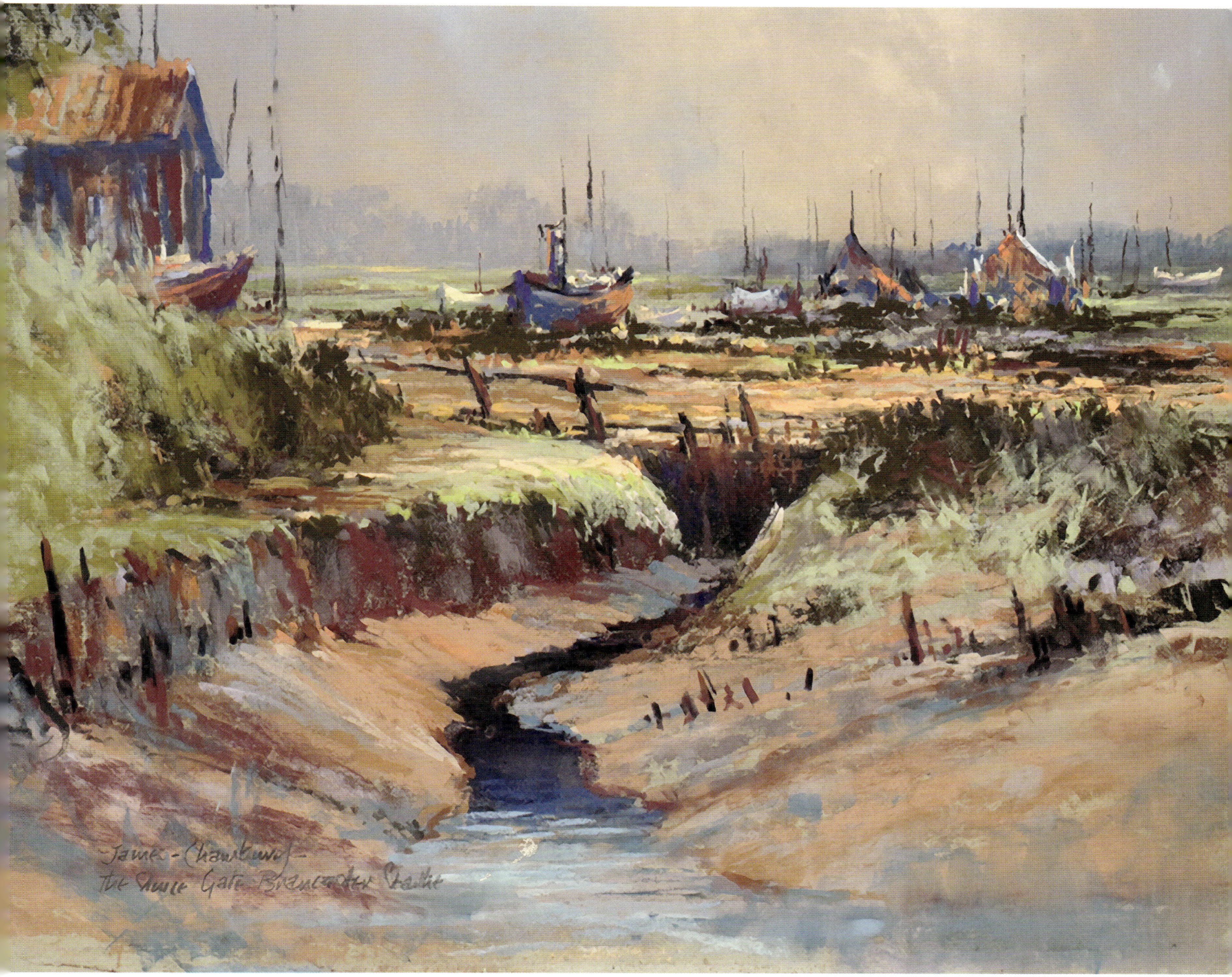

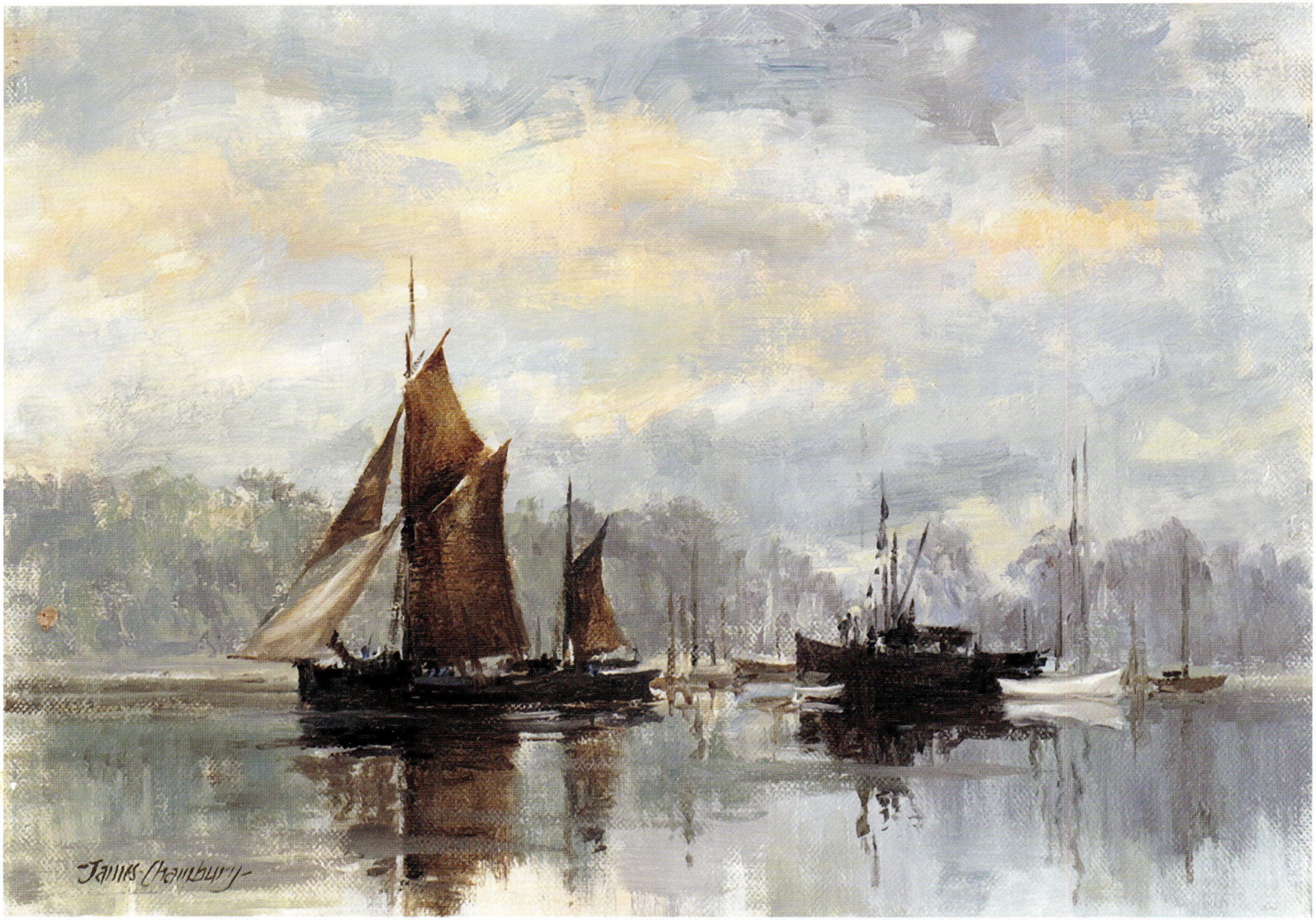

Boats on the River Orwell.
Oil 35x25cm

Opposite: Wells-next-the-Sea, Norfolk.
Watercolour

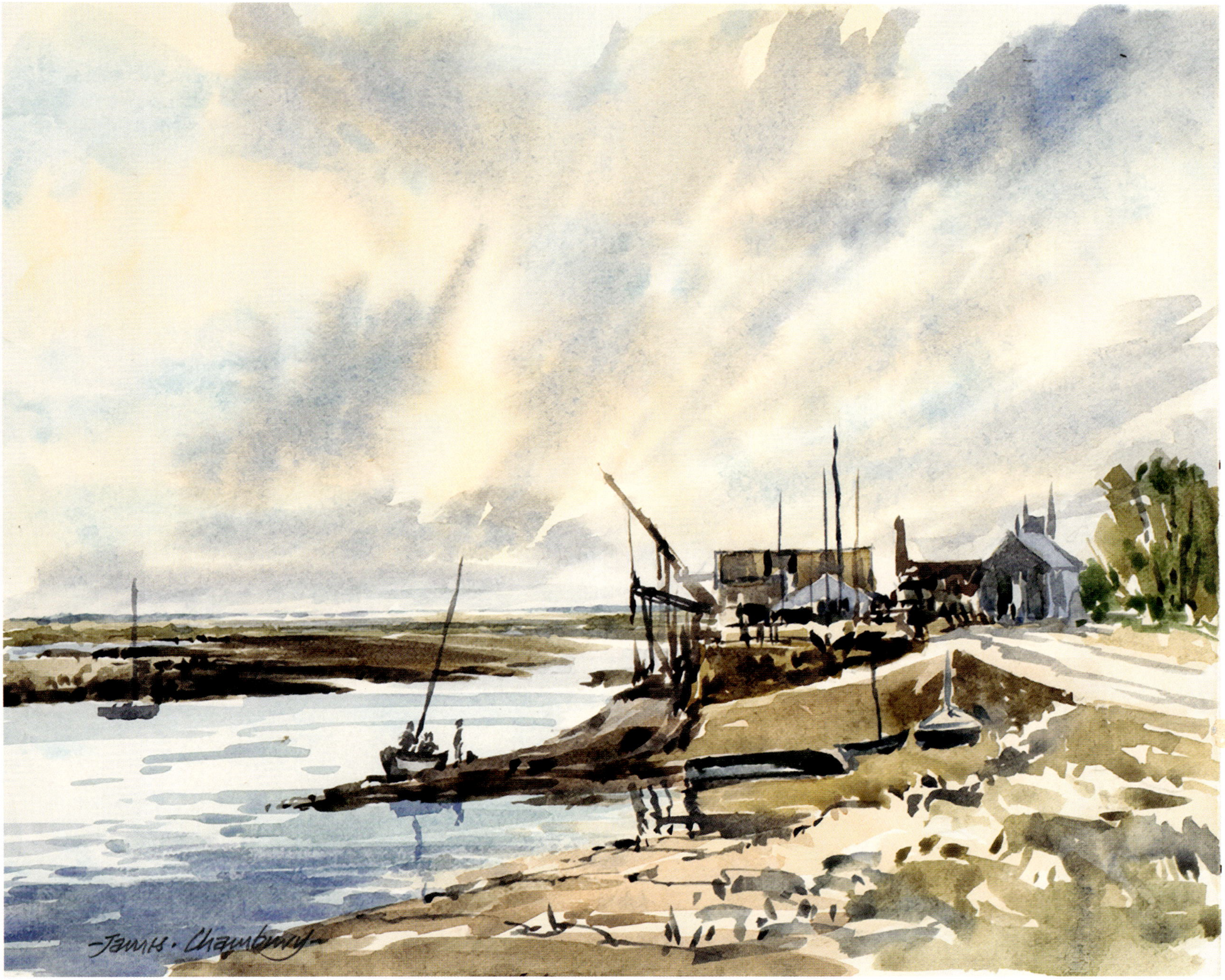
James · Chambury

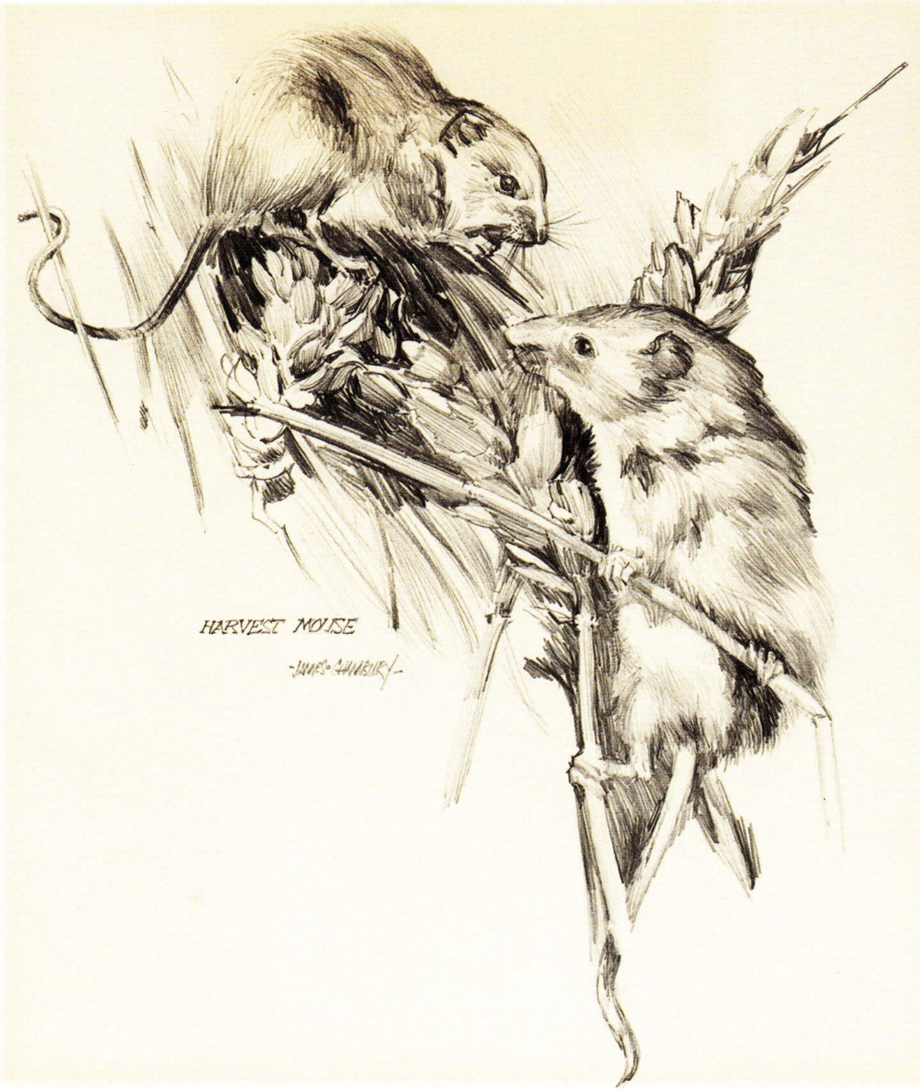
HARVEST MOUSE
-JAMES CHAMBURY-

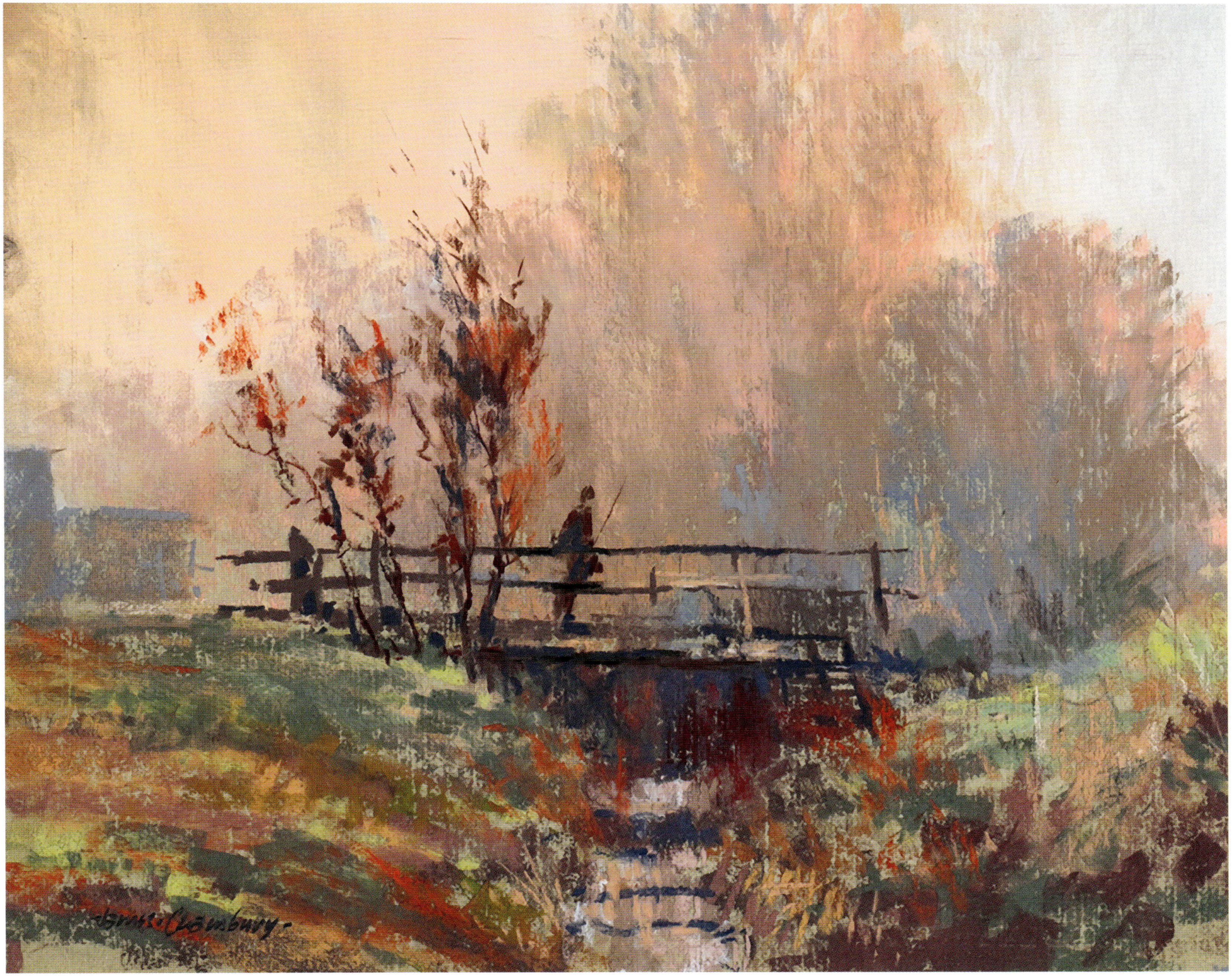

Opposite: Harvest Mice.
Pencil sketch

Hadleigh, Suffolk.
Pastel 24x20cm

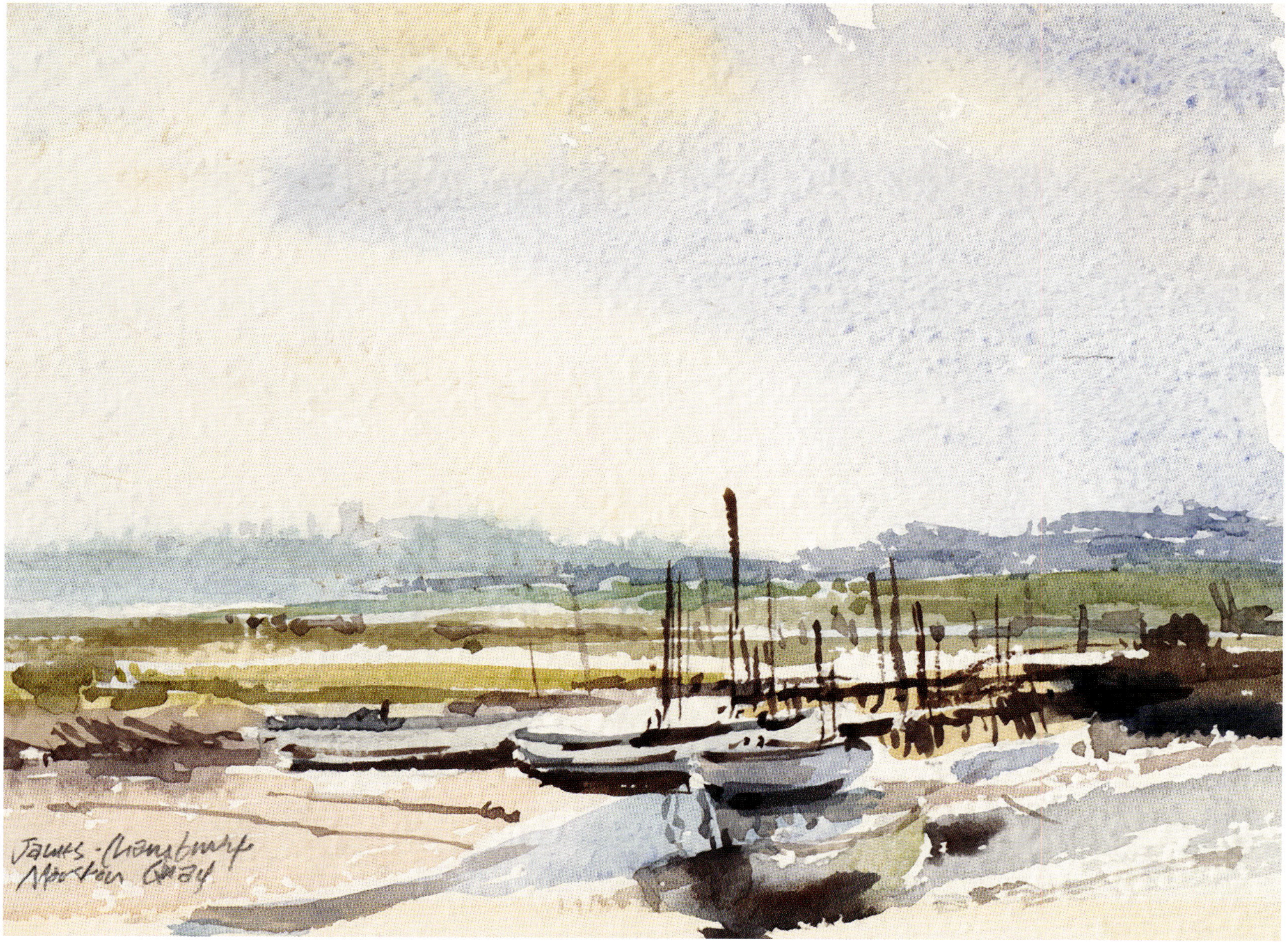

Morston Quay, Norfolk.
Watercolour

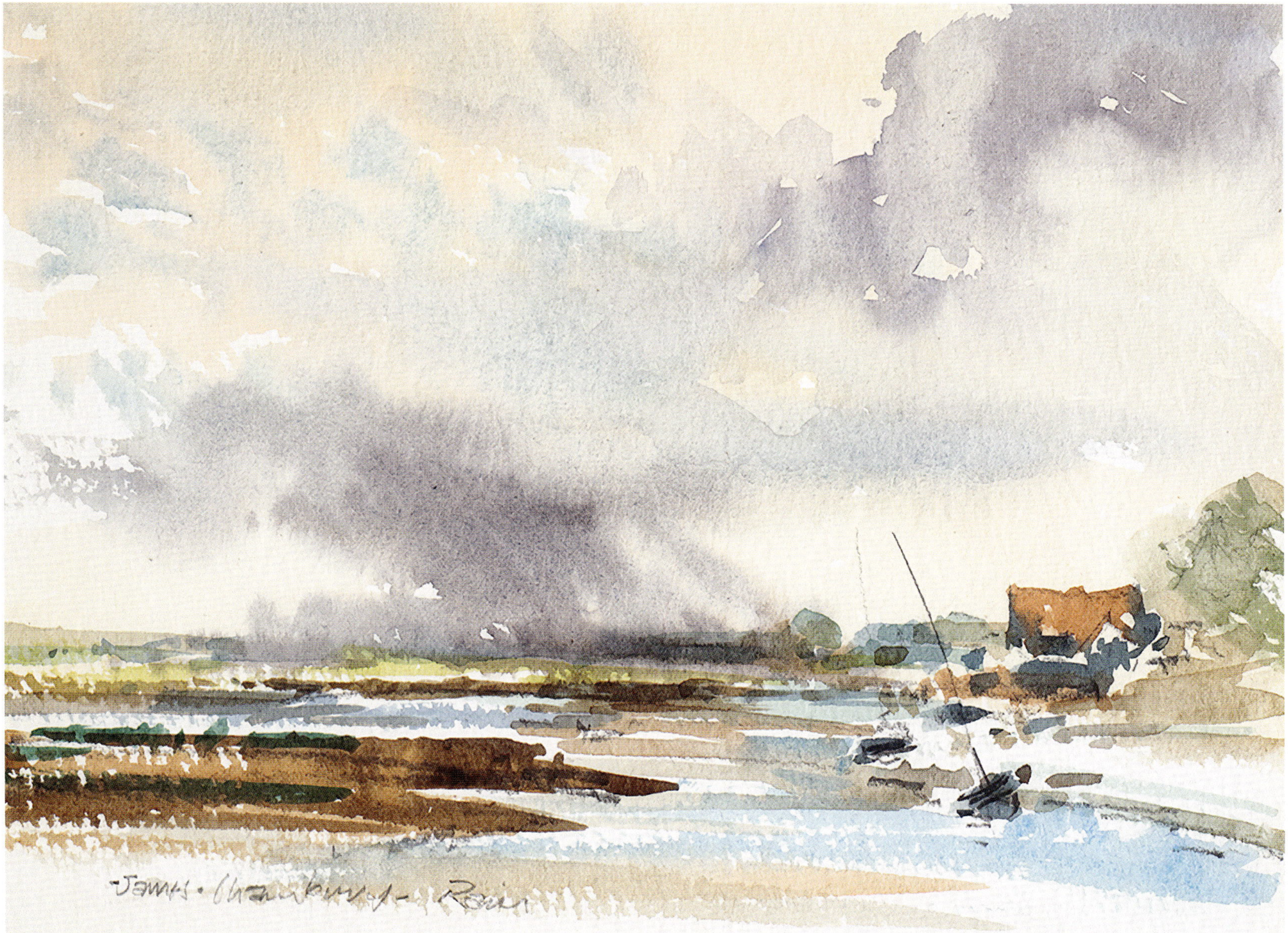

Rain, Norfolk.
Watercolour

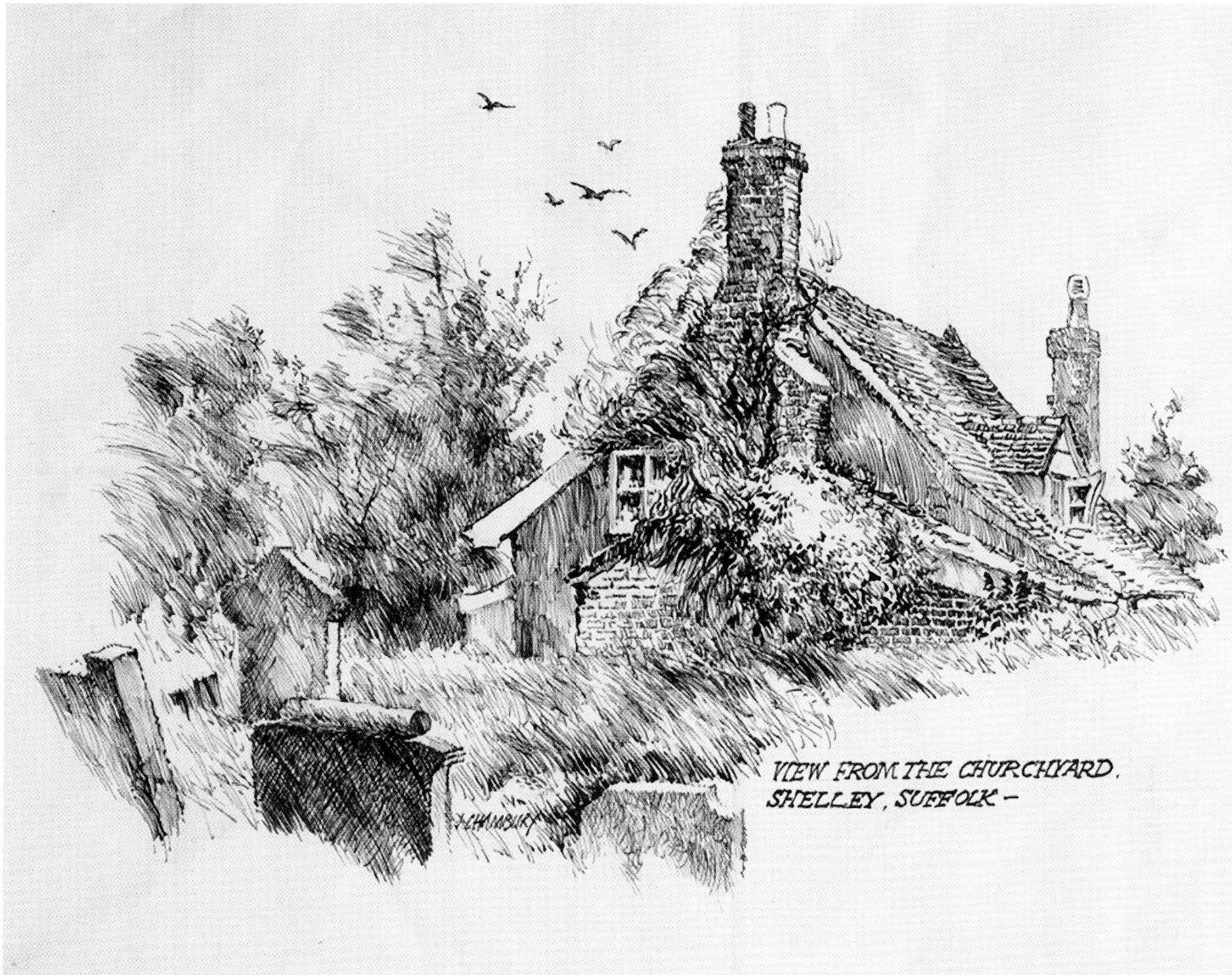

View from the Churchyard, Shelley, Suffolk.
Pen and ink 22x19cm

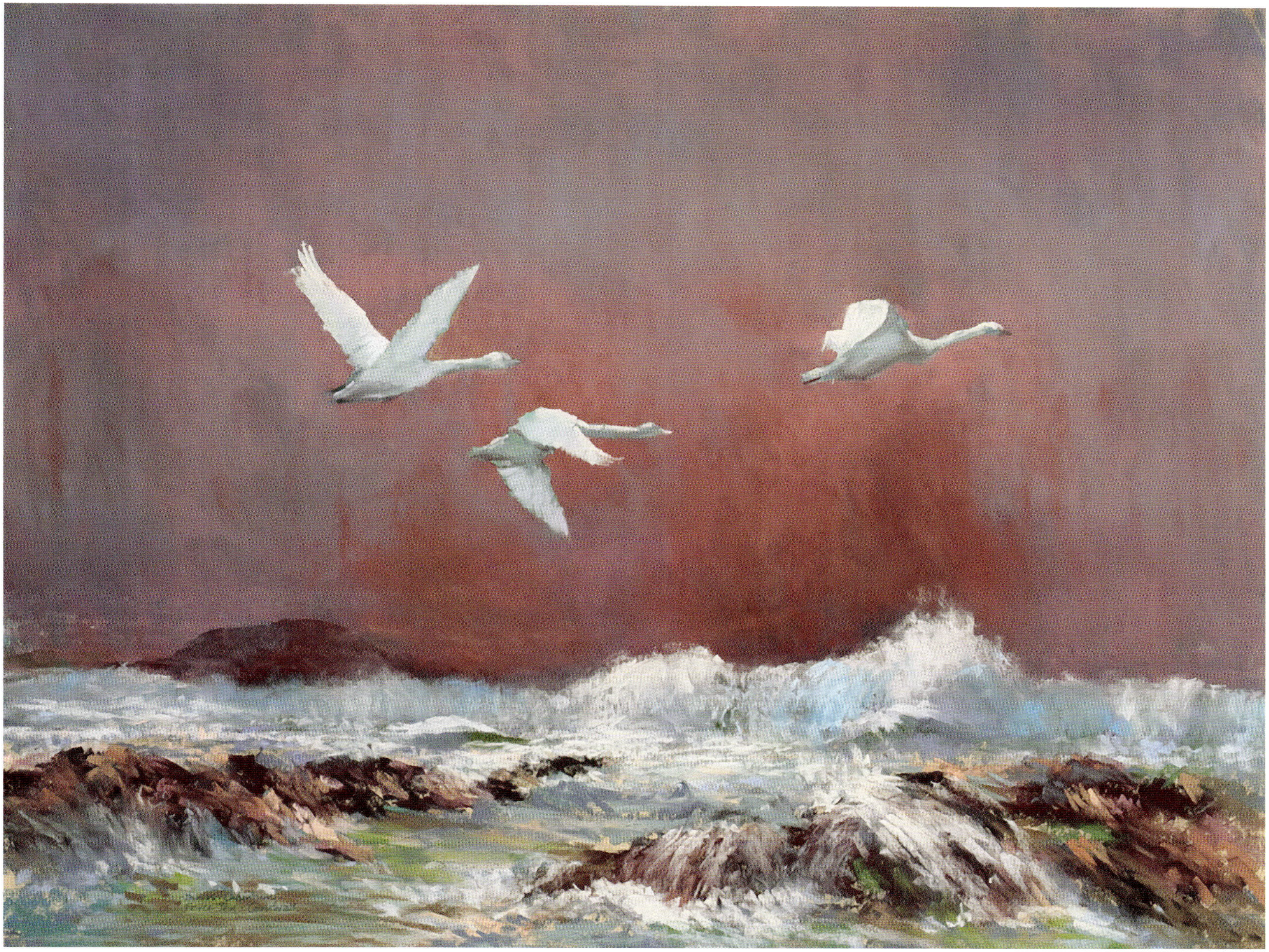

Force Ten, Cornwall.
Pastel 52x38cm

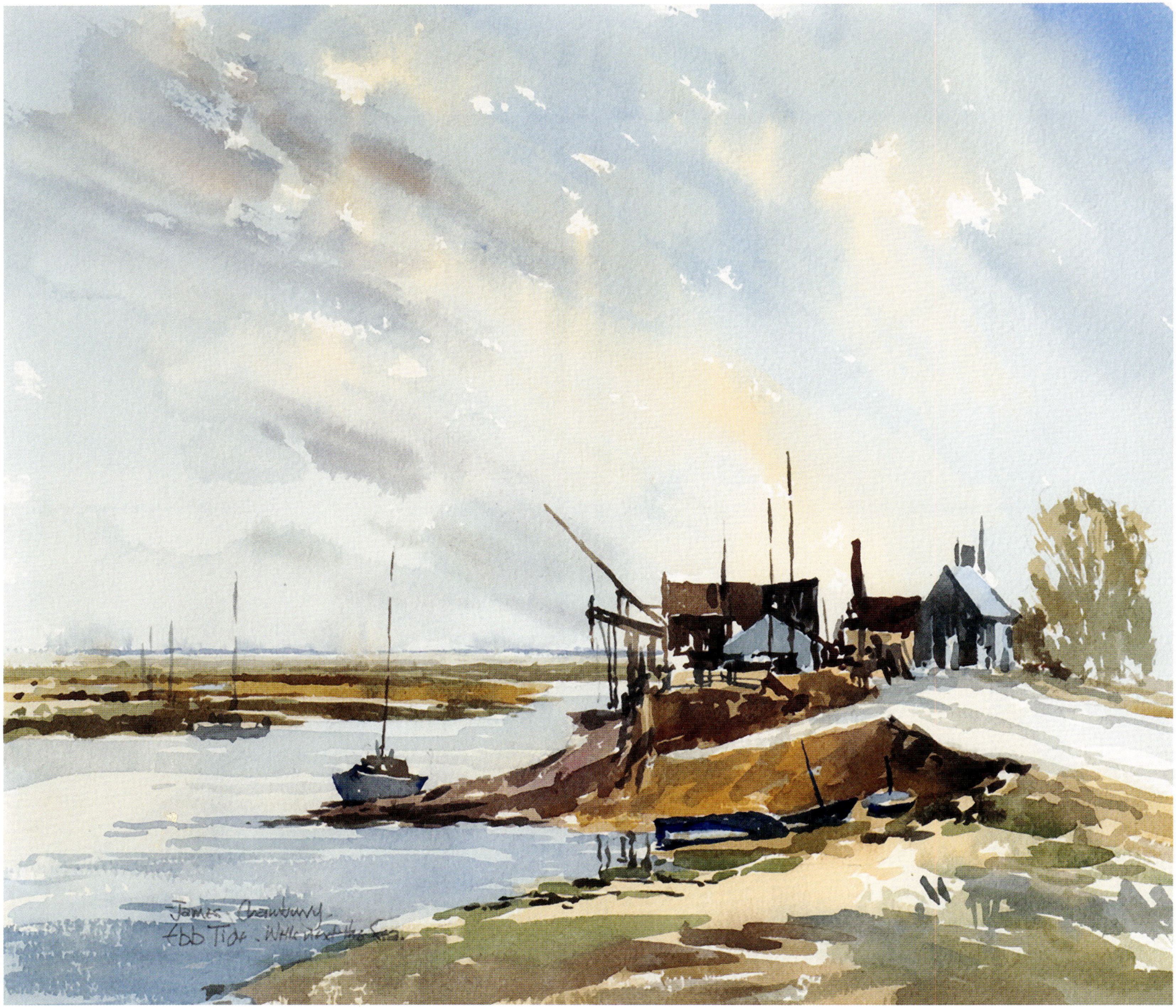
James Chambury
Ebb Tide

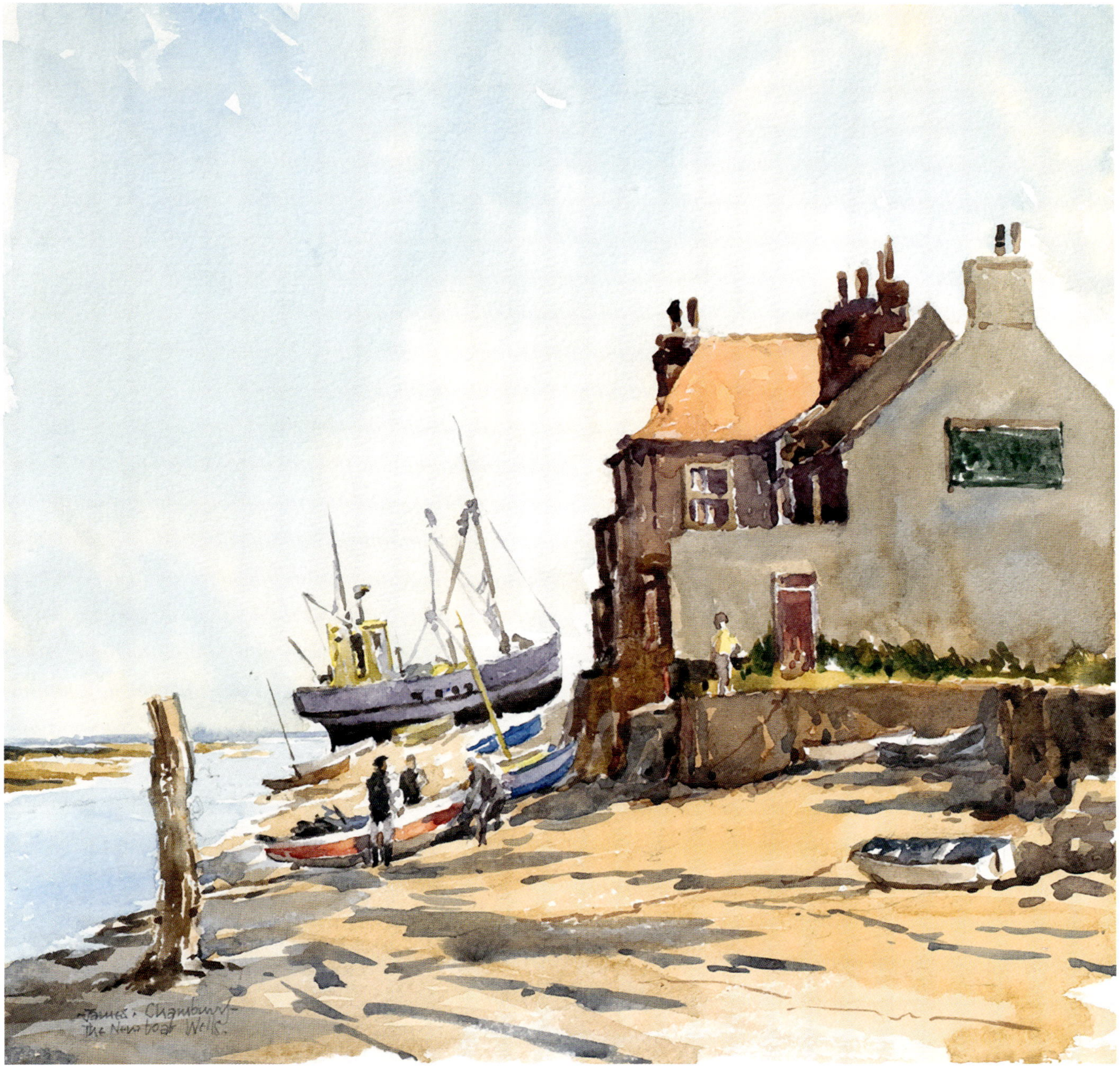

Opposite: Ebb Tide, Wells-next-the-Sea, Norfolk. Watercolour 26x23cm

The New Boat, Wells-next-the-Sea, Norfolk. Watercolour 26x22cm

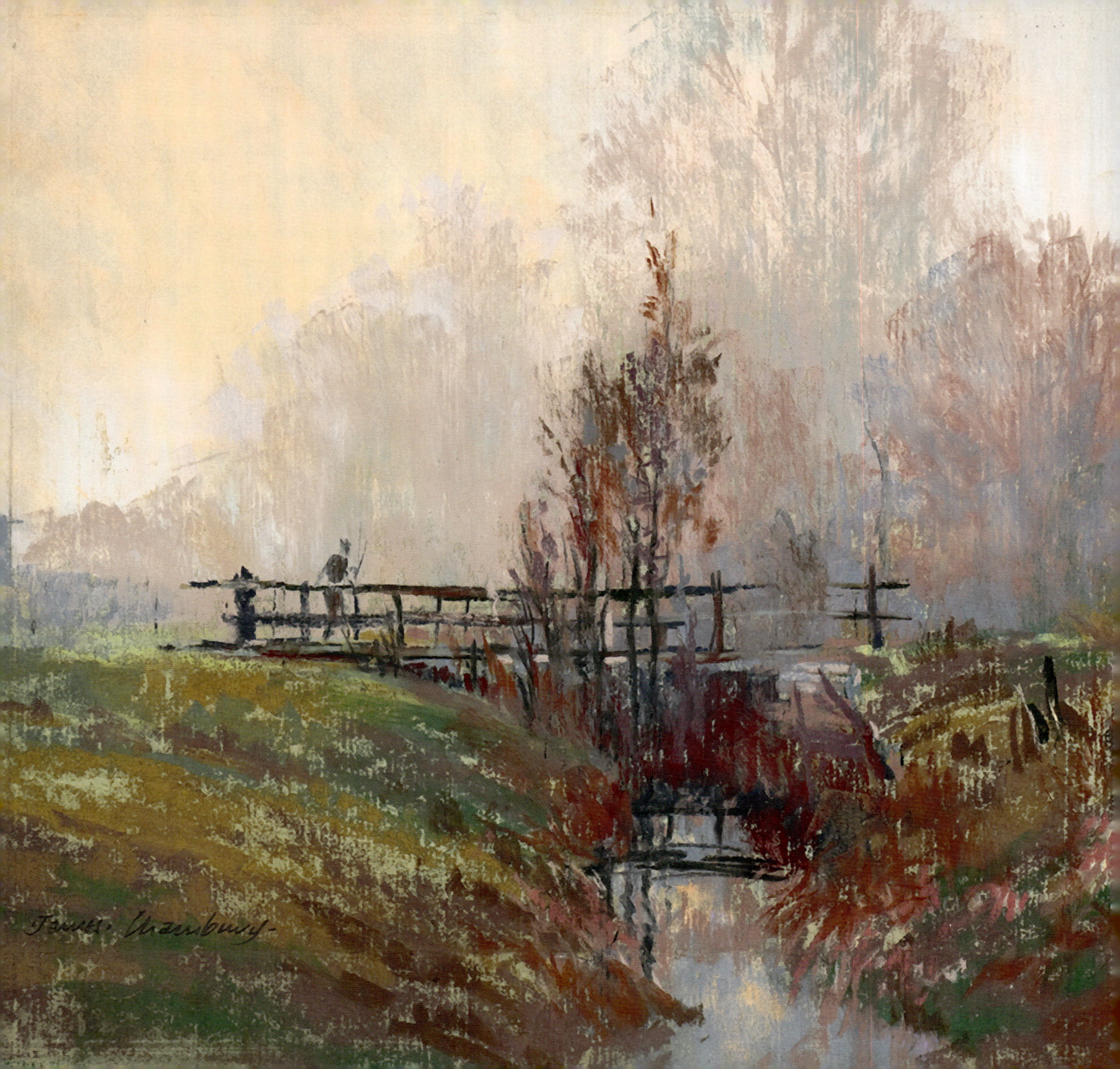

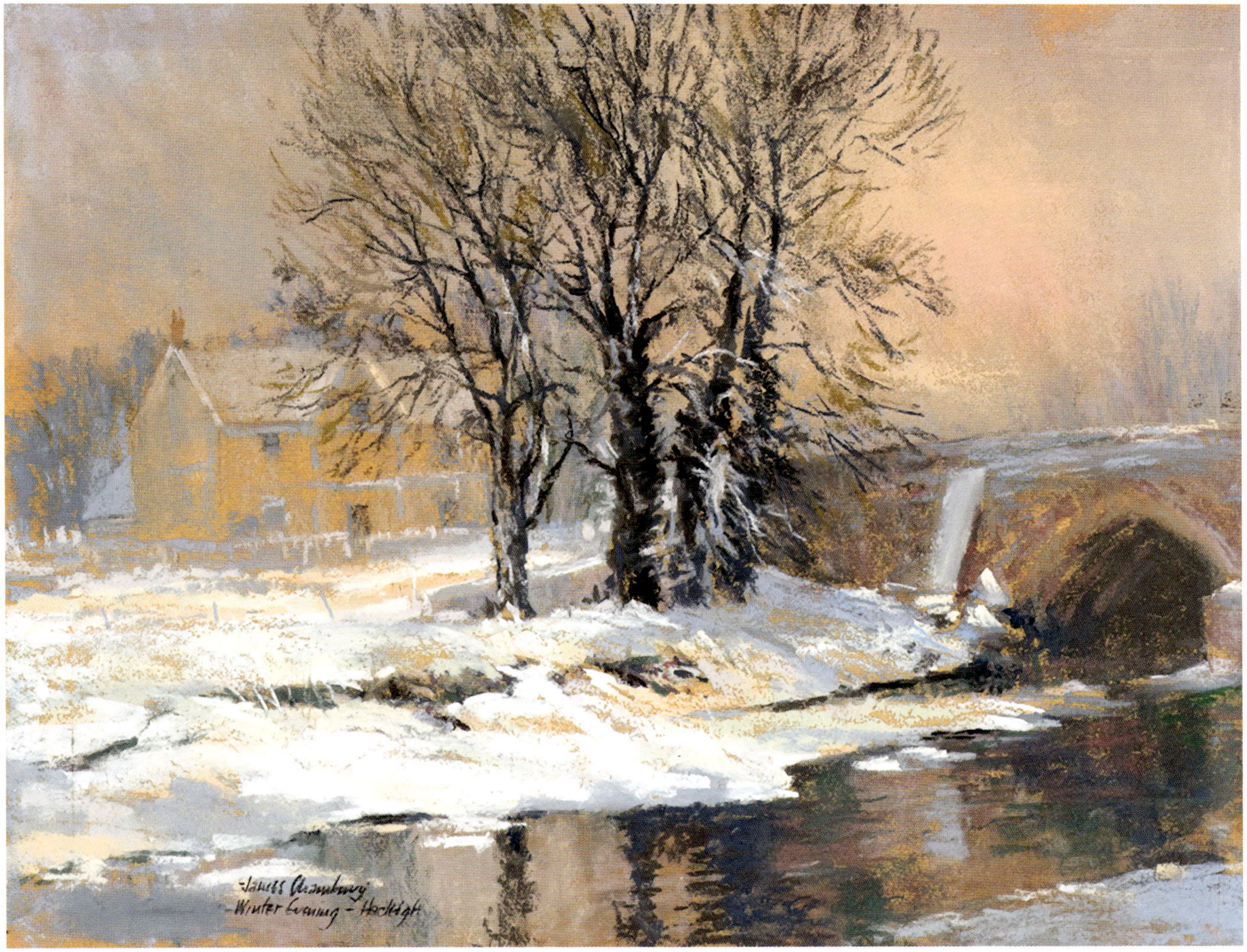

Opposite: Misty Morning by the Footbridge, Hadleigh. Watercolour 26x23cm

Winter Evening, Hadleigh, Suffolk. Pastel

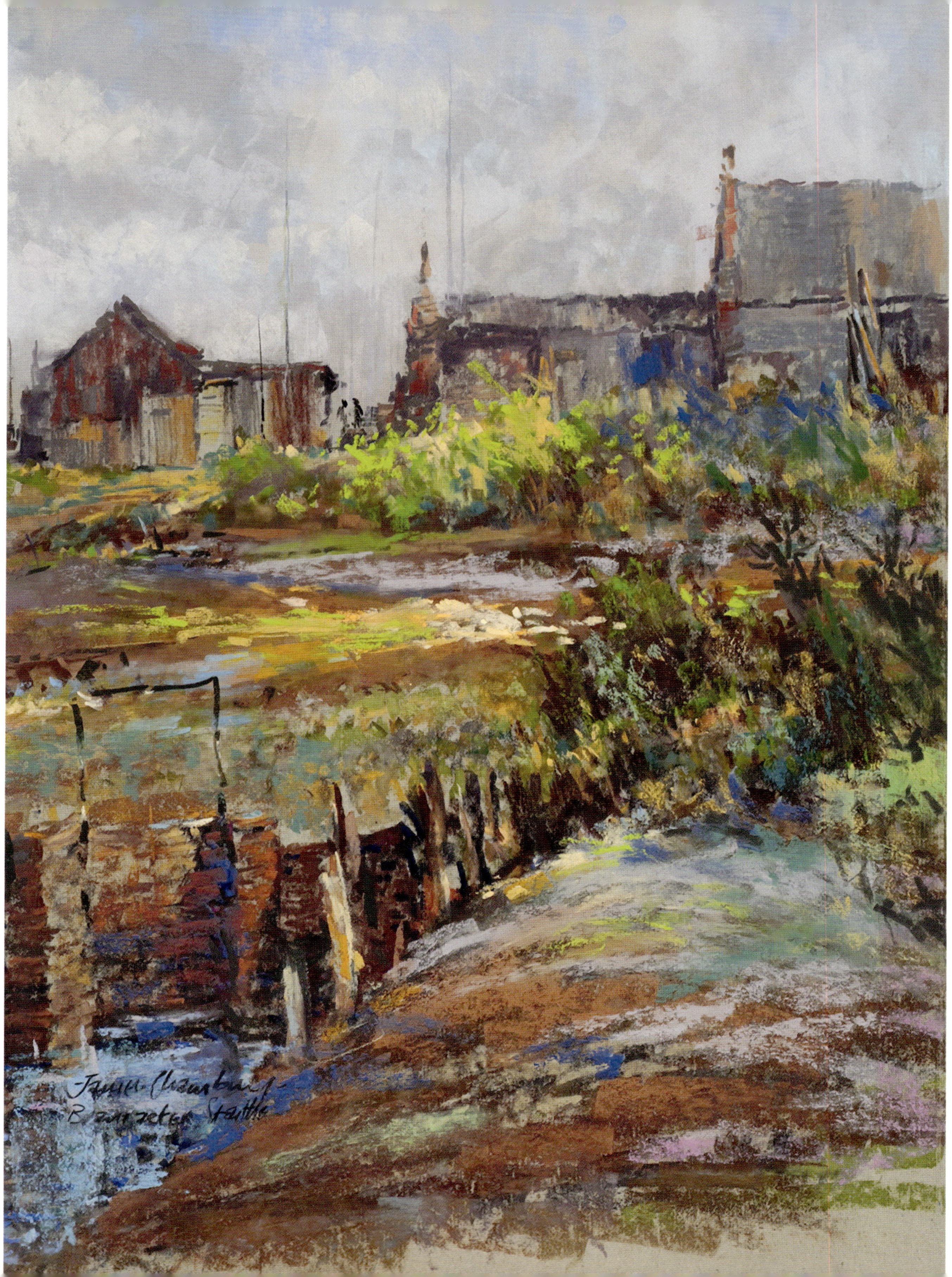

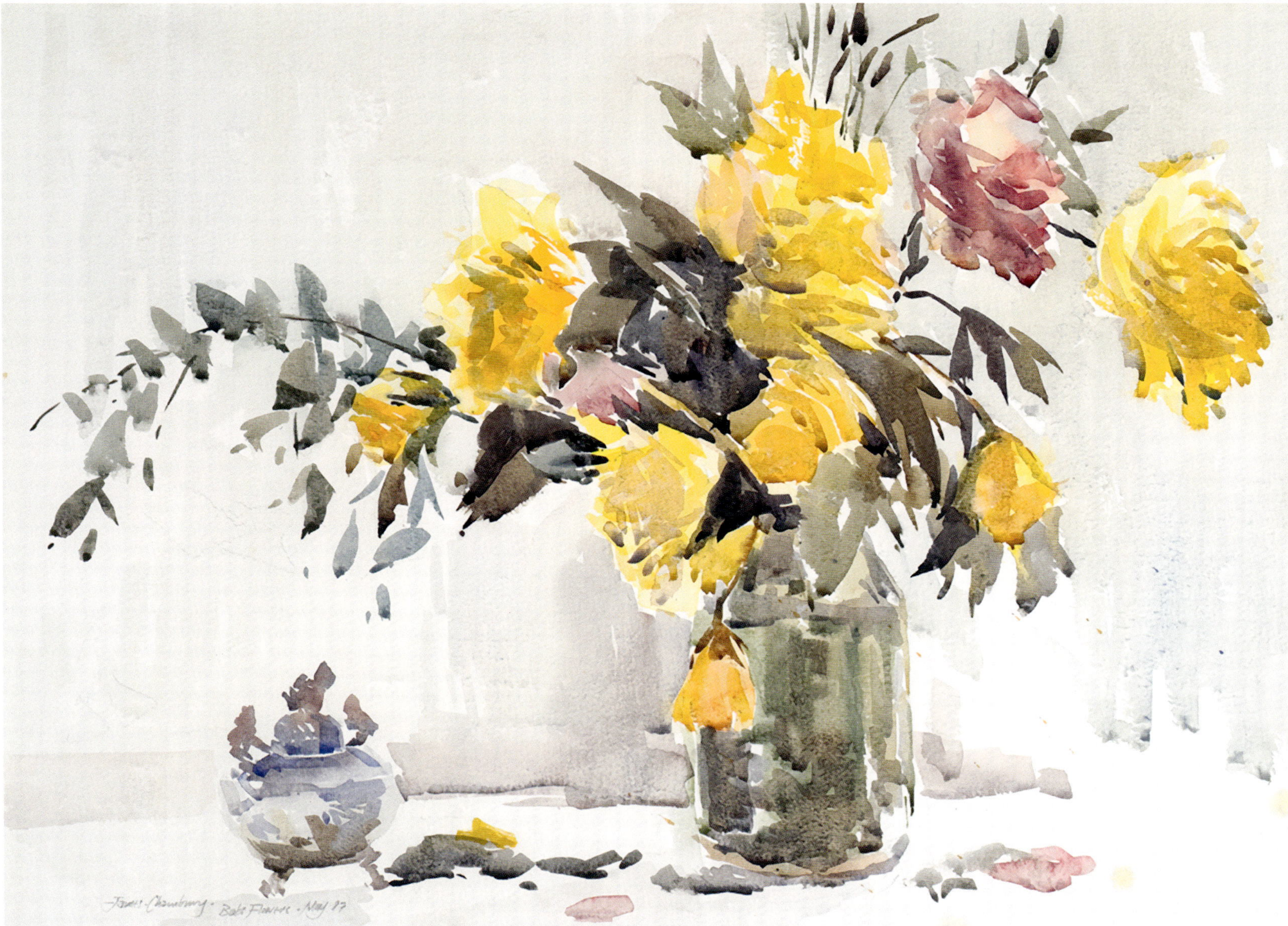

Opposite: Brancaster Staithe, Norfolk.
Pastel

Babs' Flowers.
Watercolour 53x38cm

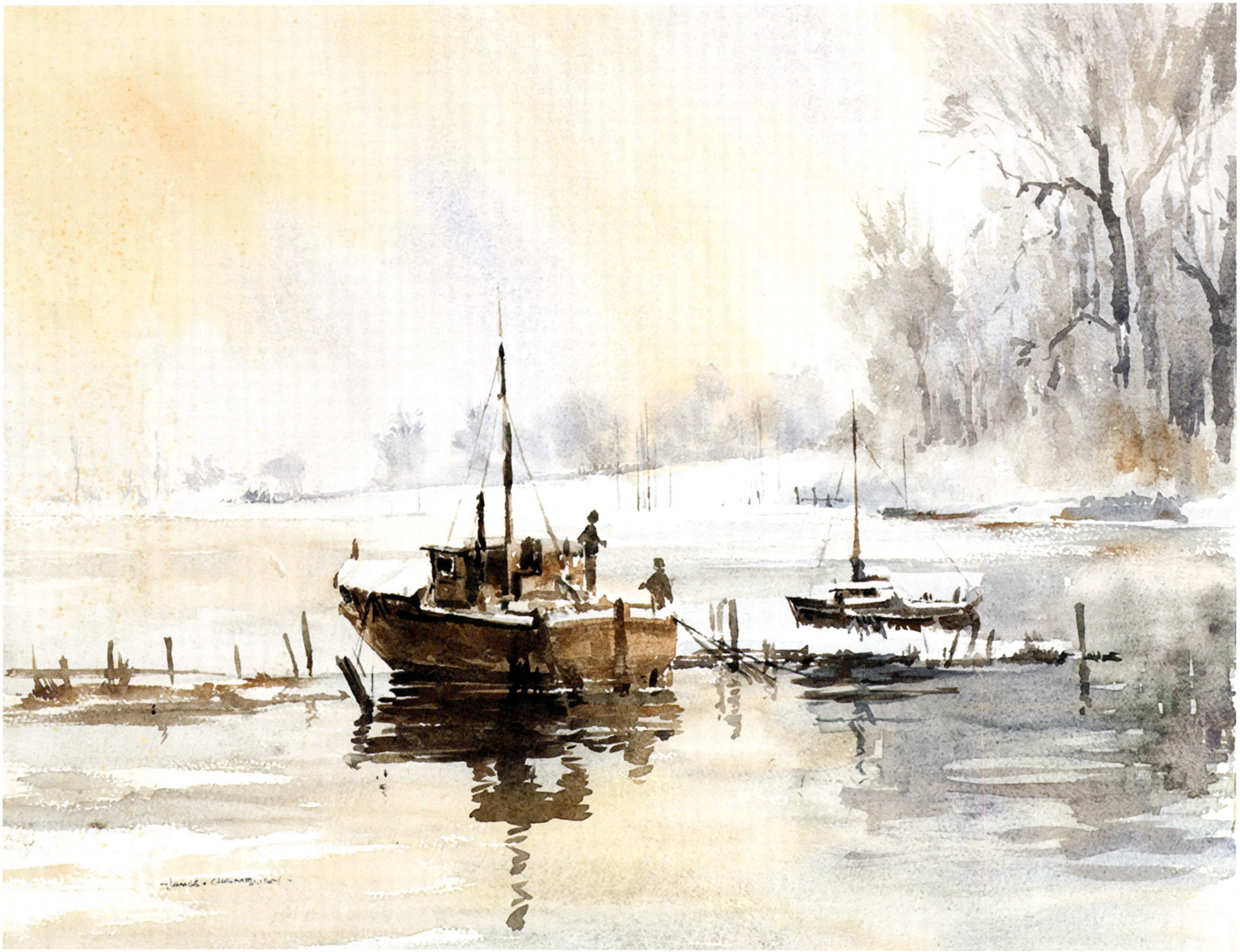

Boats on the River Deben in the Snow.
Watercolour 50x43cm

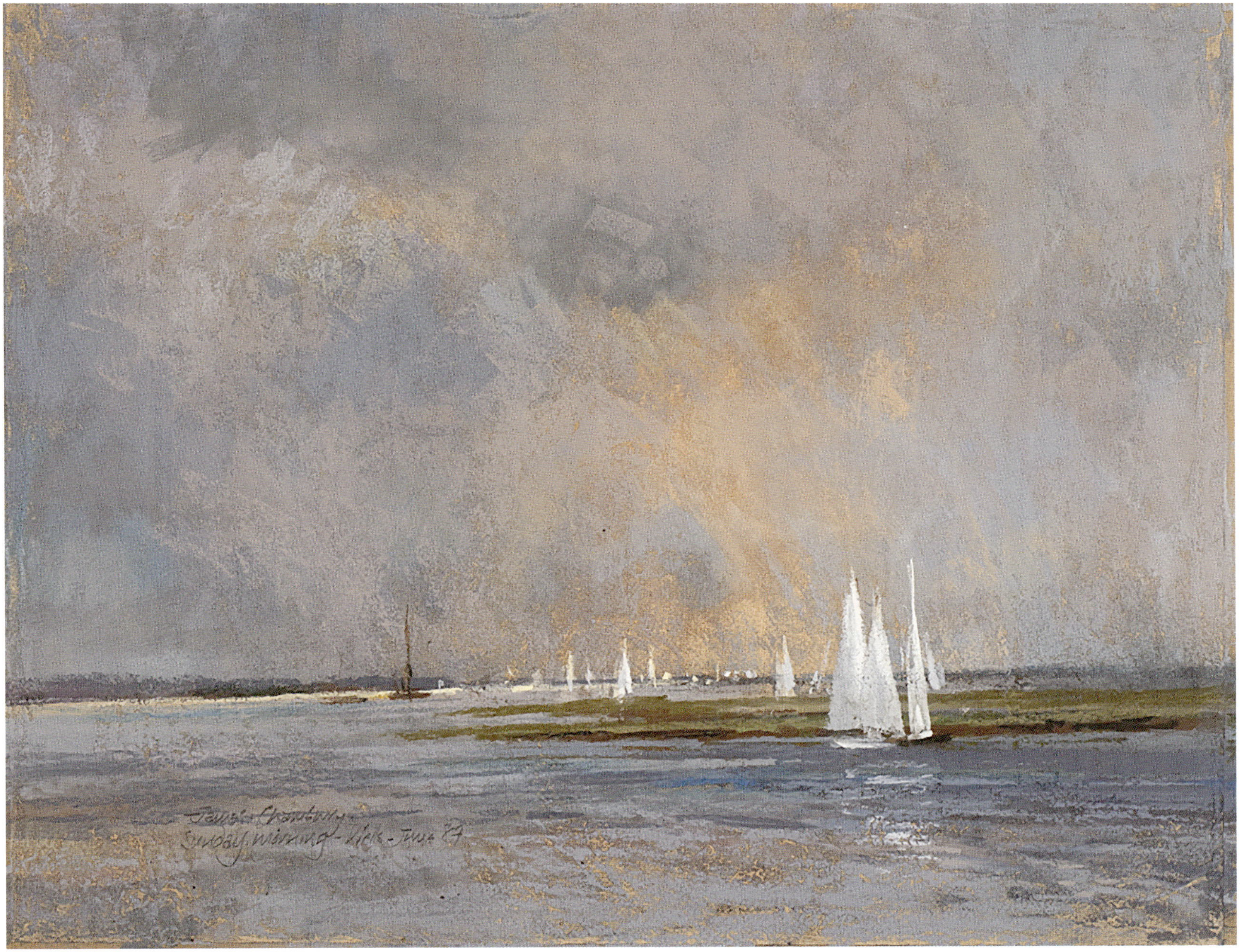

Sunday Morning, Wells.
Pastel 34x2cm

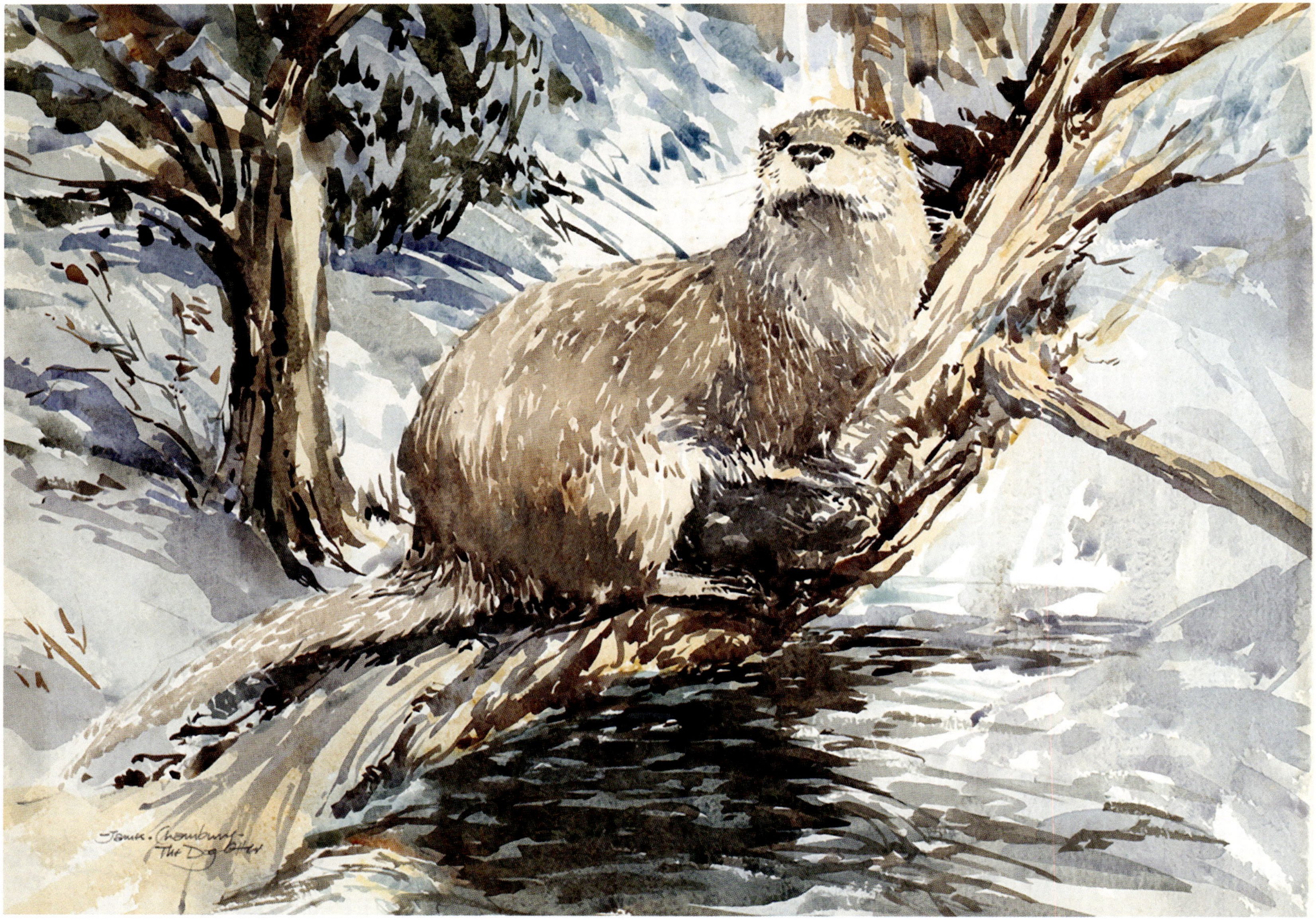

The Dog Otter.
Watercolour

Opposite: Ashness Bridge and Derwentwater.
Pastel 34x27cm

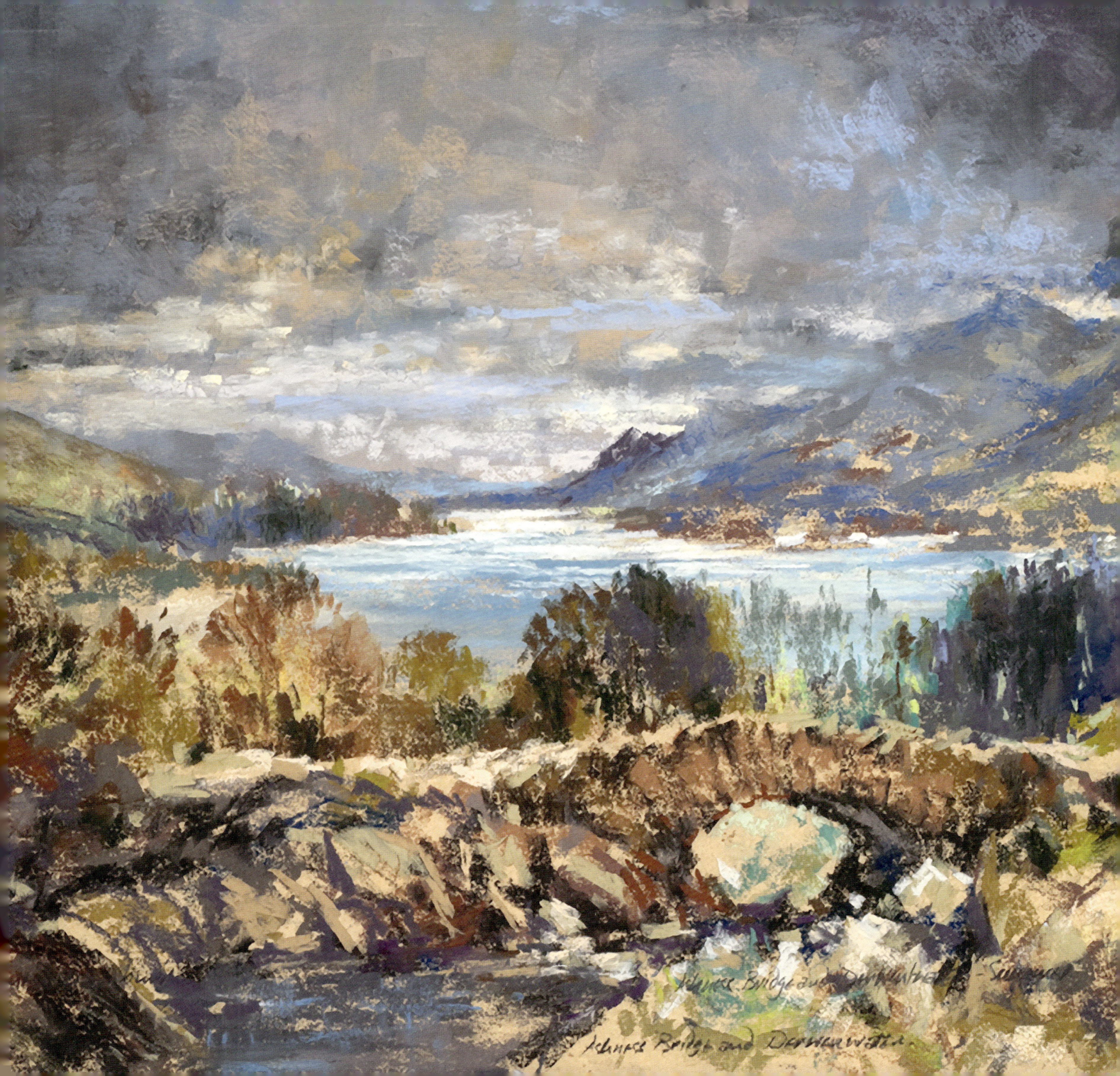
Ashness Bridge and Derwentwater.

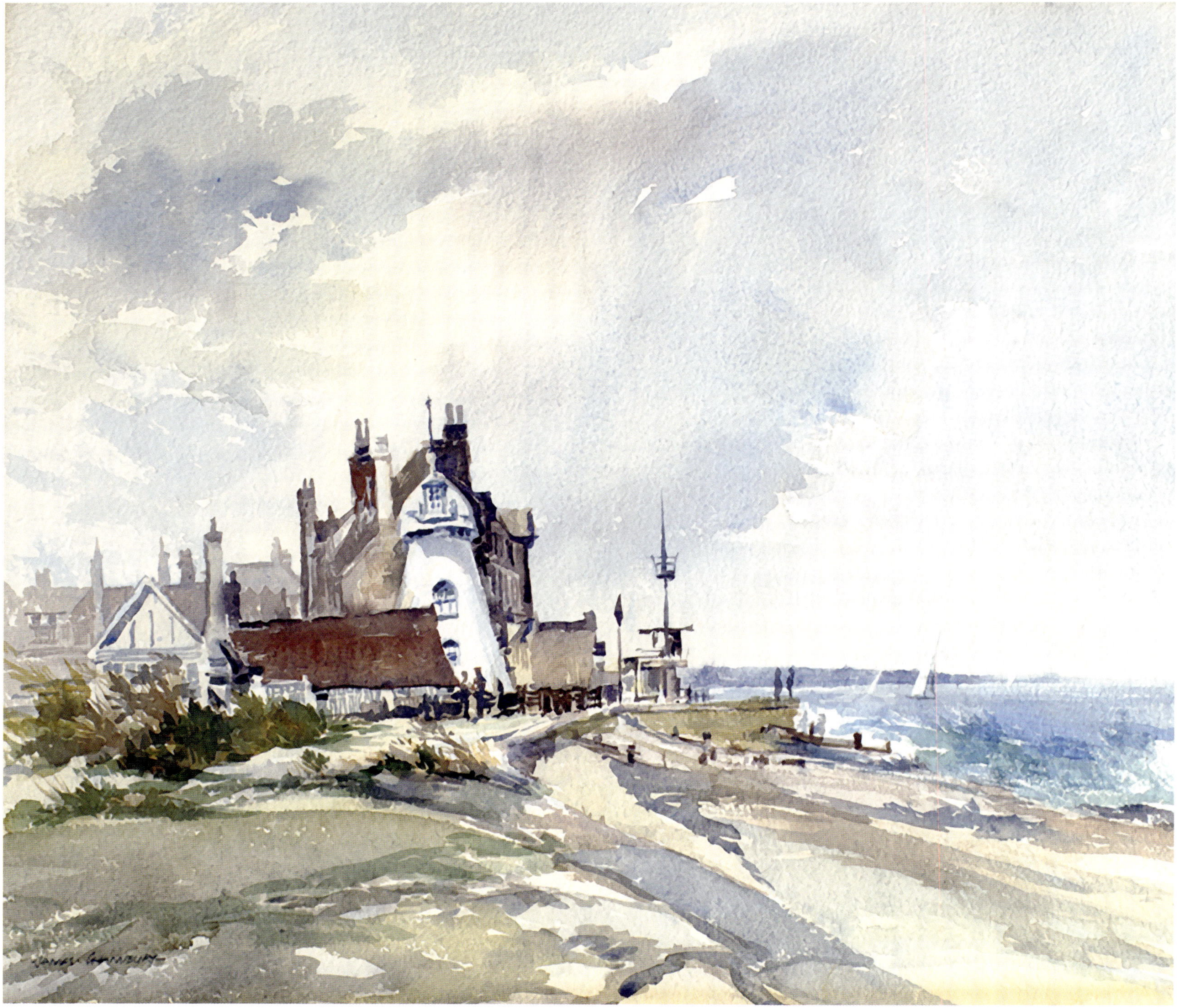

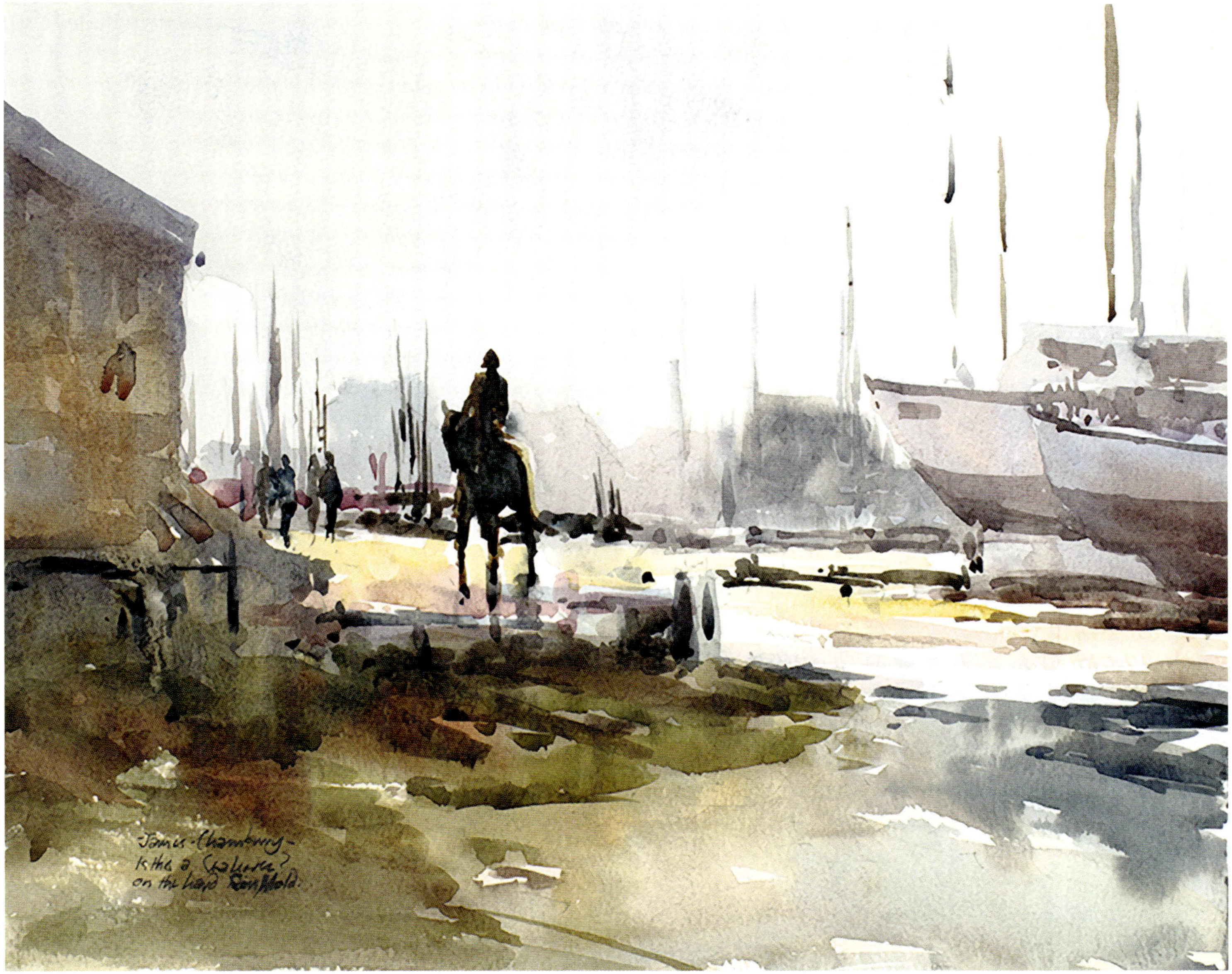

Opposite: Aldeburgh Lighthouse from the Spit.
Watercolour

Is this a seahorse?
Watercolour

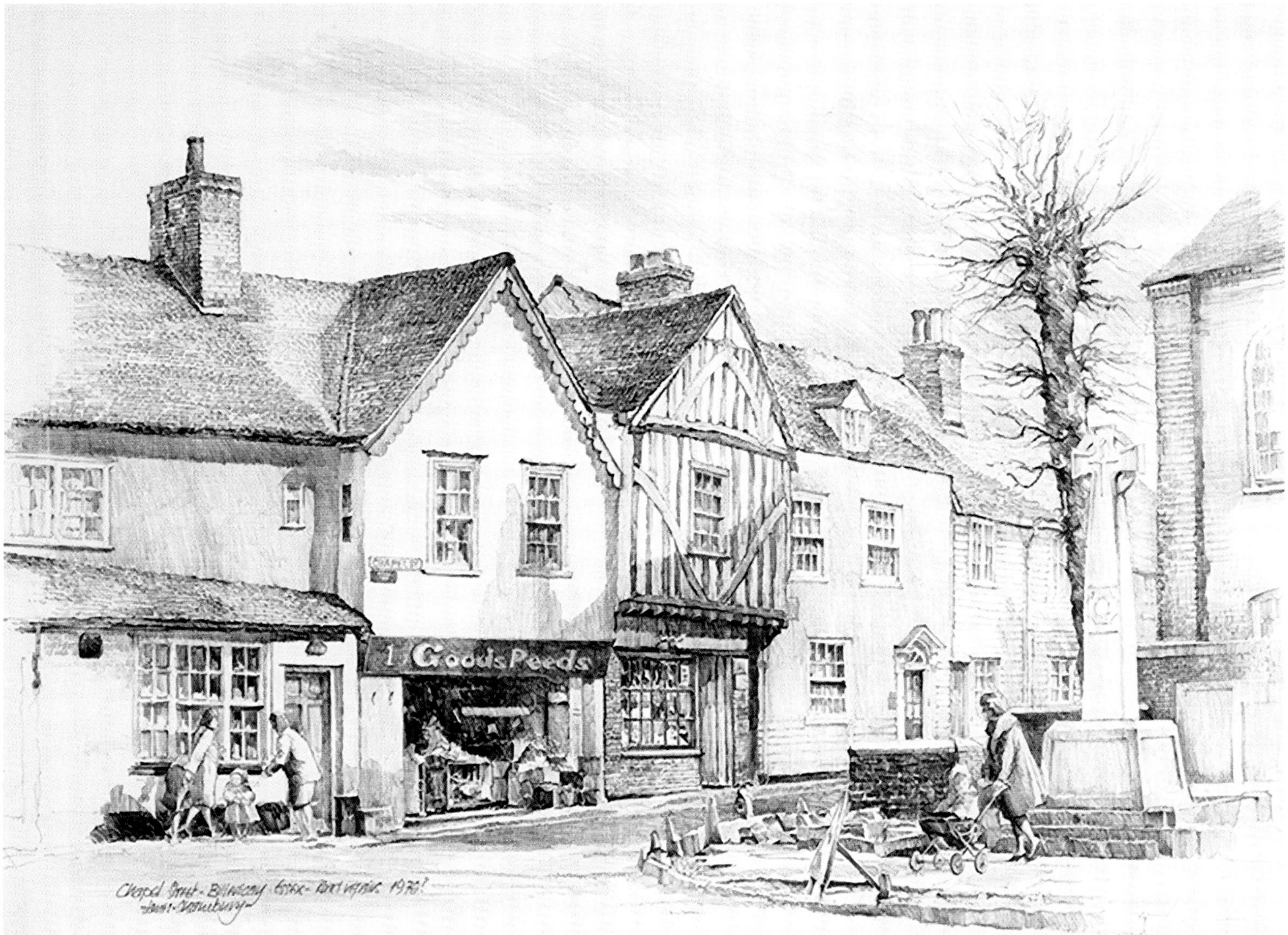

GoodsPeeds, Billericay.
Pencil drawing 38x30cm

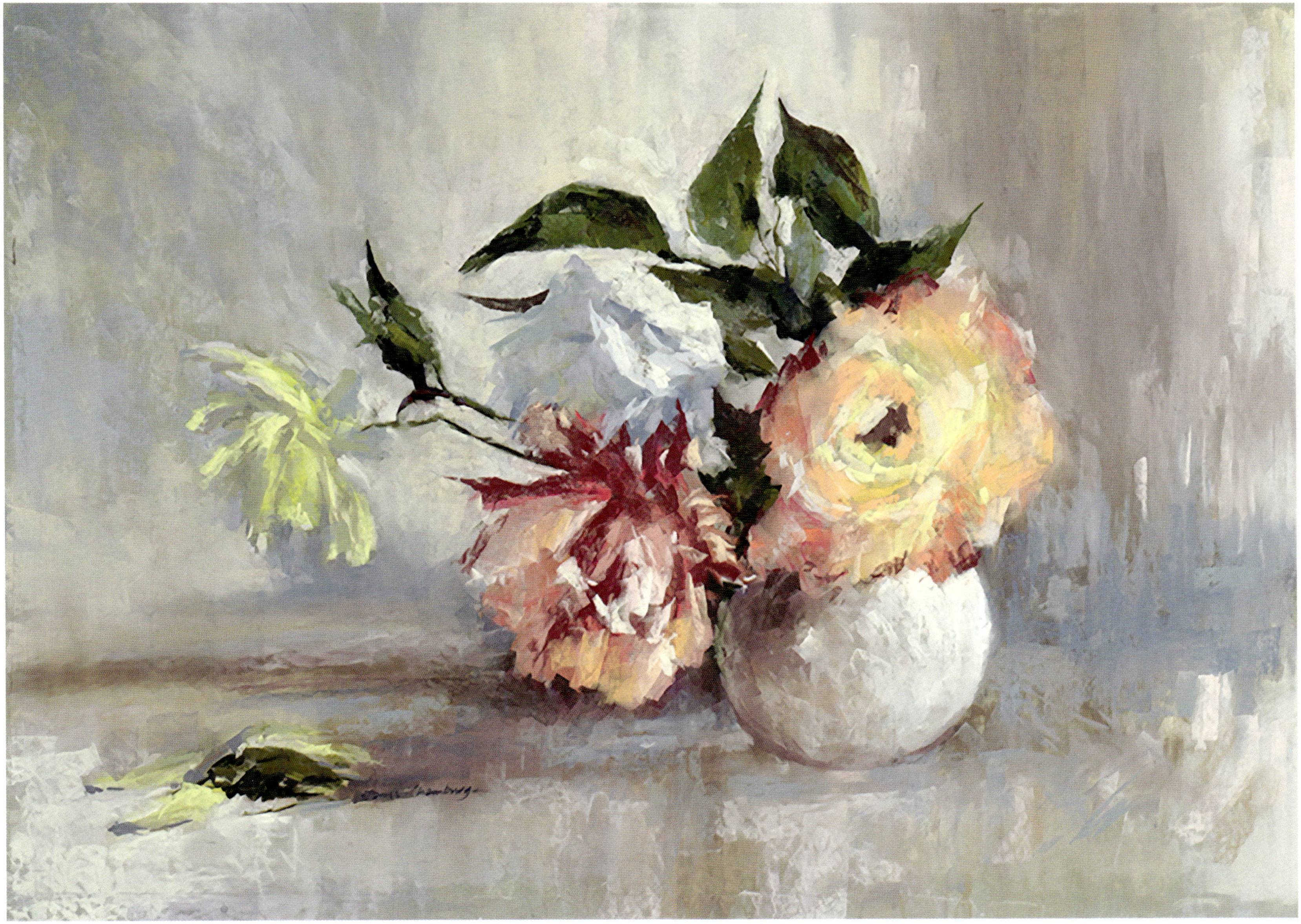

Four Dropping Roses in a Round White Bowl.
Pastel 51x36cm

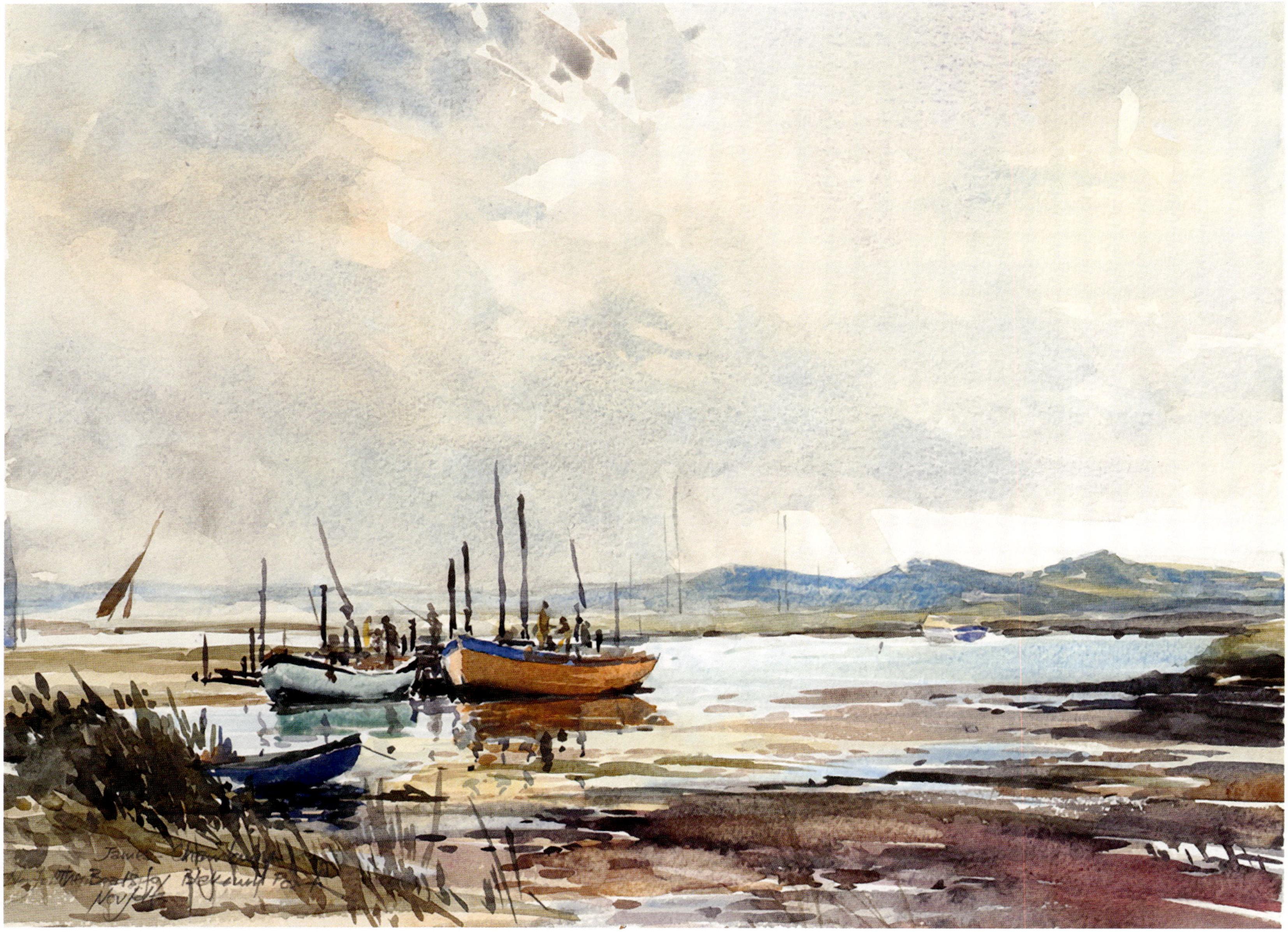

The Boats for Blakeney Point, Norfolk.
Watercolour

Sunday Morning Mevagissey, Cornwall.
Oil 50x39cm

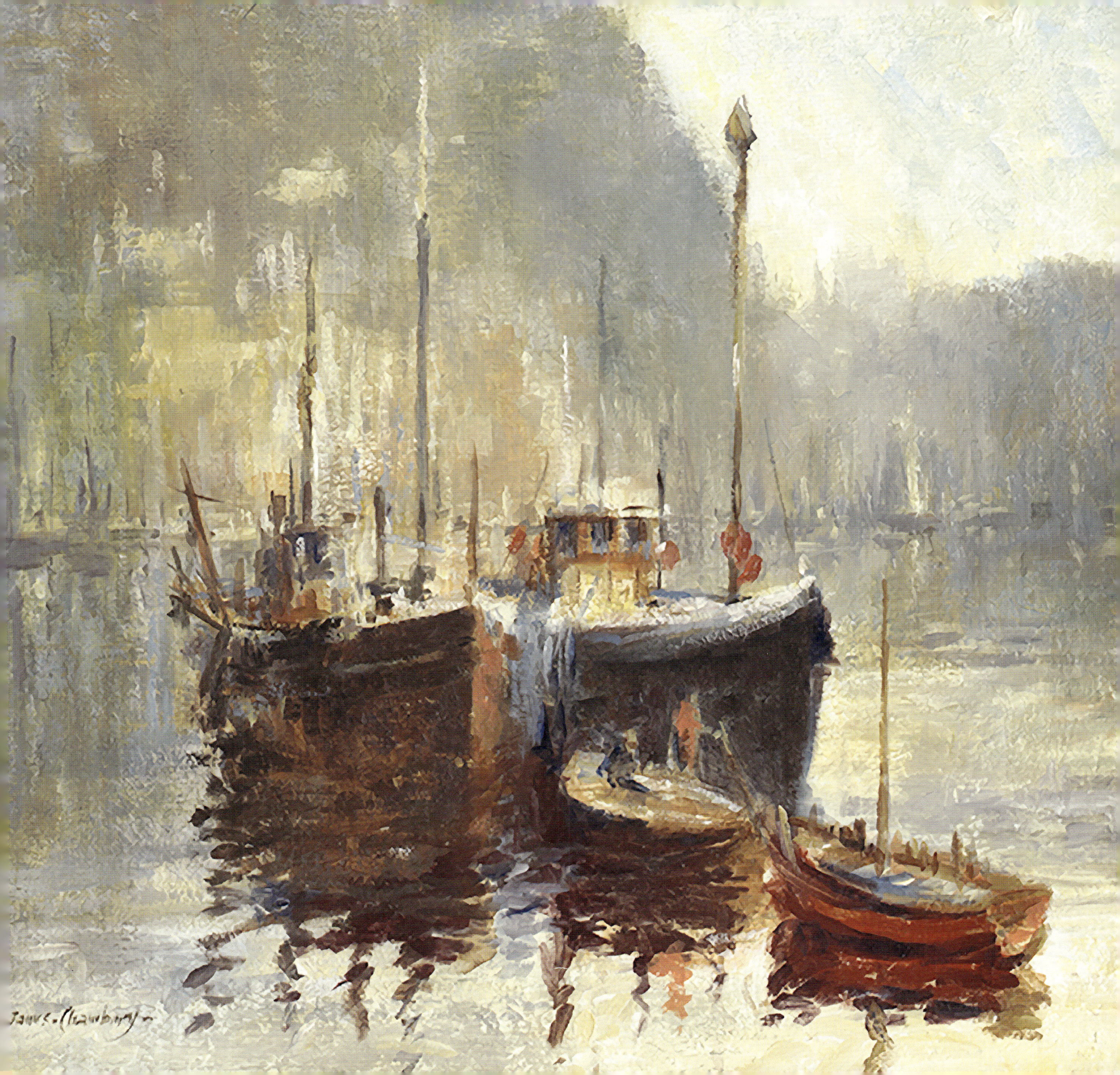

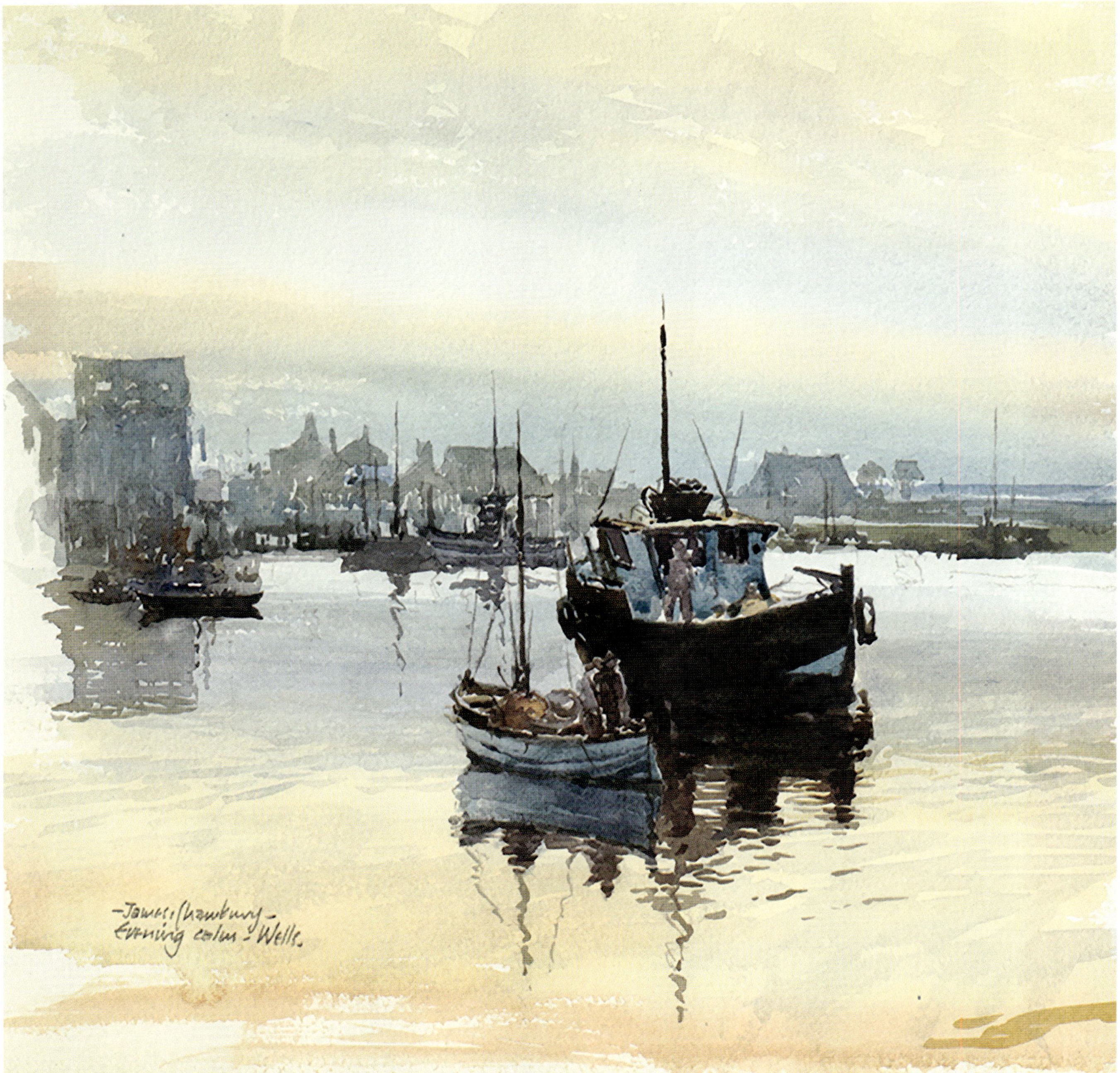

Evening Calm Wells, Norfolk.
Watercolour

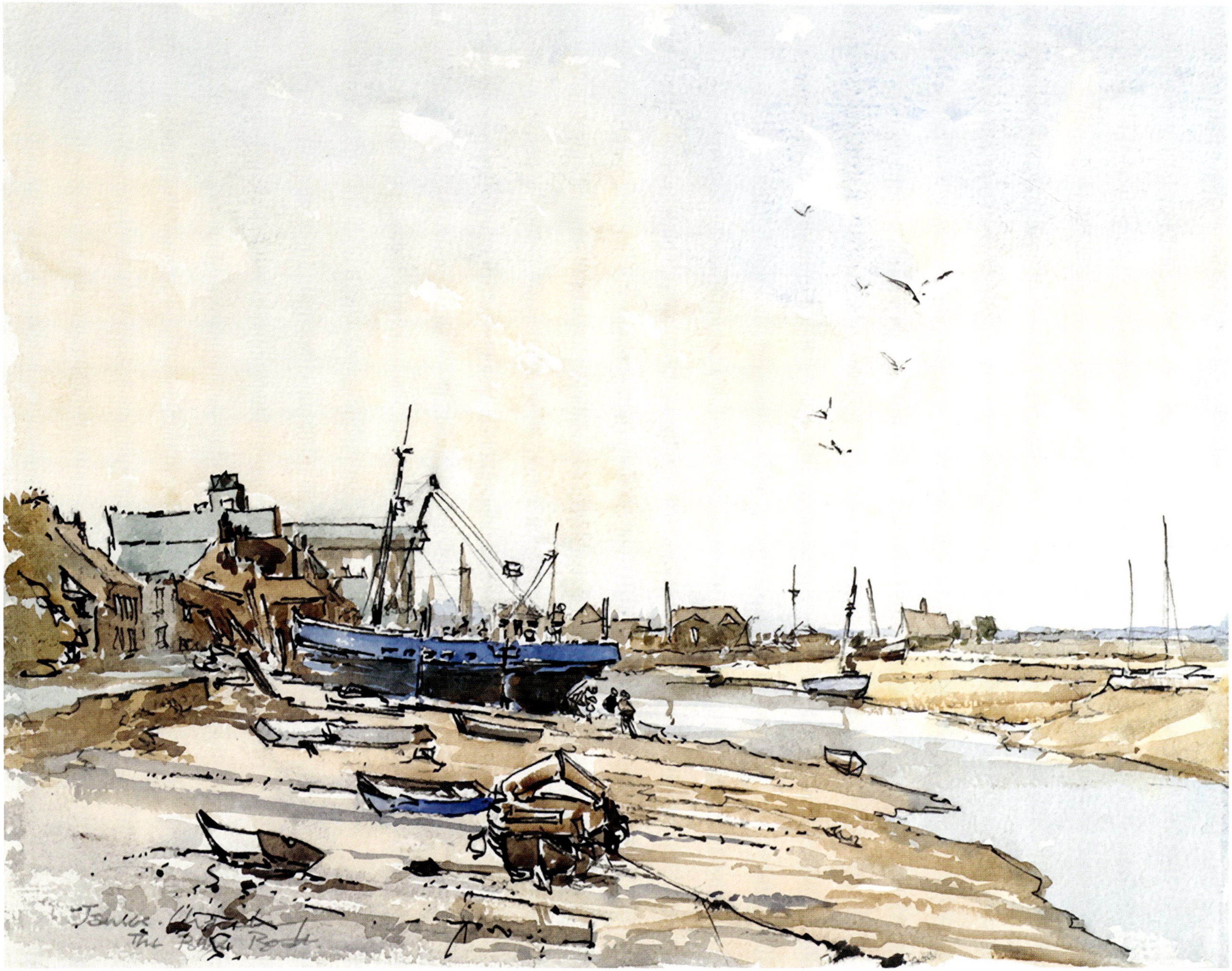

The Blue Boats, Wells, Norfolk.
Line and wash 34x27cm

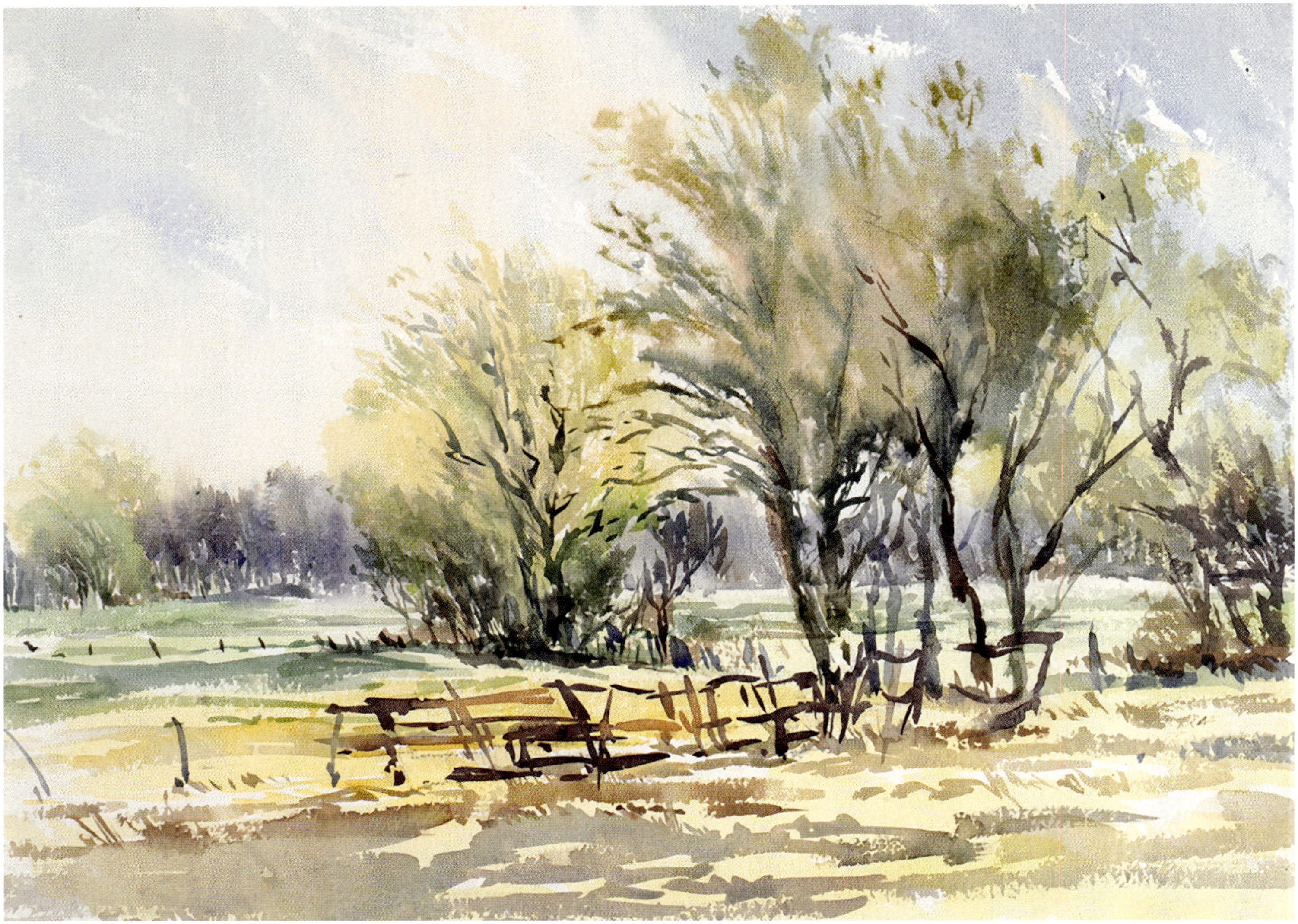

The Dandelion Field, Keukenlaan, Holland.
Watercolour 58x44cm

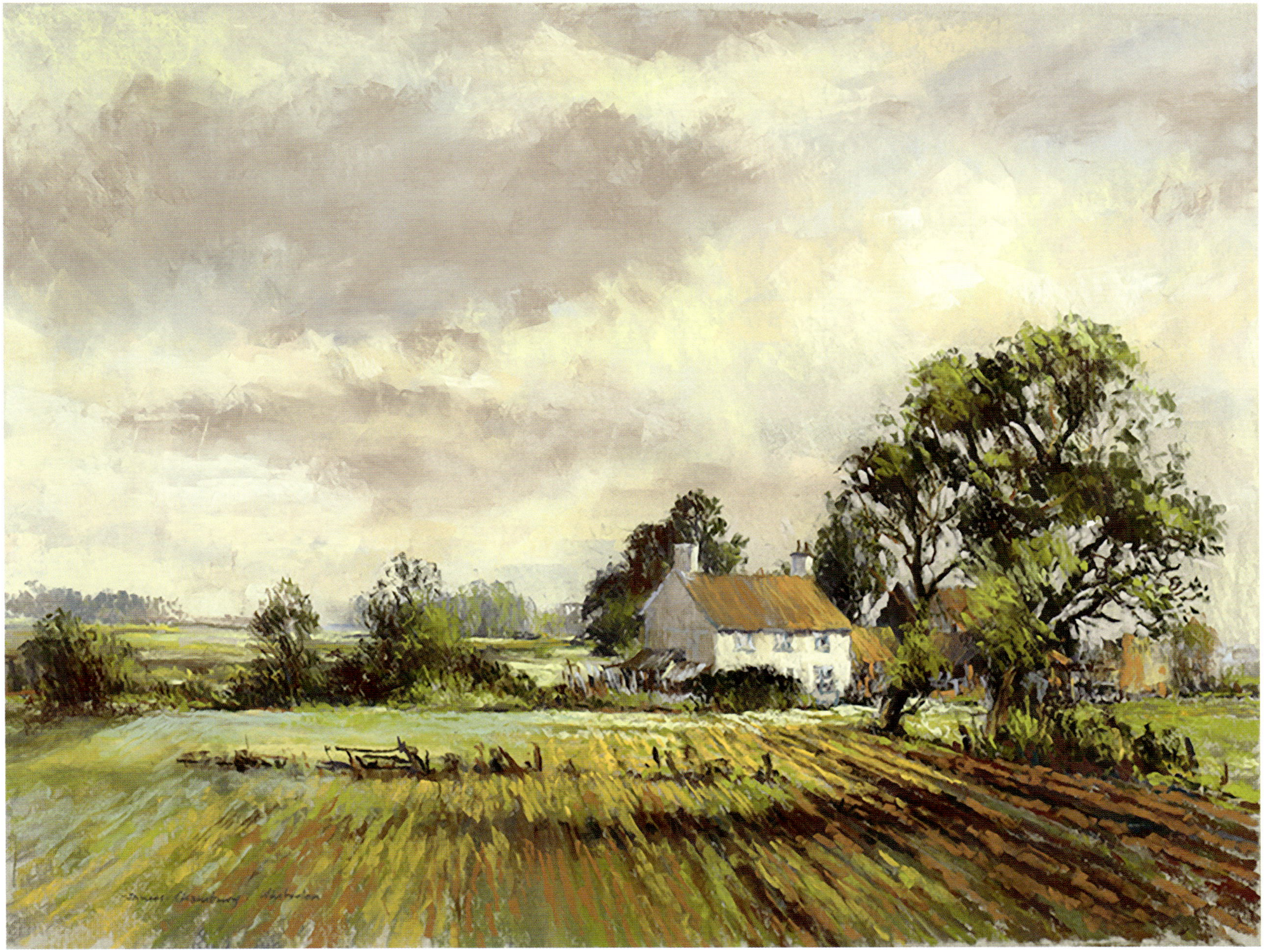

Winterton, Norfolk.
Pastel

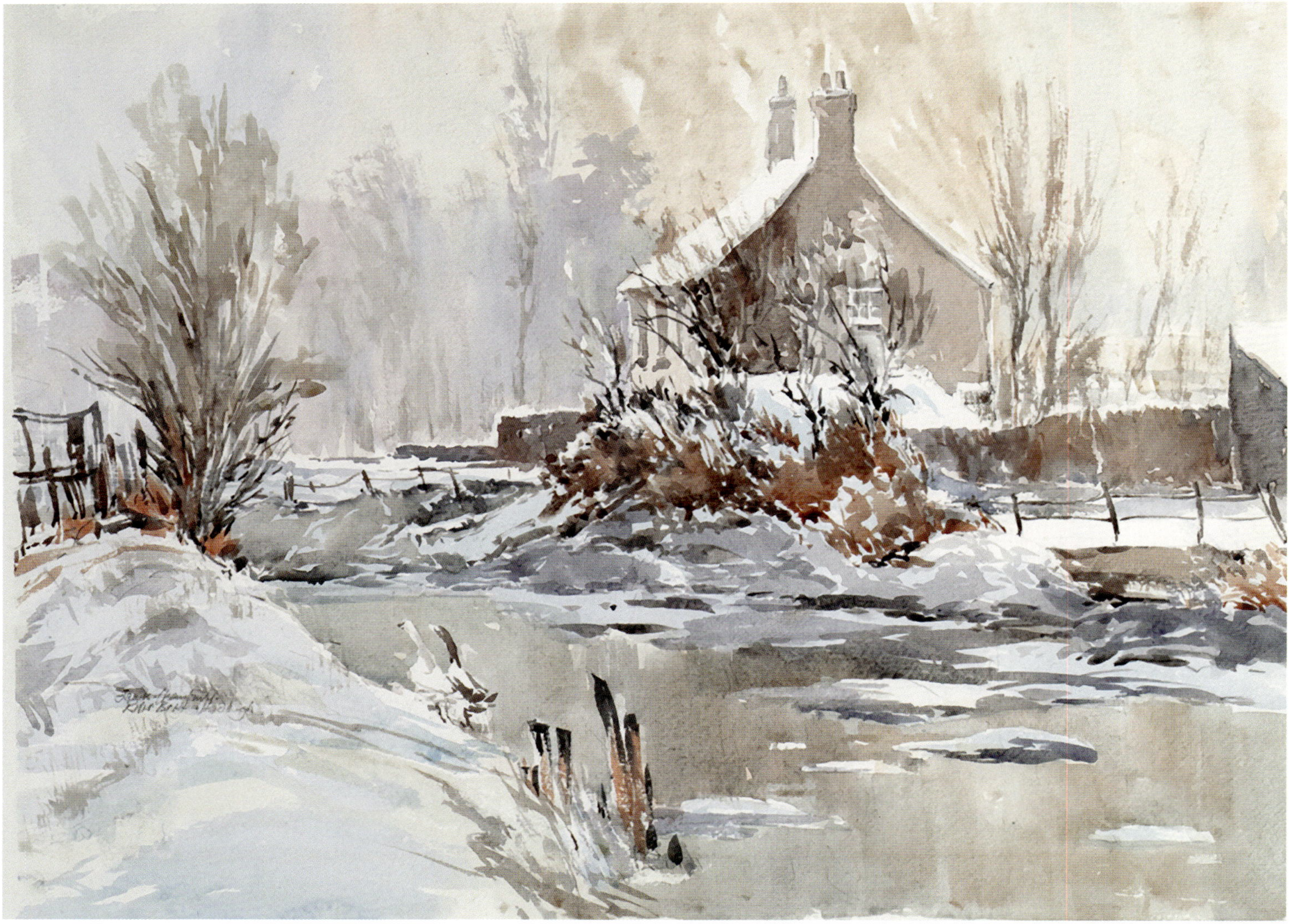

The River Brett in Snow, Hadleigh.
Watercolour

Basket of flowers.
Watercolour

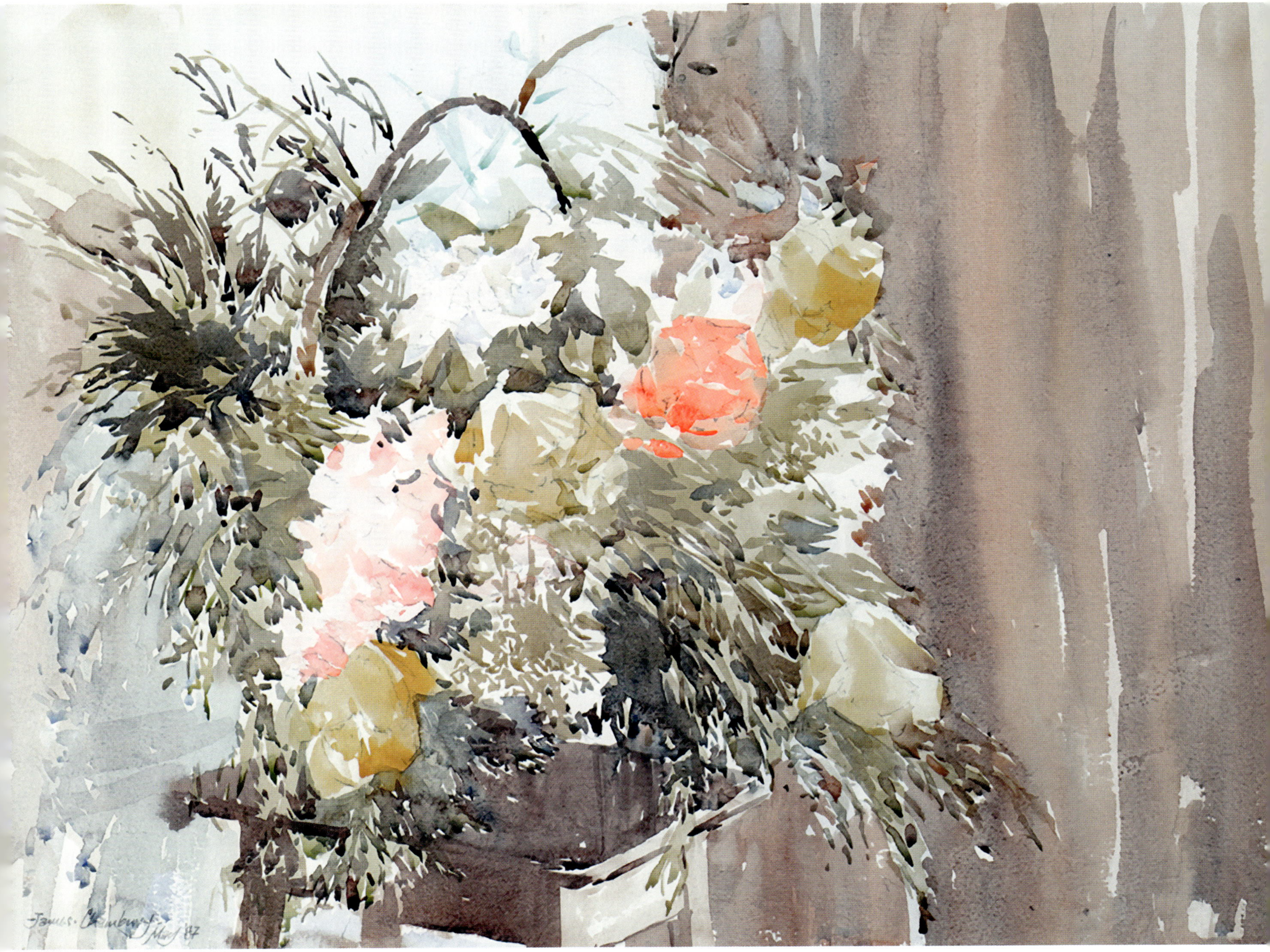

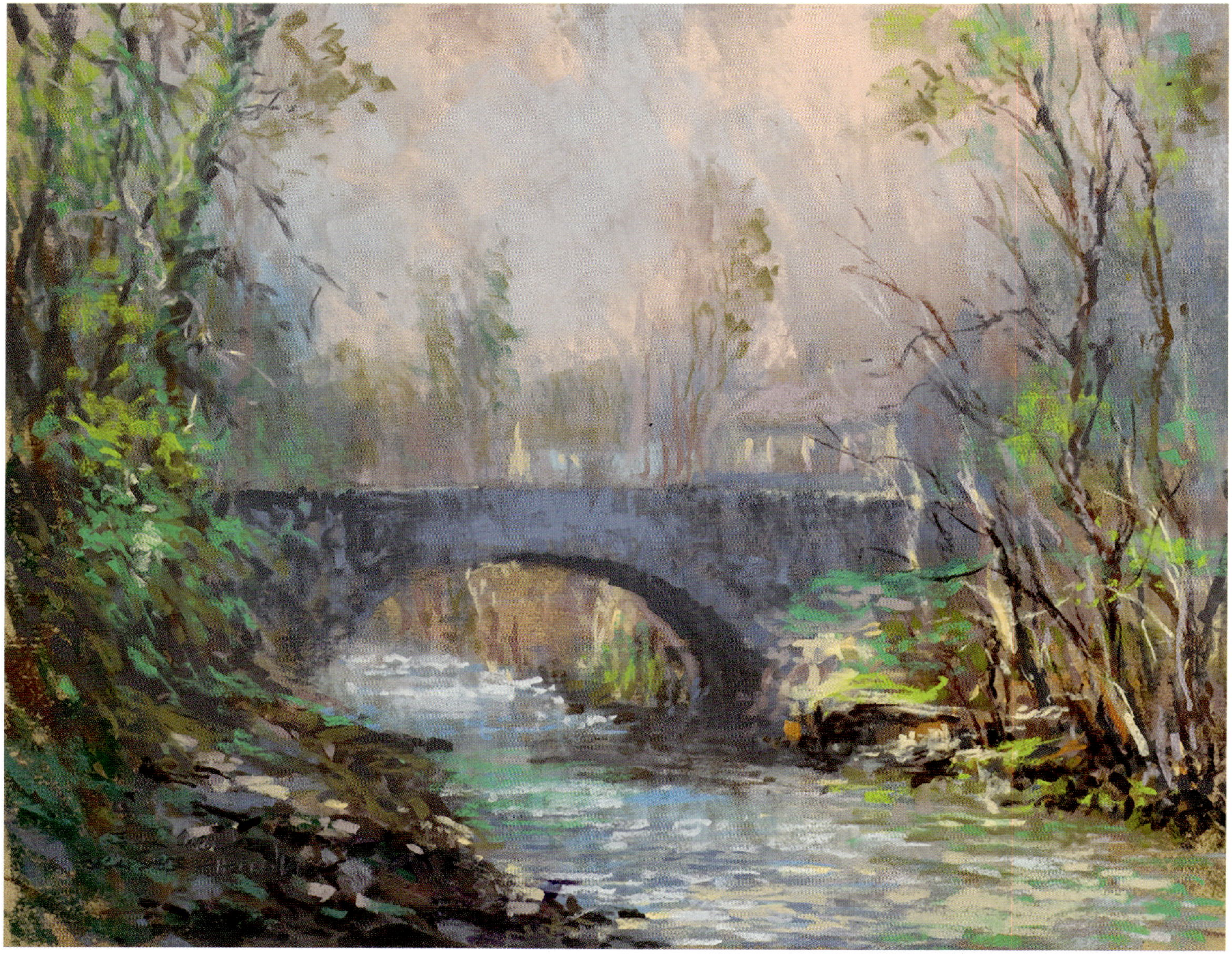

Beck Steps Elterwater, Lake District.
Pastel 35x26cm

Opposite: Fisherman at Toppesfield Bridge, Suffolk.
Pastel 37x28cm

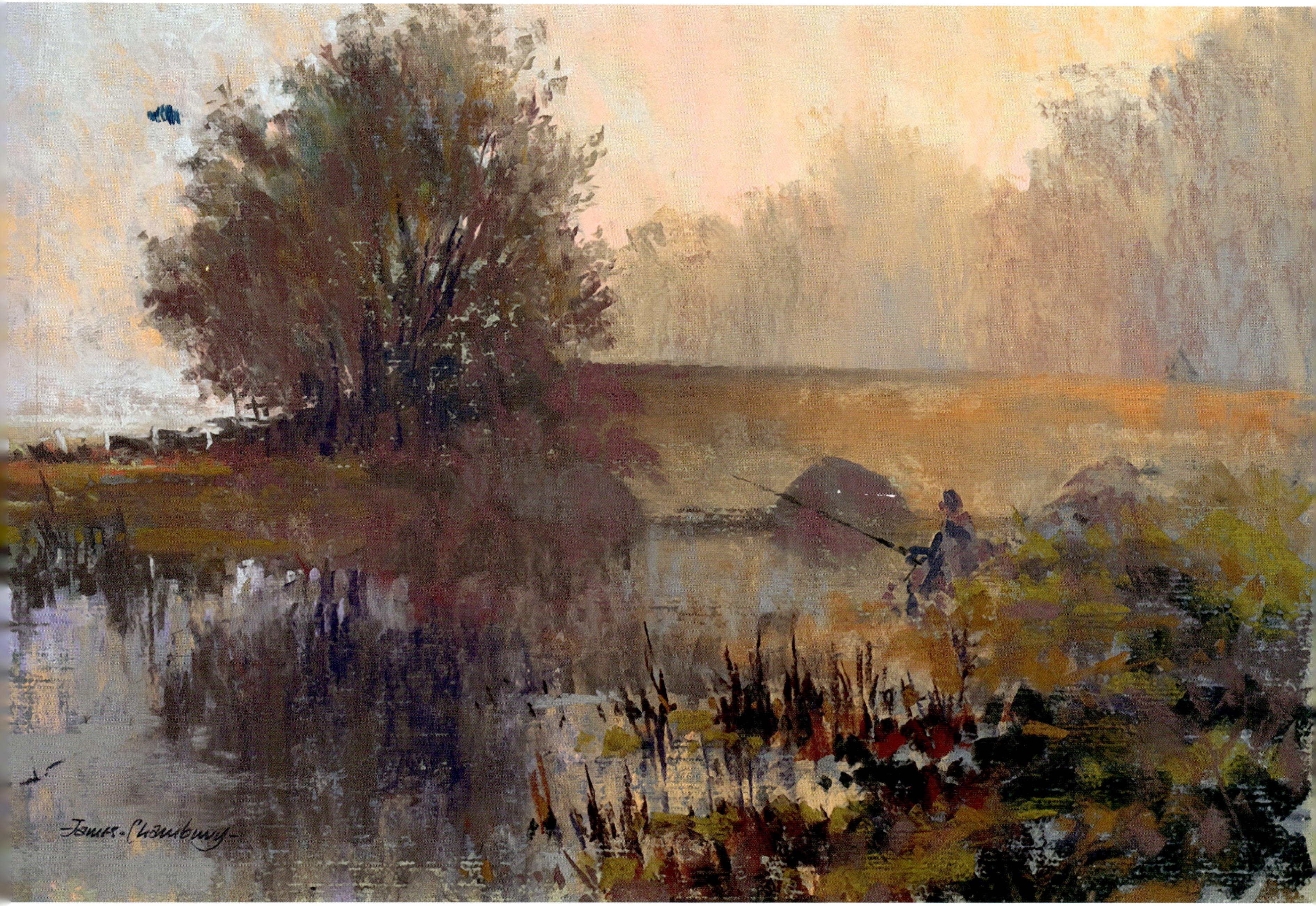
James Chambury

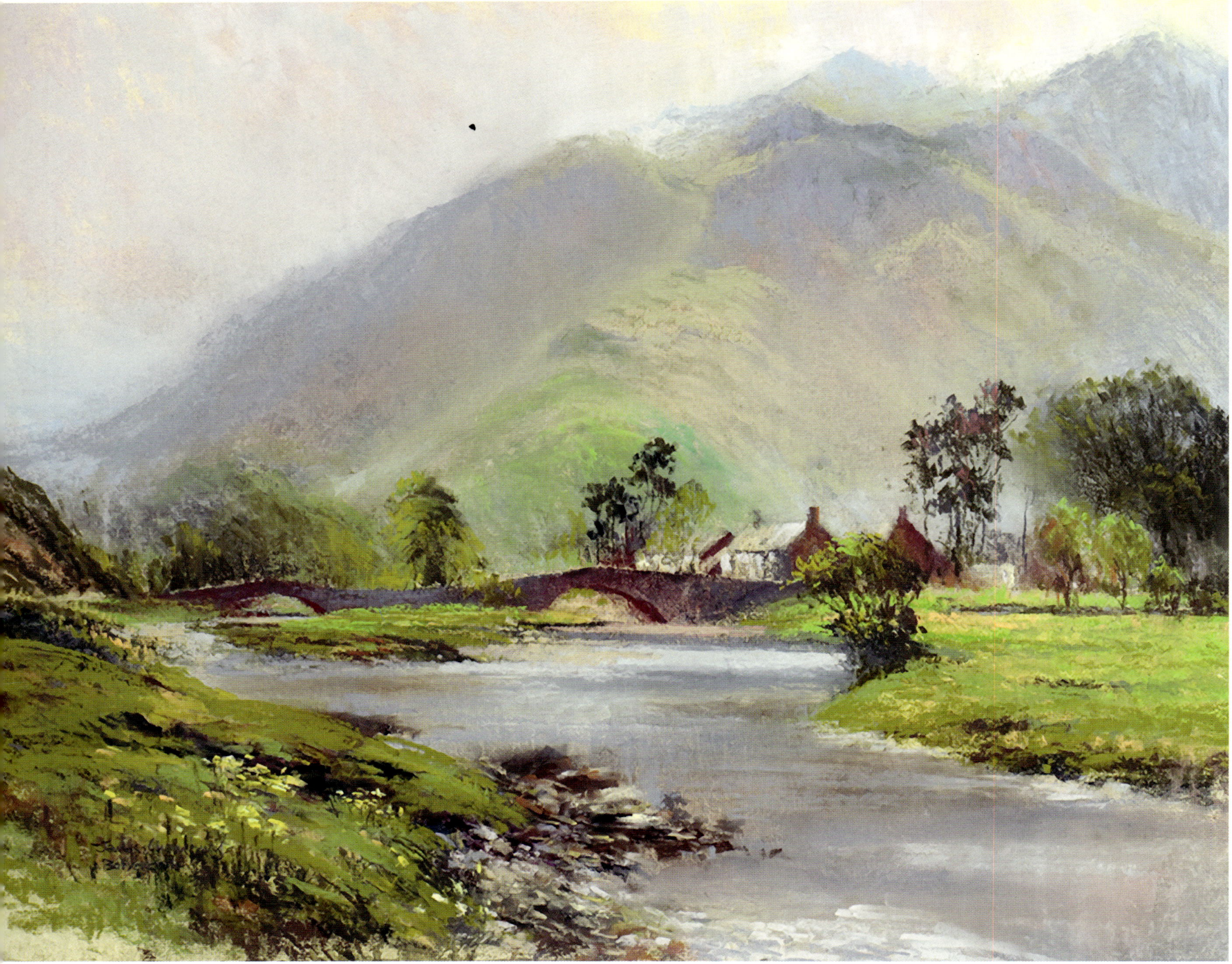

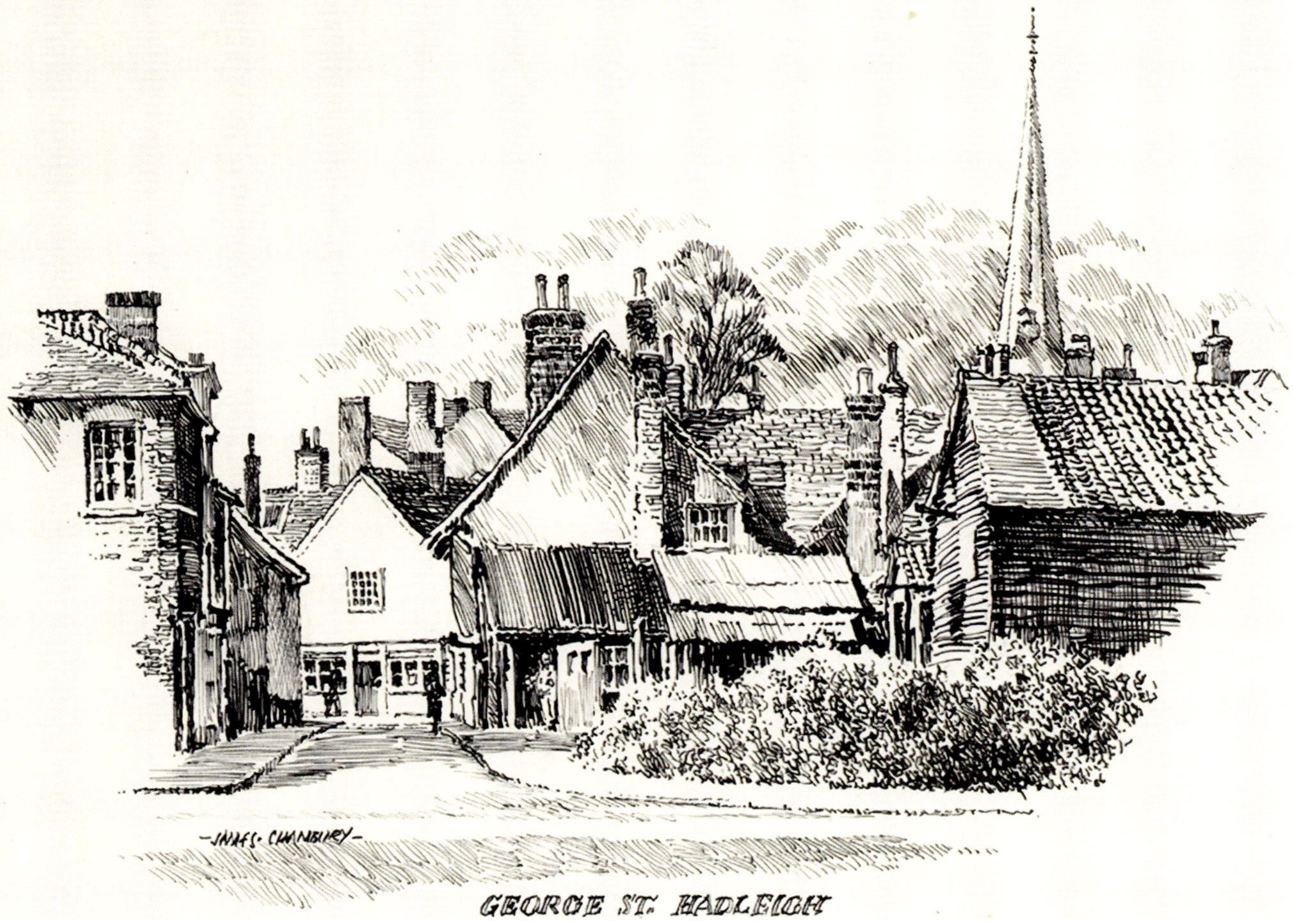

Opposite: Scene near Borrowdale.
Pastel 57x41cm

George Street, Hadleigh.
Pen and ink sketch 19x14cm

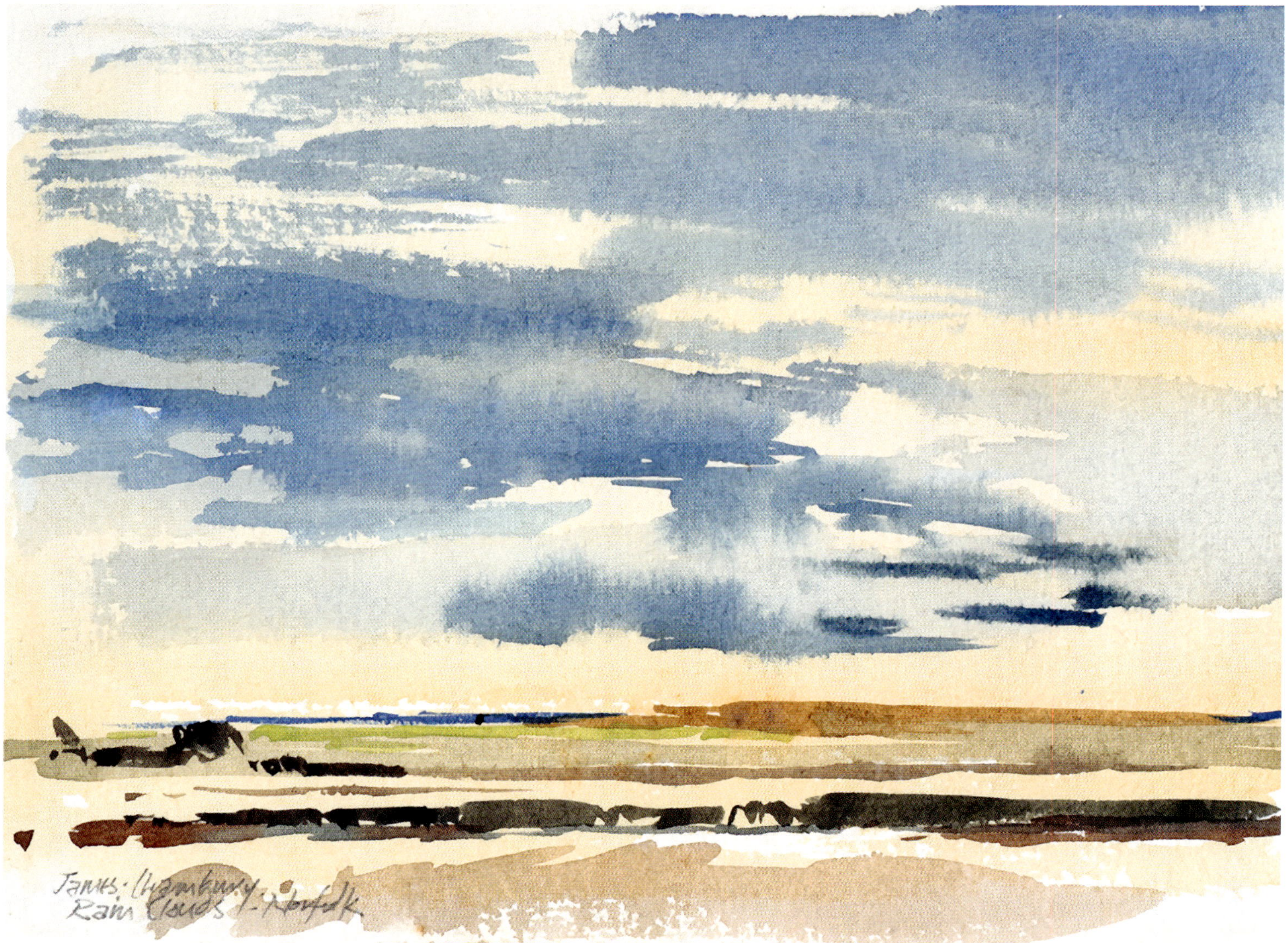

Rain Clouds, Norfolk.
Watercolour 17x12cm

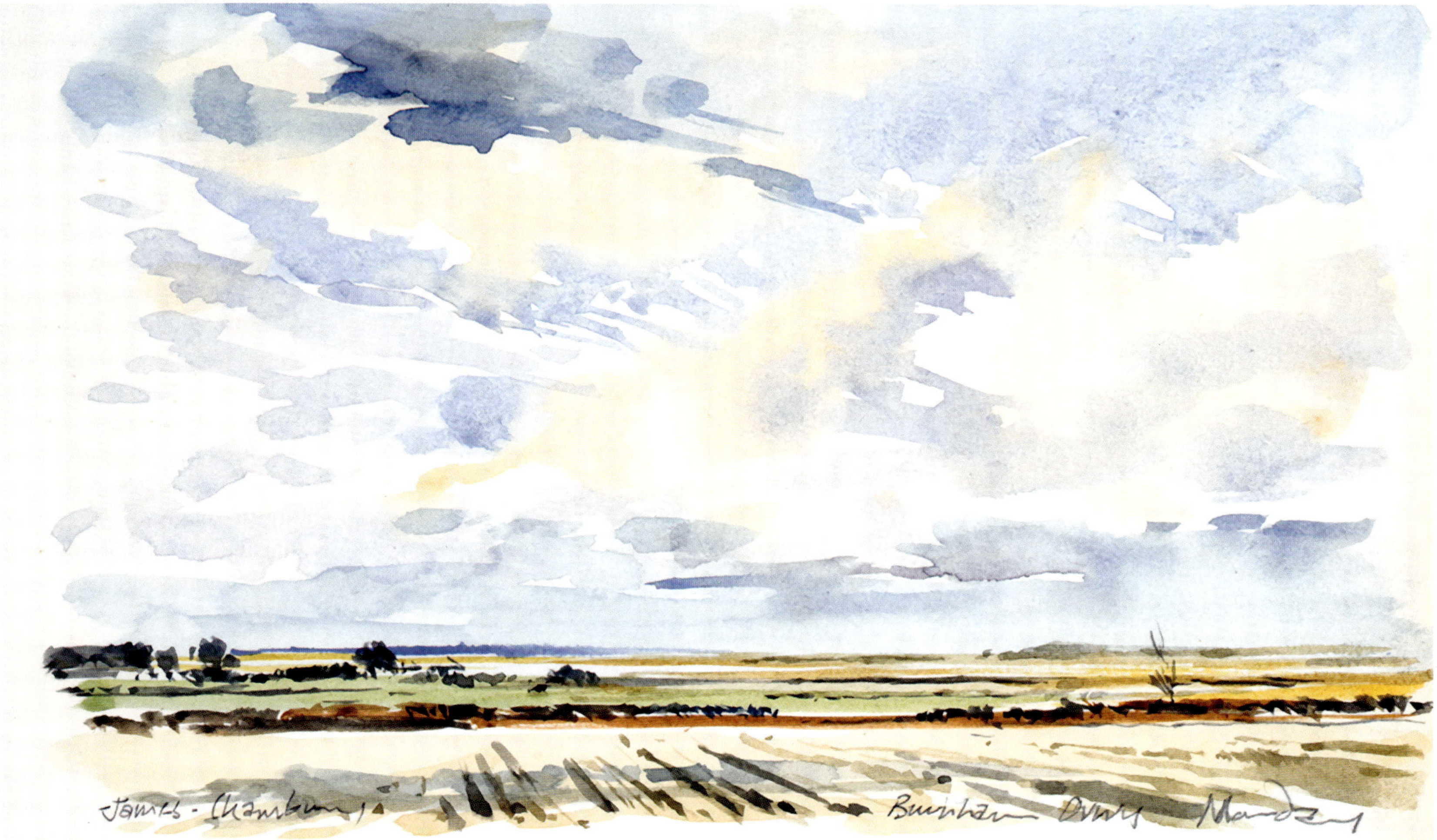

Burnham Overy Monday, Norfolk.
Watercolour

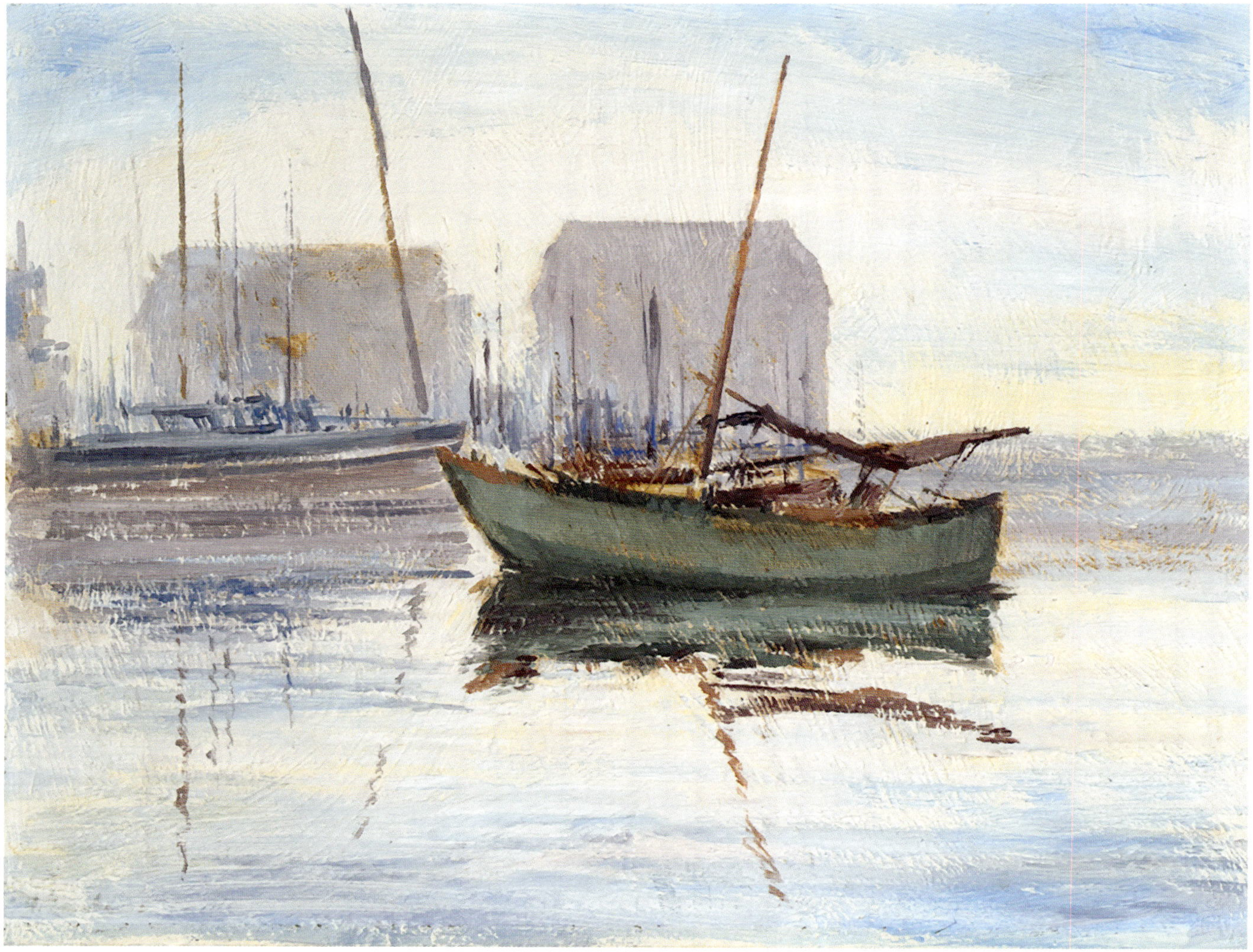

Tide Mill at Woodbridge, Suffolk.
Oil 30x22cm

Sunrise Aldeburgh, Suffolk.
Watercolour 16x13cm

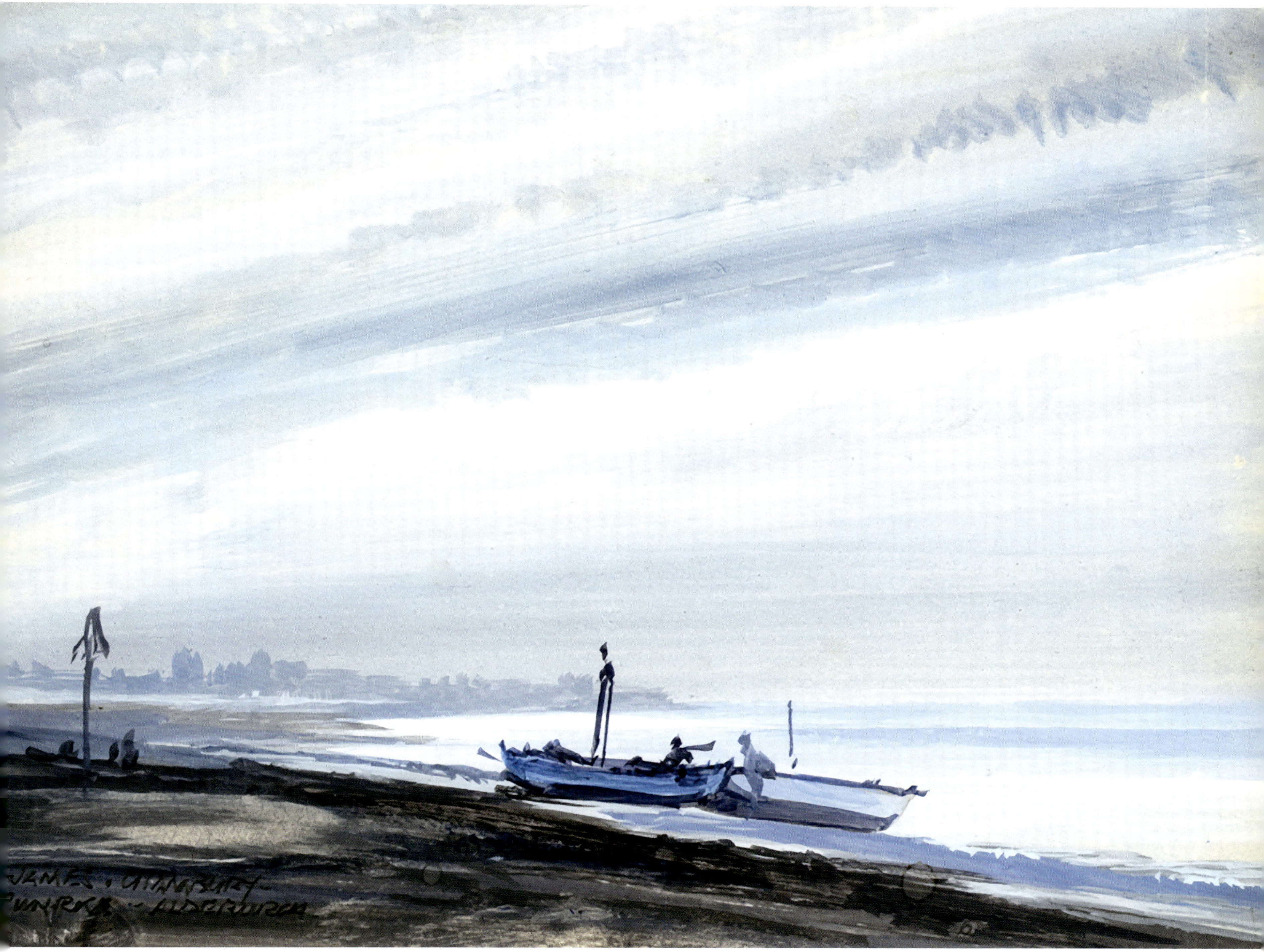

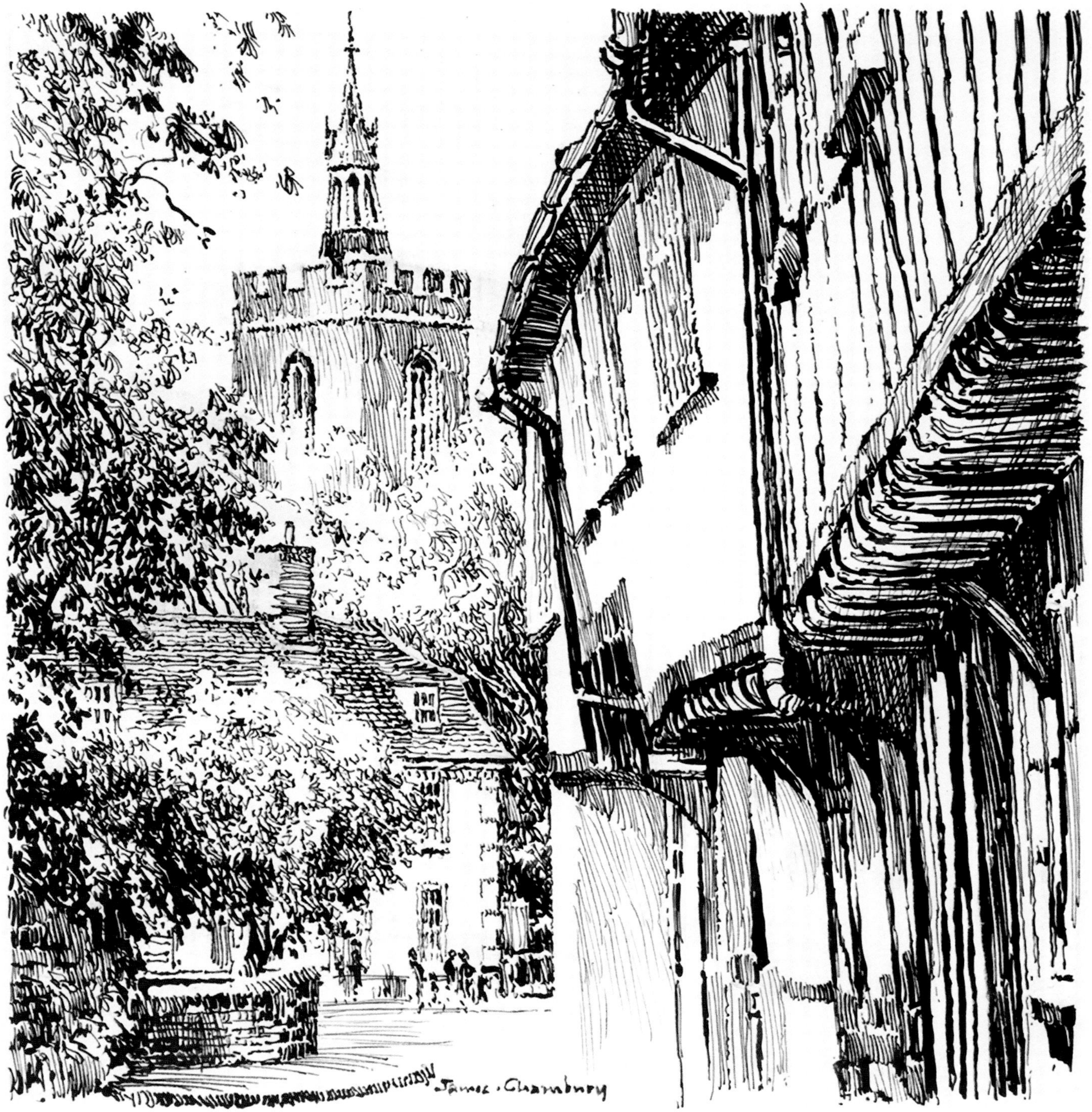
James Chambury

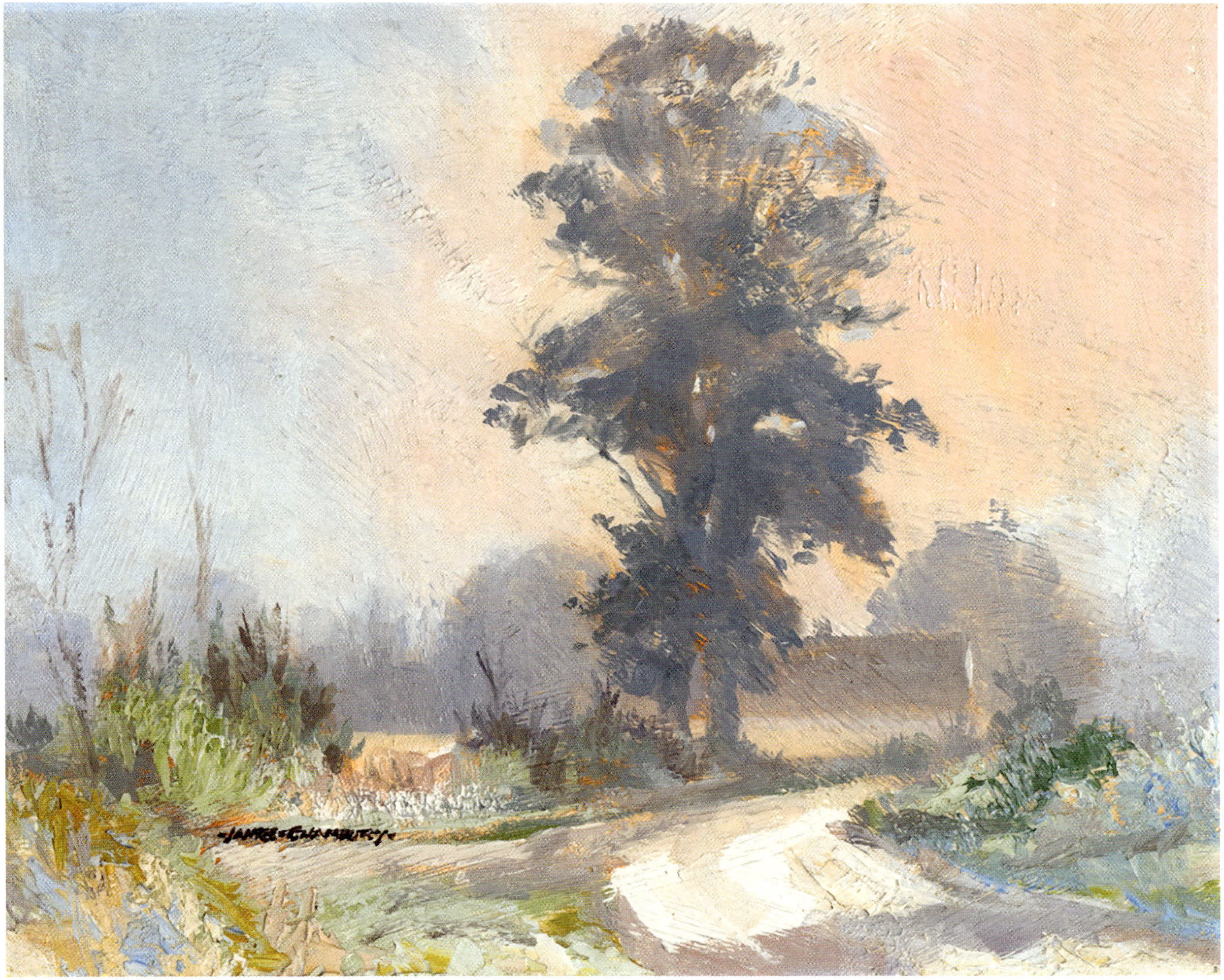

Boxford: Old Buildings and Church, Suffolk.
Pen and ink 14x14cm

Elm Tree at Buttsbury Ford, Essex.
Oil 27x21cm

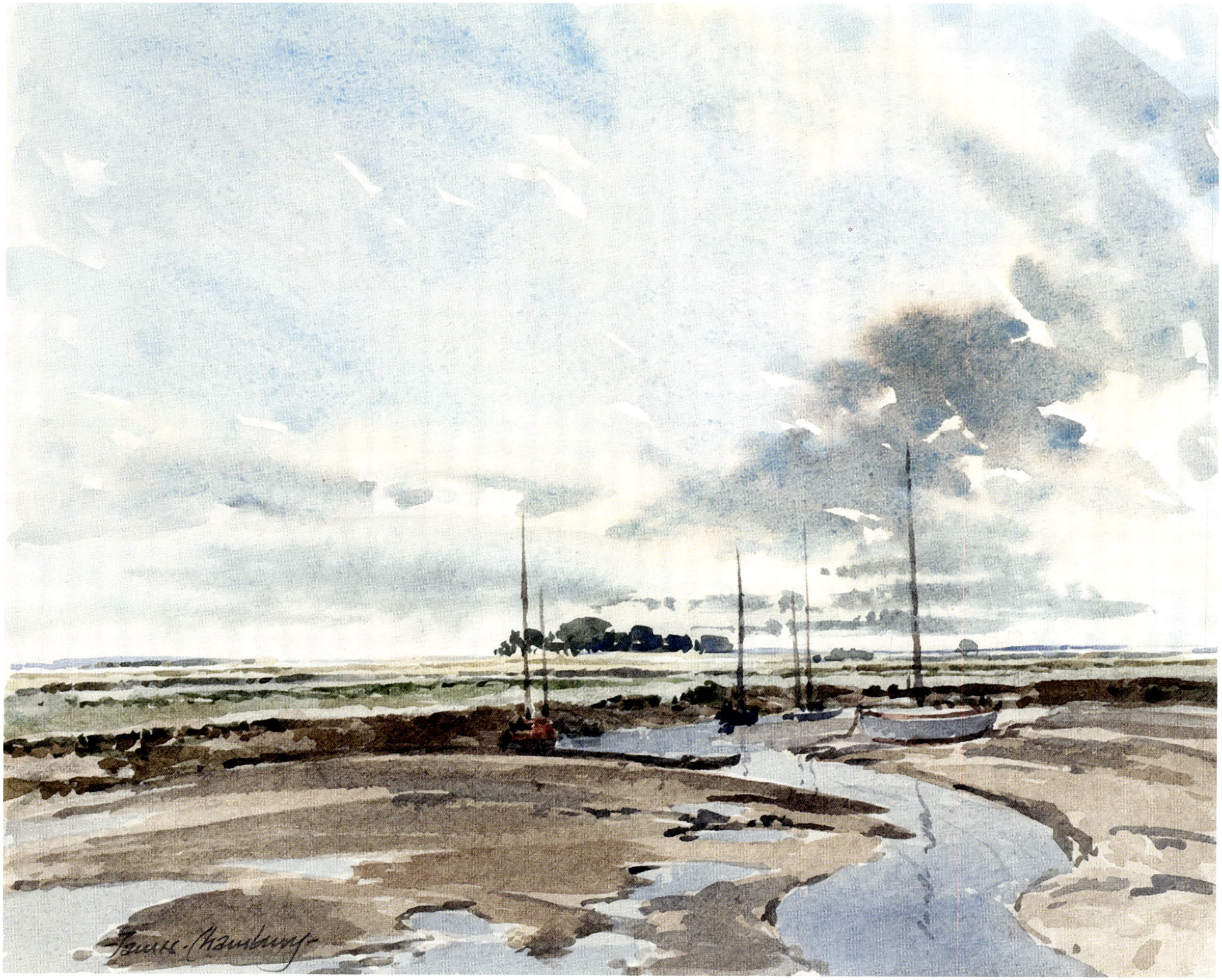

Estuary on the Norfolk Coast.
Watercolour

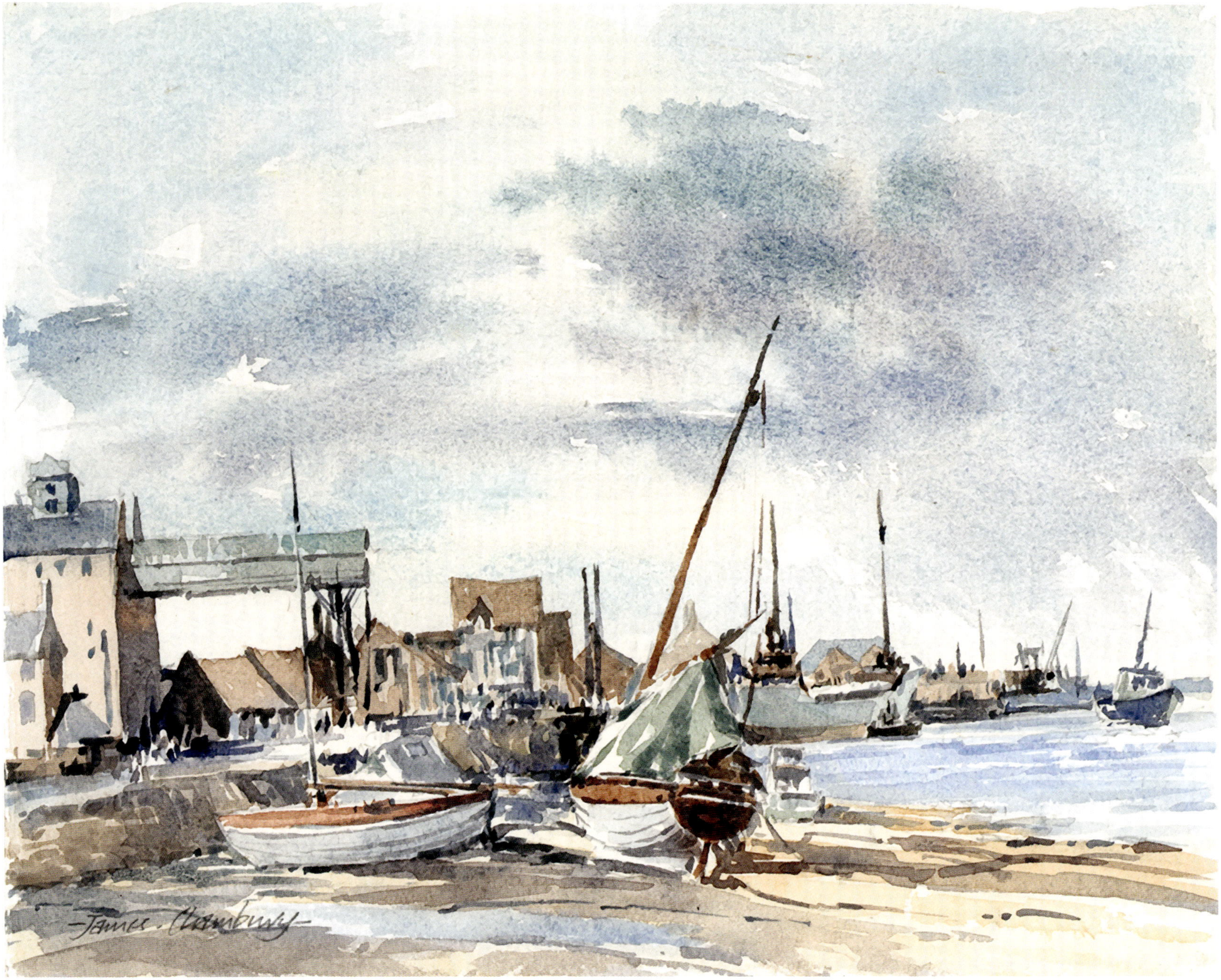

Wells at Low Tide, Norfolk.
Watercolour

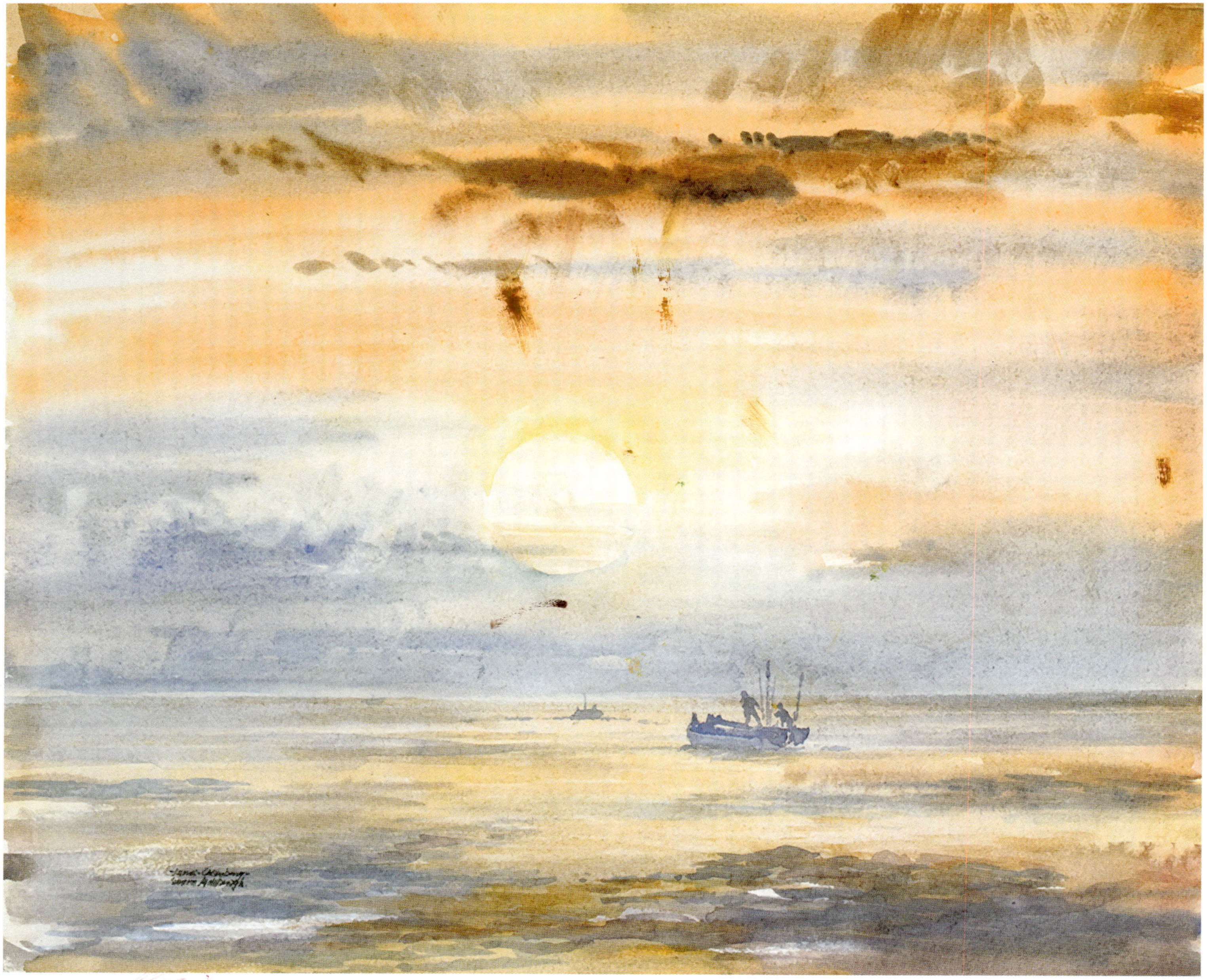

Sunrise Aldeburgh, Suffolk.
Watercolour 40x33cm

Opposite: Walberswick from Southwold.
Watercolour 40x33cm

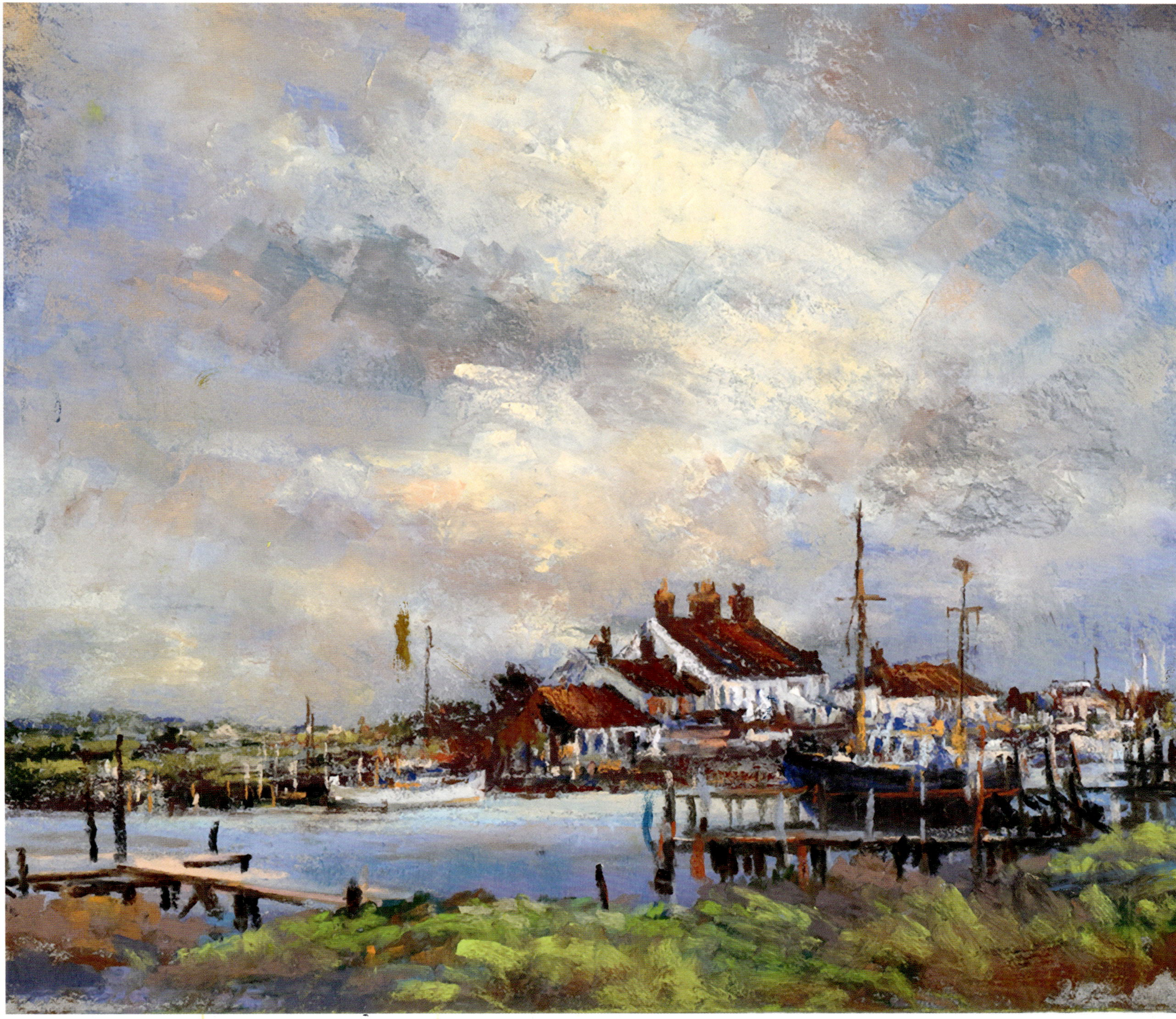

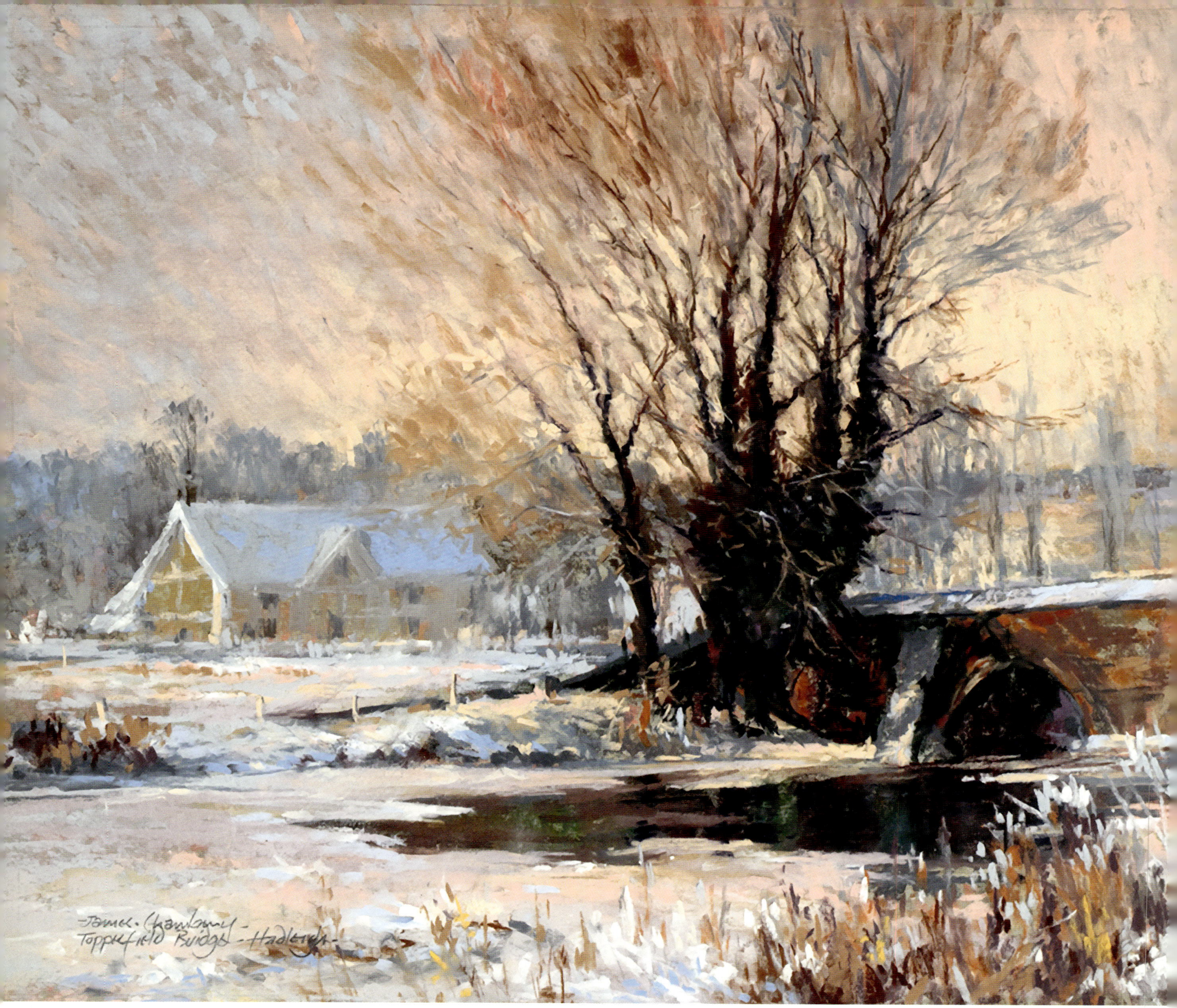
Toppesfield Bridge - Hadleigh

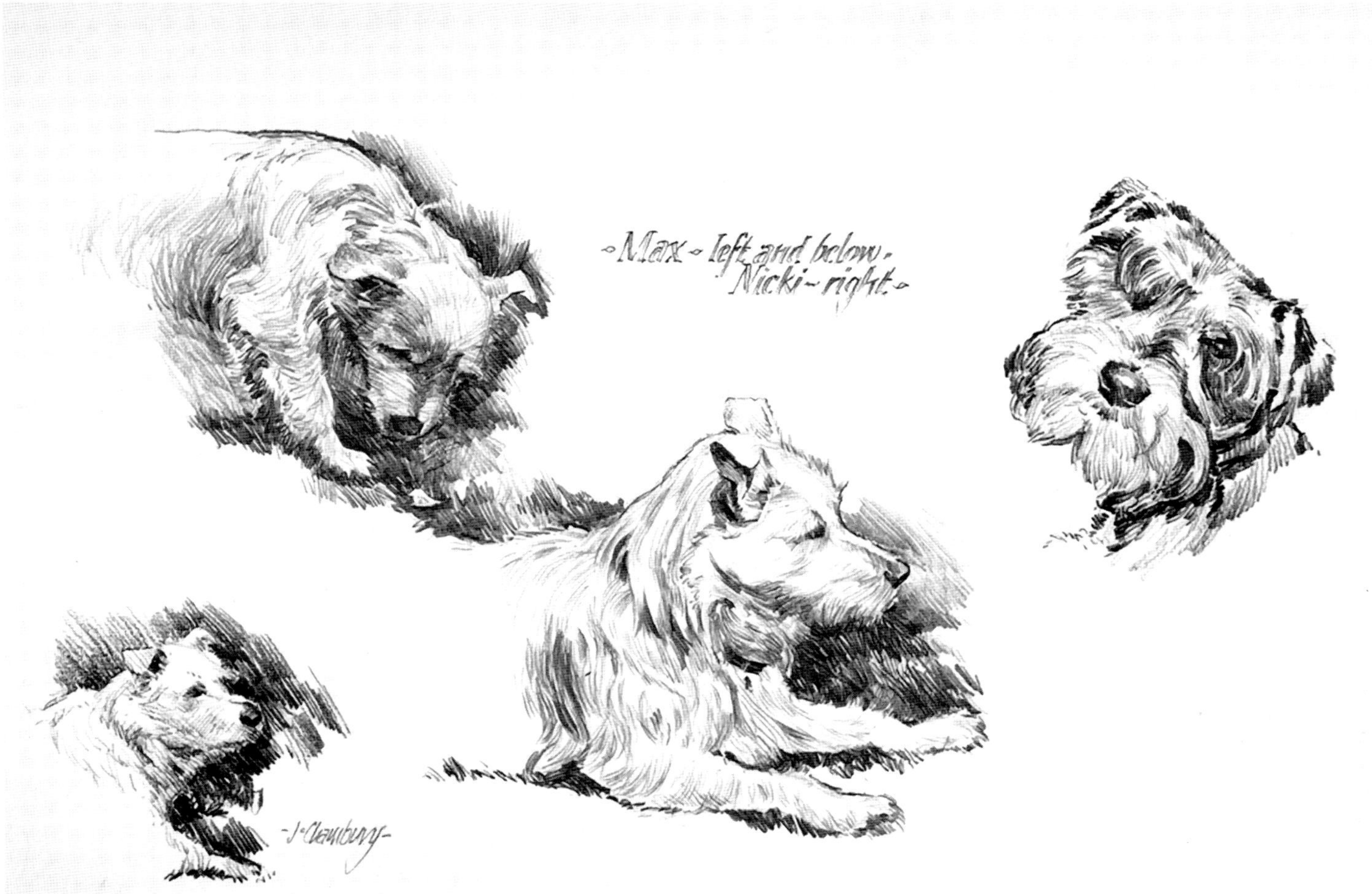

Opposite: Topplesfield Bridge, Hadleigh.
Pastel 33x27cm

Max and Nicki.
Pencil sketch

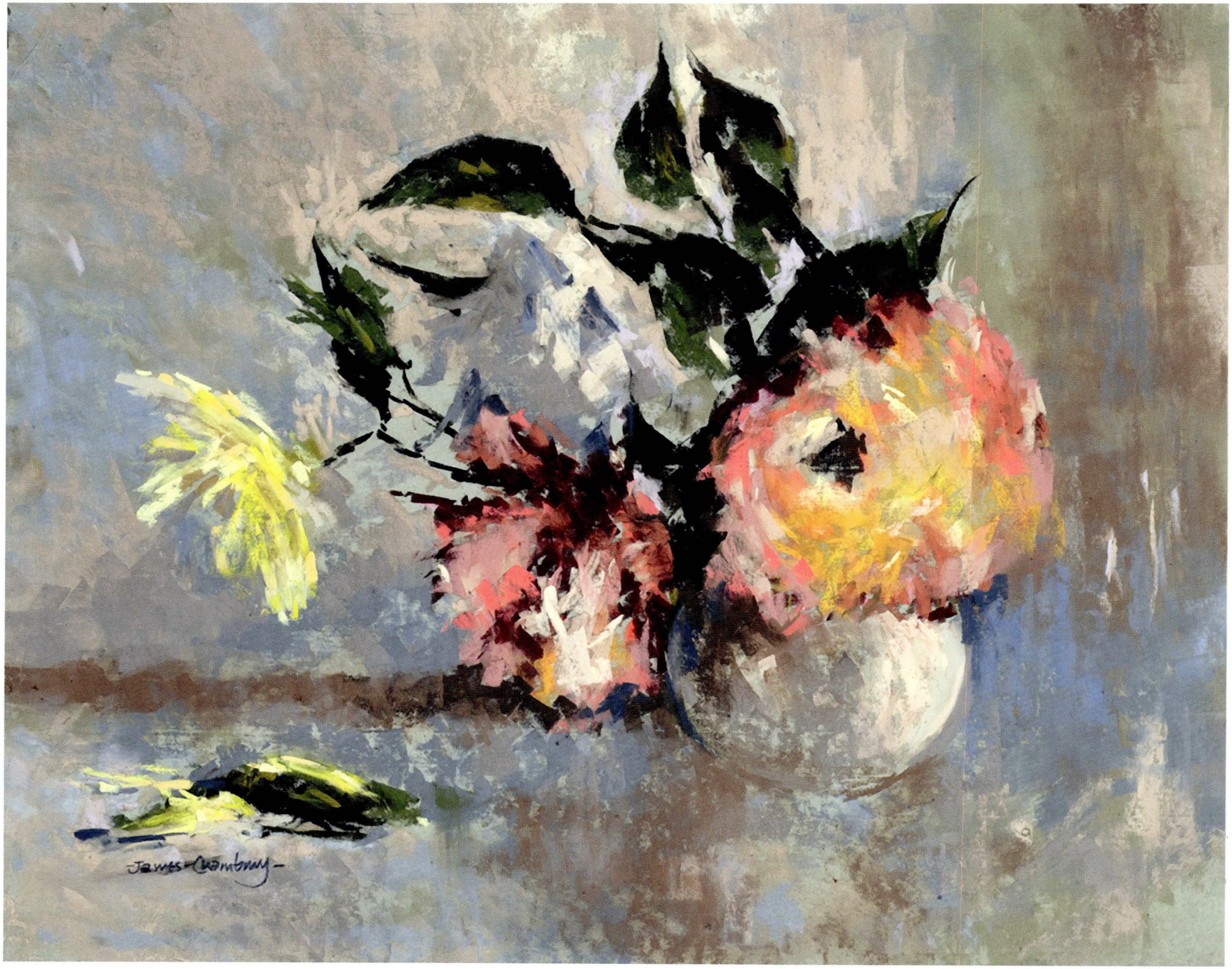

Roses.
Pastel 33x26cm

Opposite: The Deben below Woodbridge, Winter. Suffolk.
Watercolour

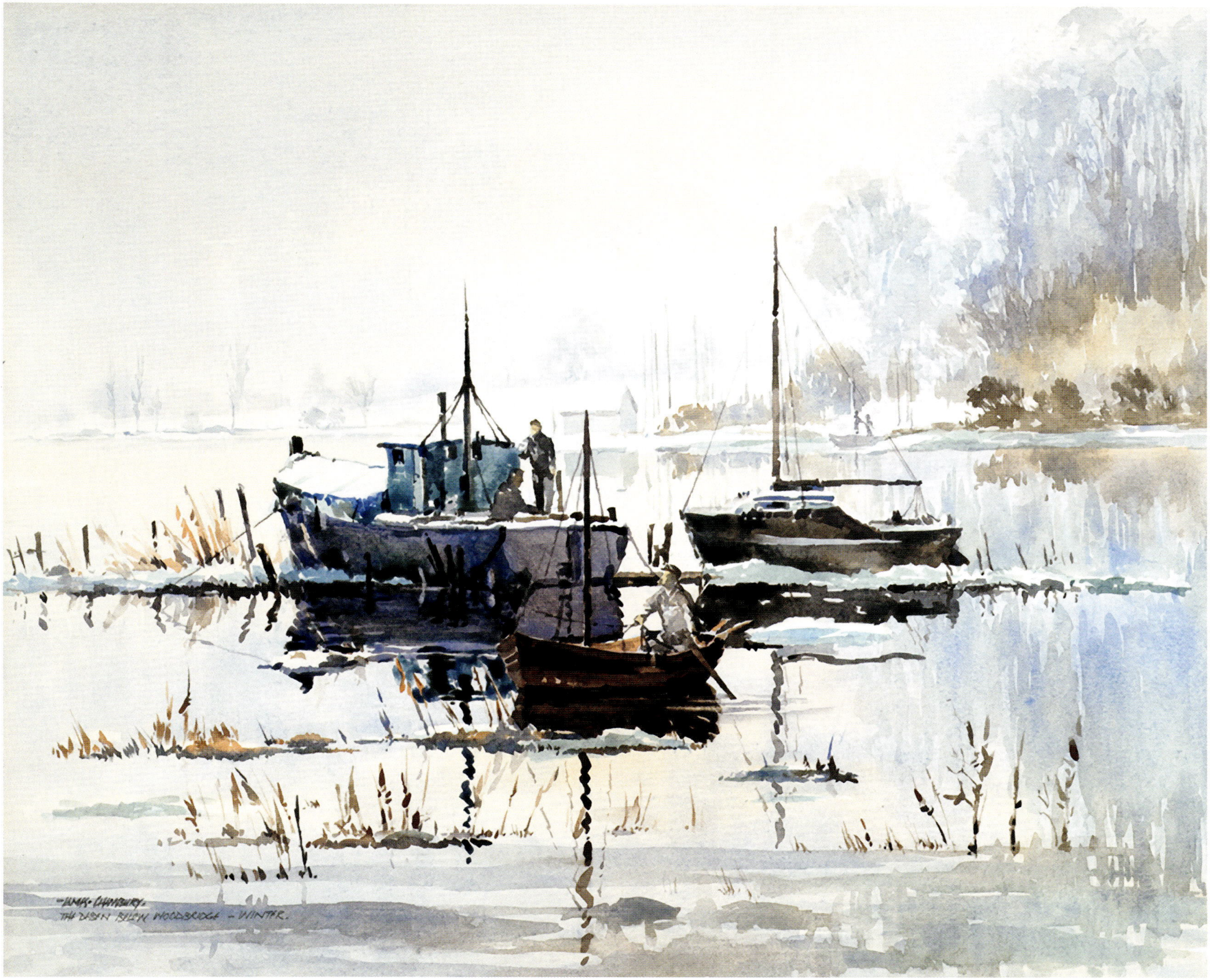

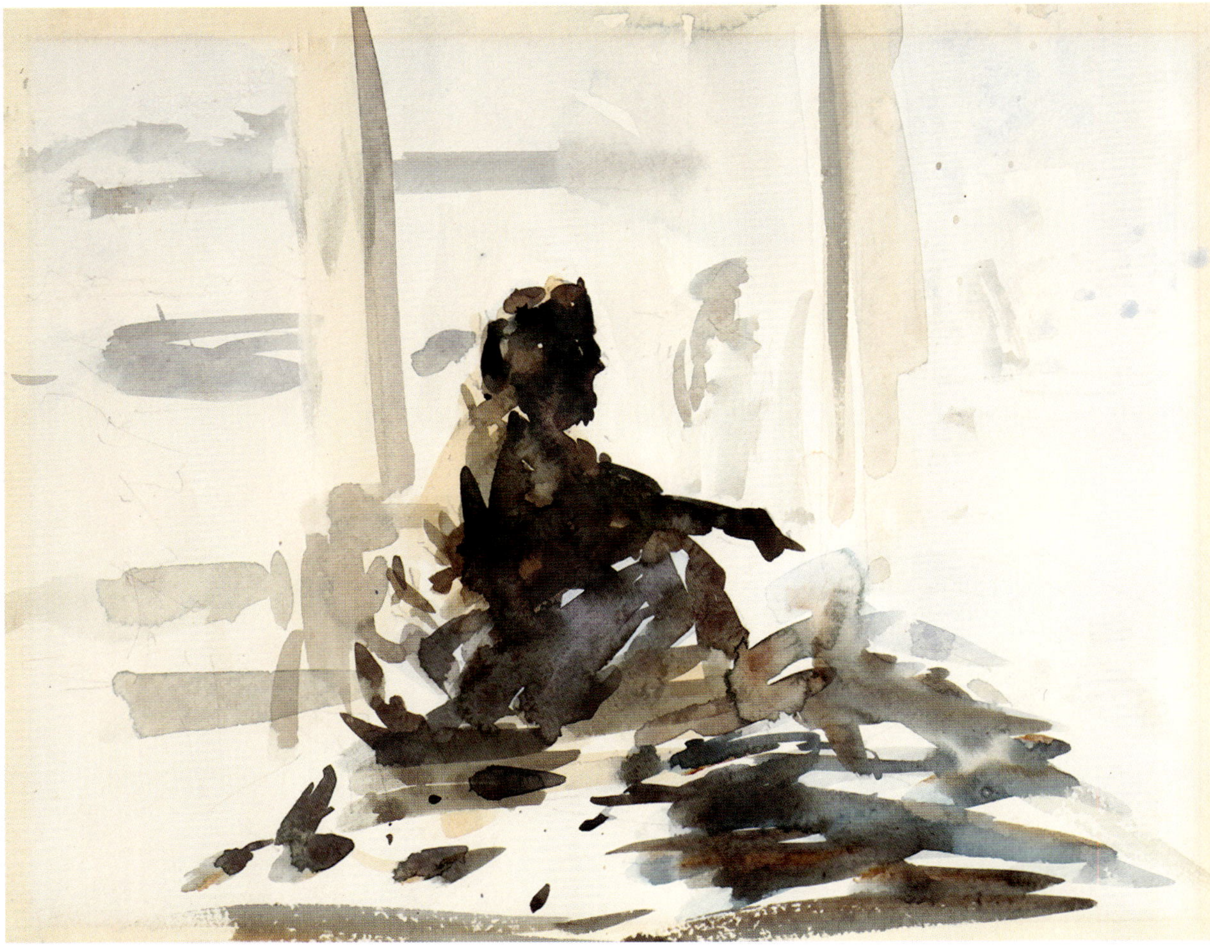

Omani Figure.
Watercolour sketch 34x26cm

Opposite:Autumn Scene River Brett, Hadleigh.
Pastel 33x27cm

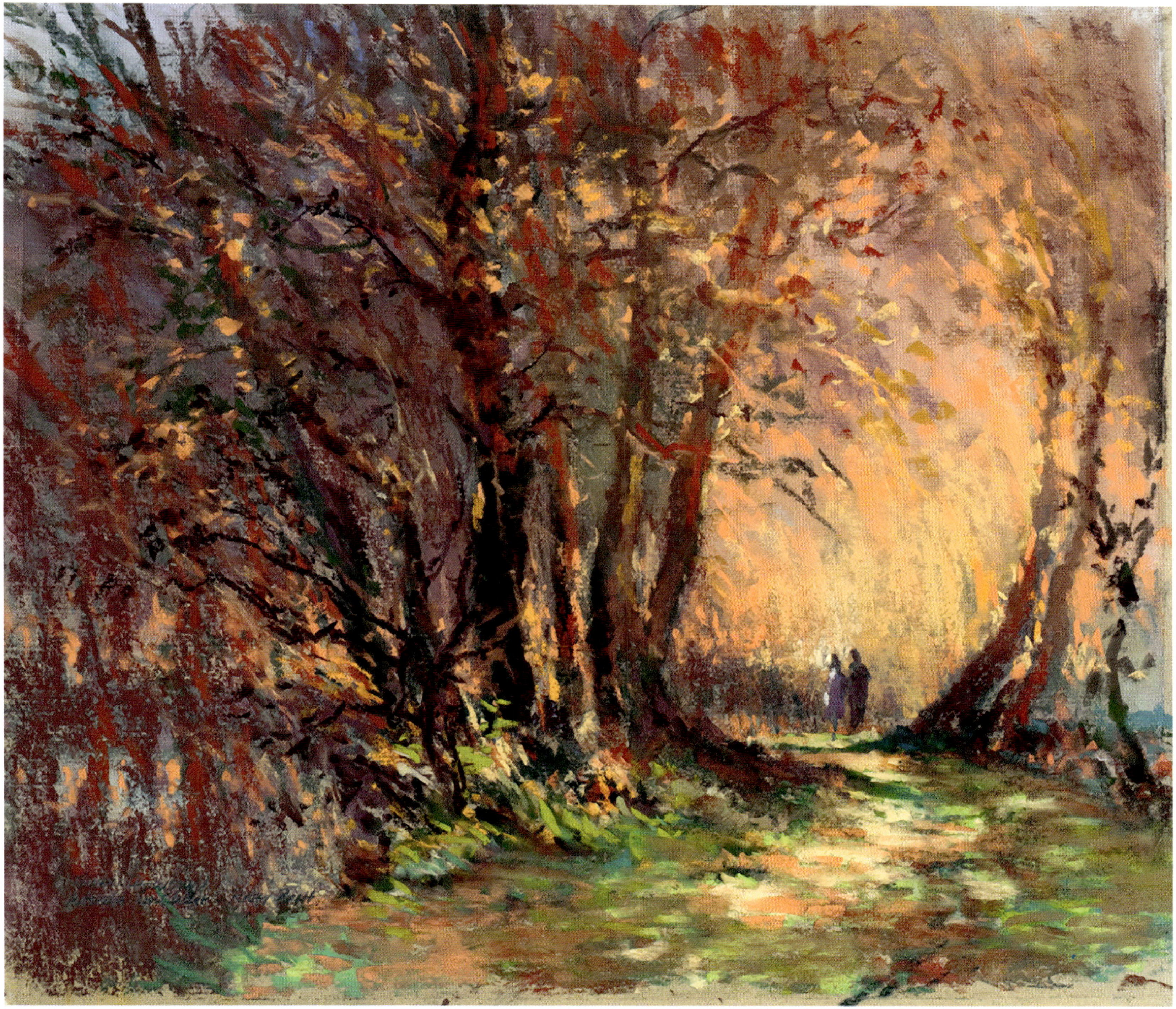

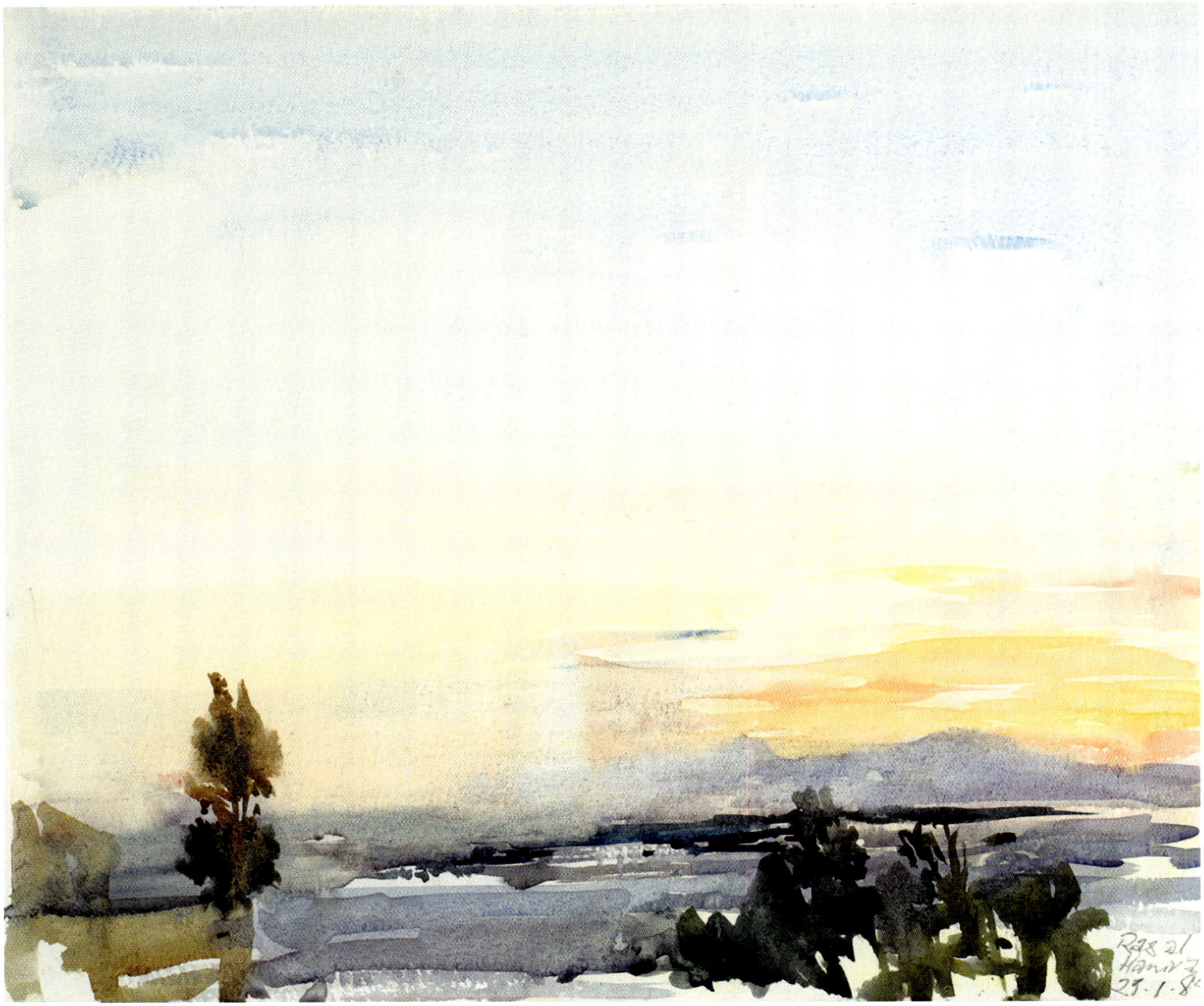

Ras al Hamra, Sunset, Oman.
Watercolour 33x27cm

Opposite: Snow, the Footbridge, Hadleigh, Suffolk.
Line and wash 34x26cm

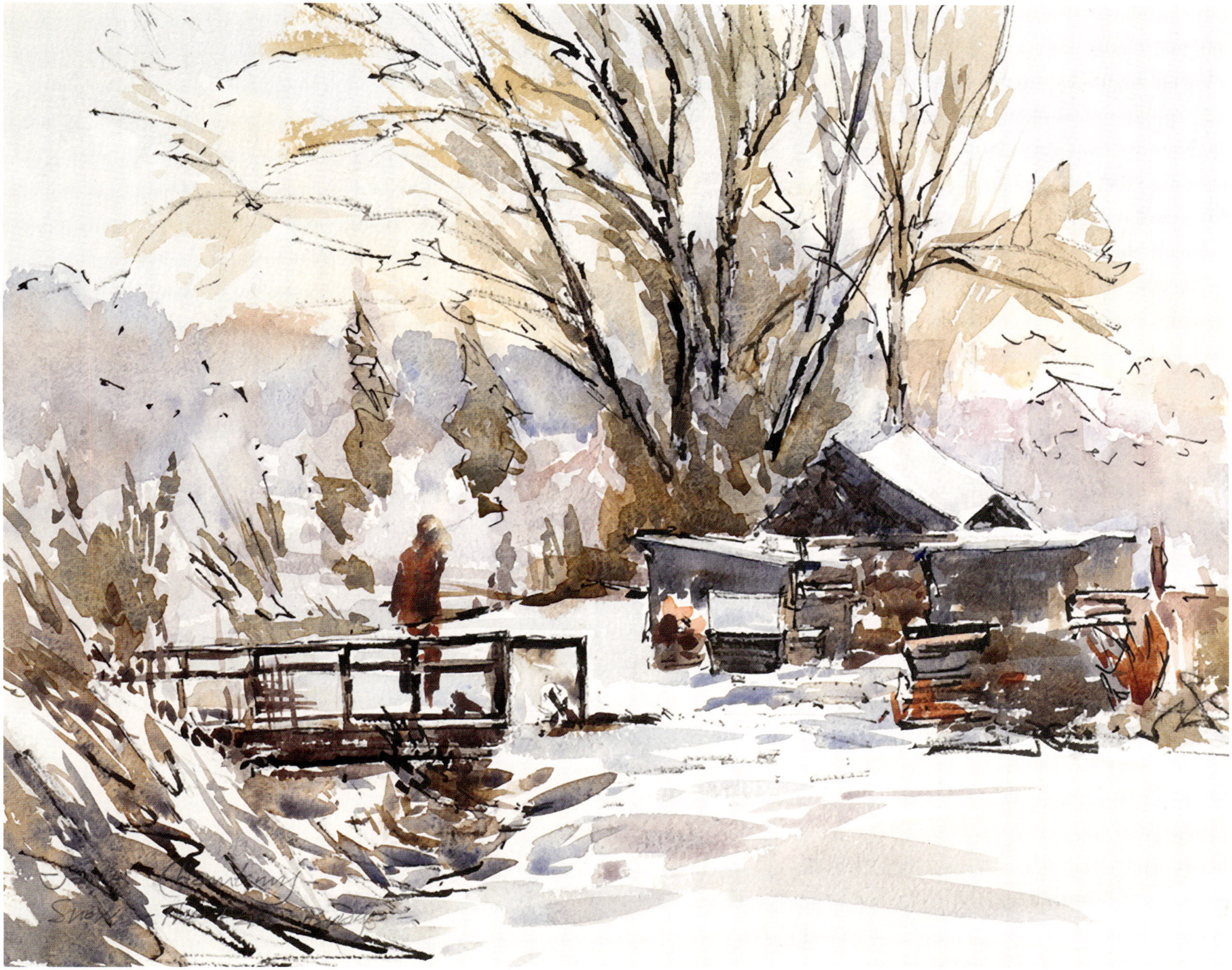

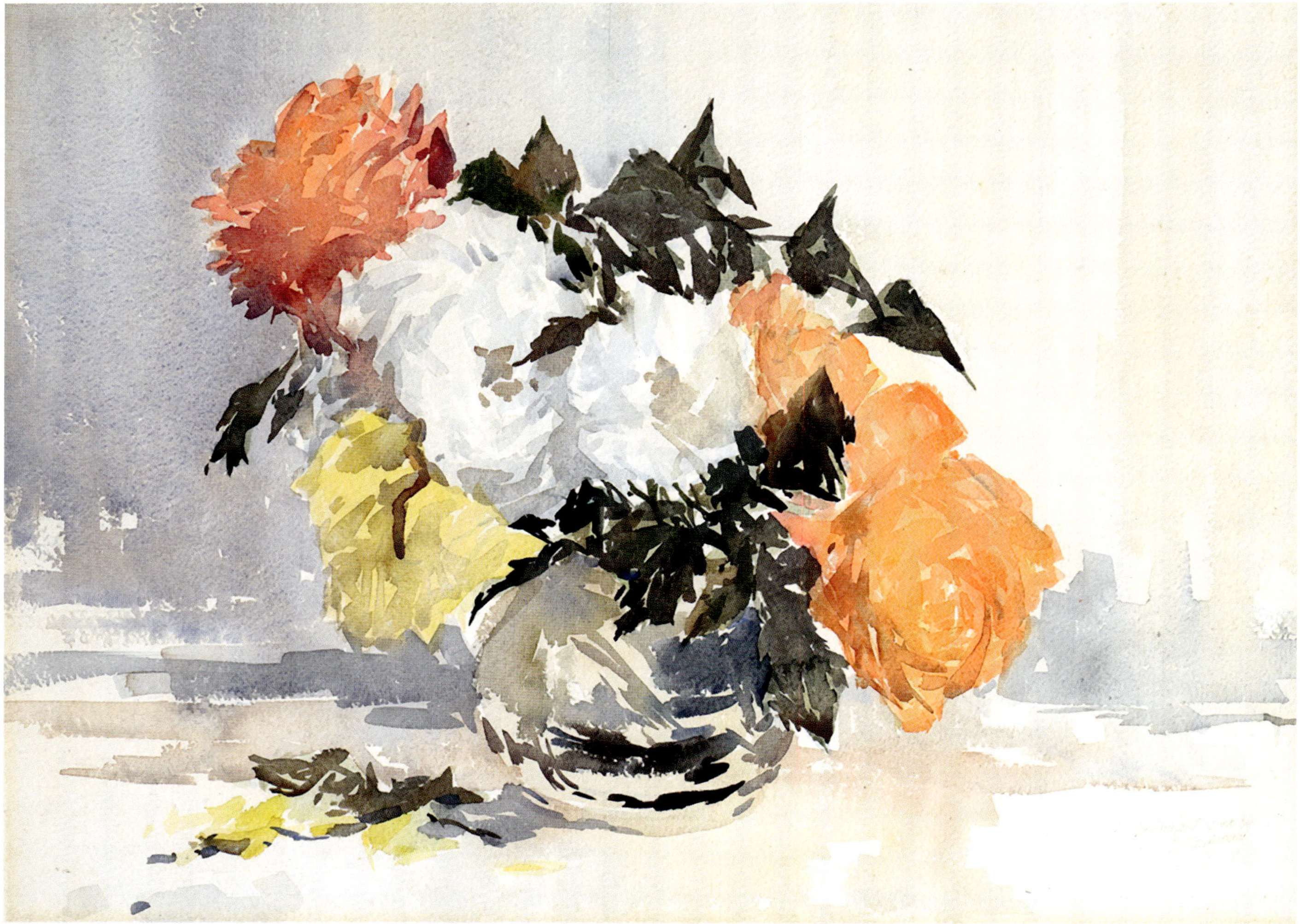

Jose's Roses.
Watercolour 52x37cm

Opposite: Near Kersey Mill. Birds Following the Plough.
Pastel 33x25cm

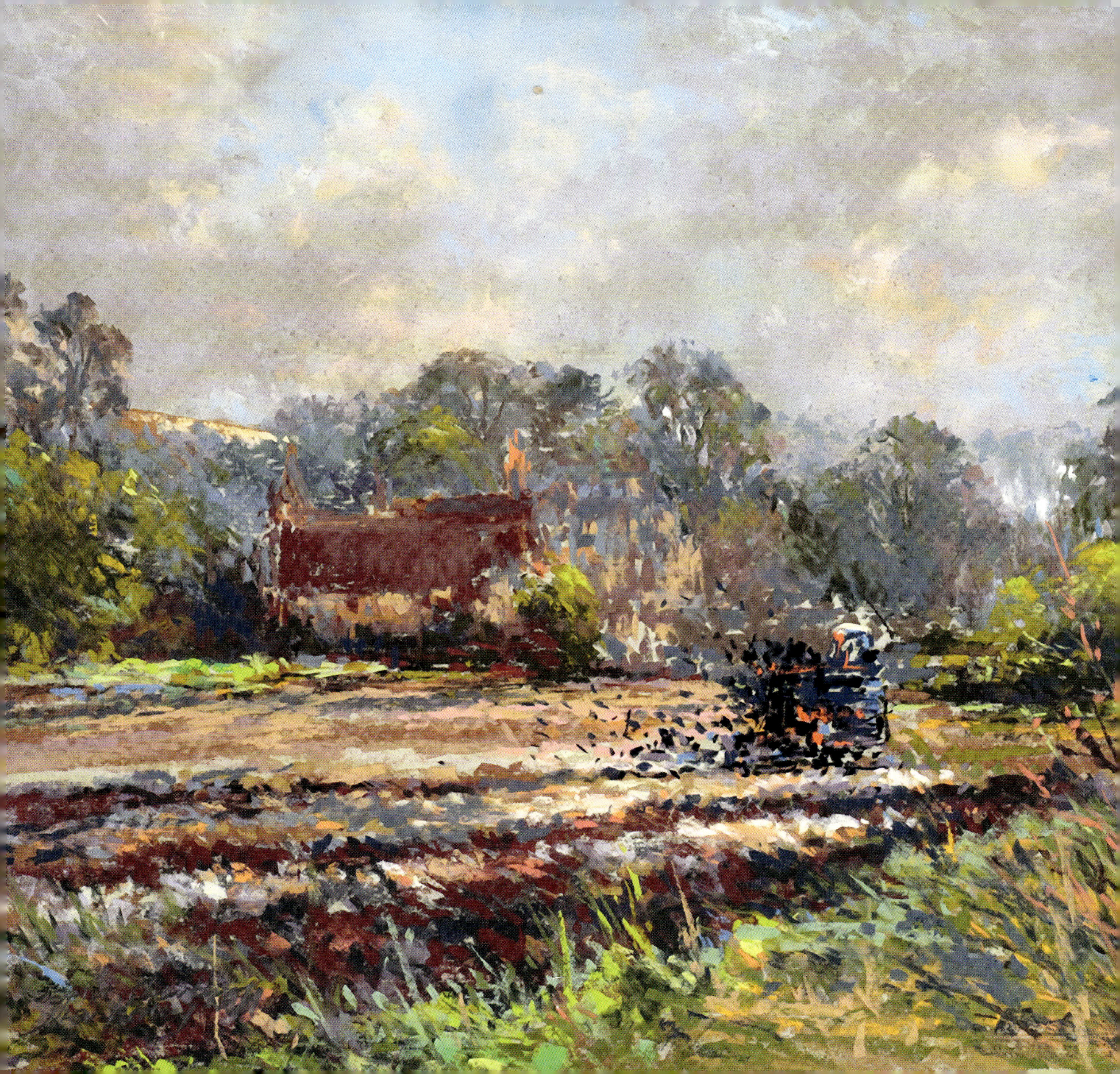

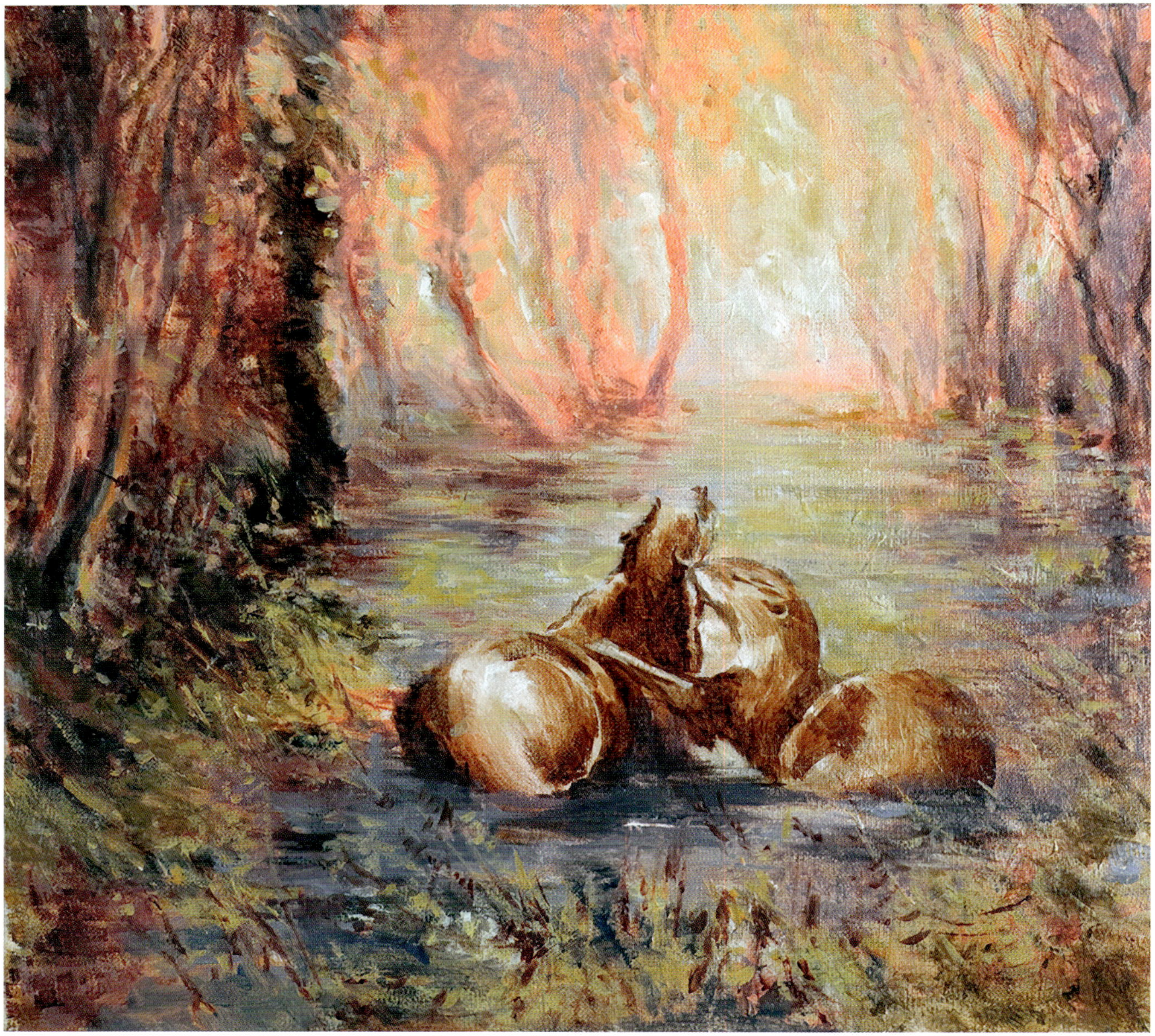

Two otters, Norfolk.
Watercolour 38x35cm

Opposite: Estuary Scene, Norfolk.
Watercolour

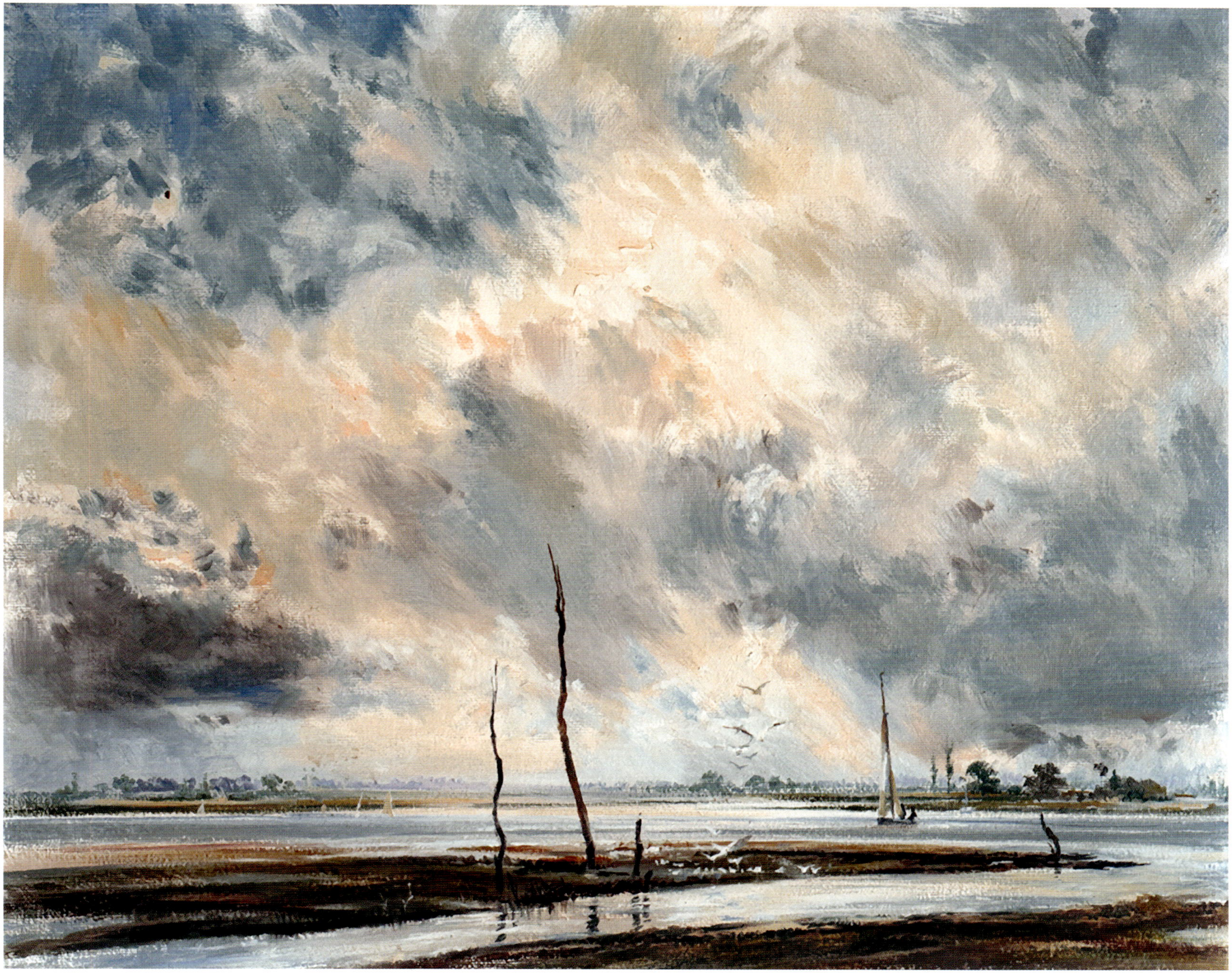

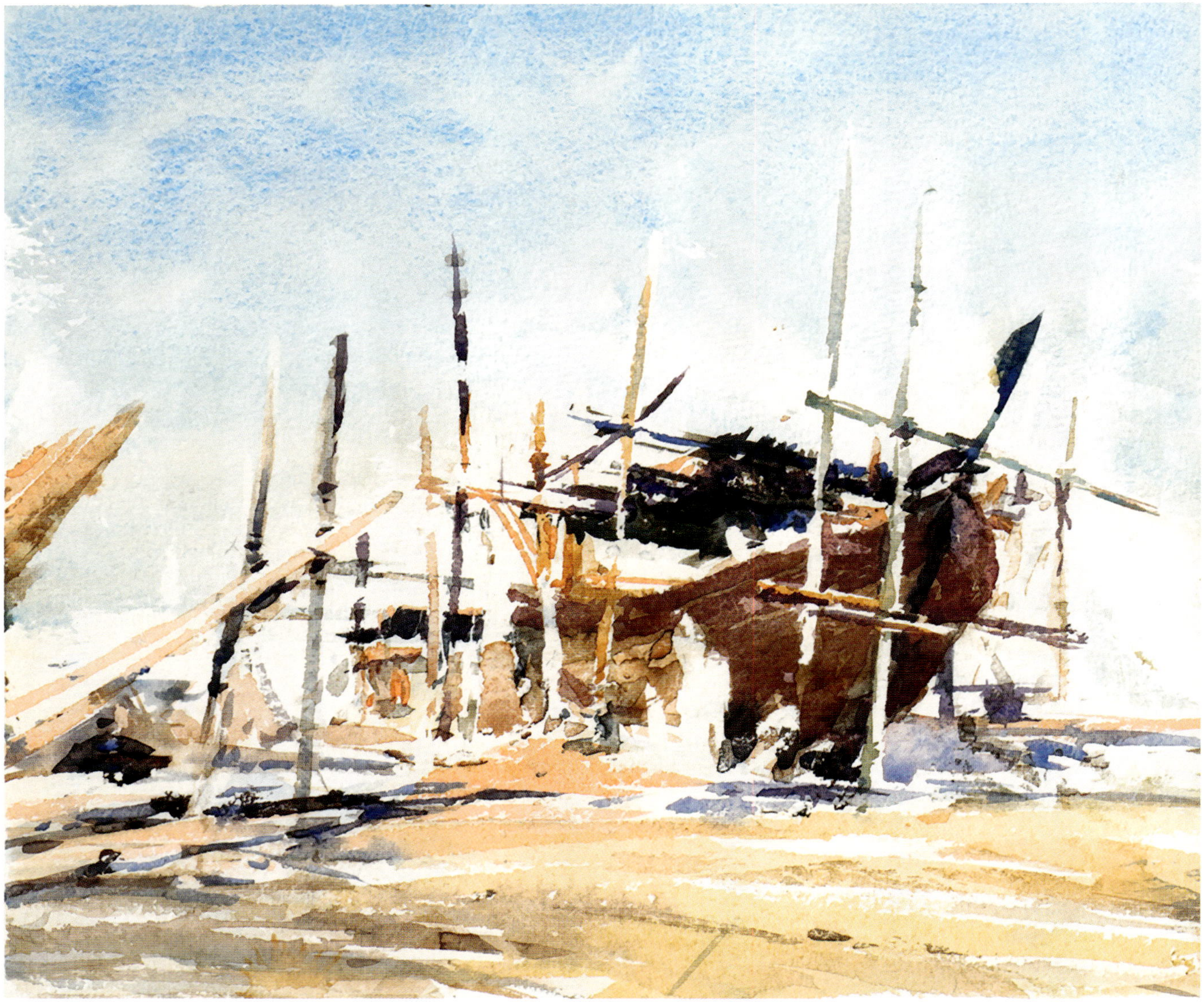

Dhow Building in Oman (unfinished).
Watercolour 22x18cm

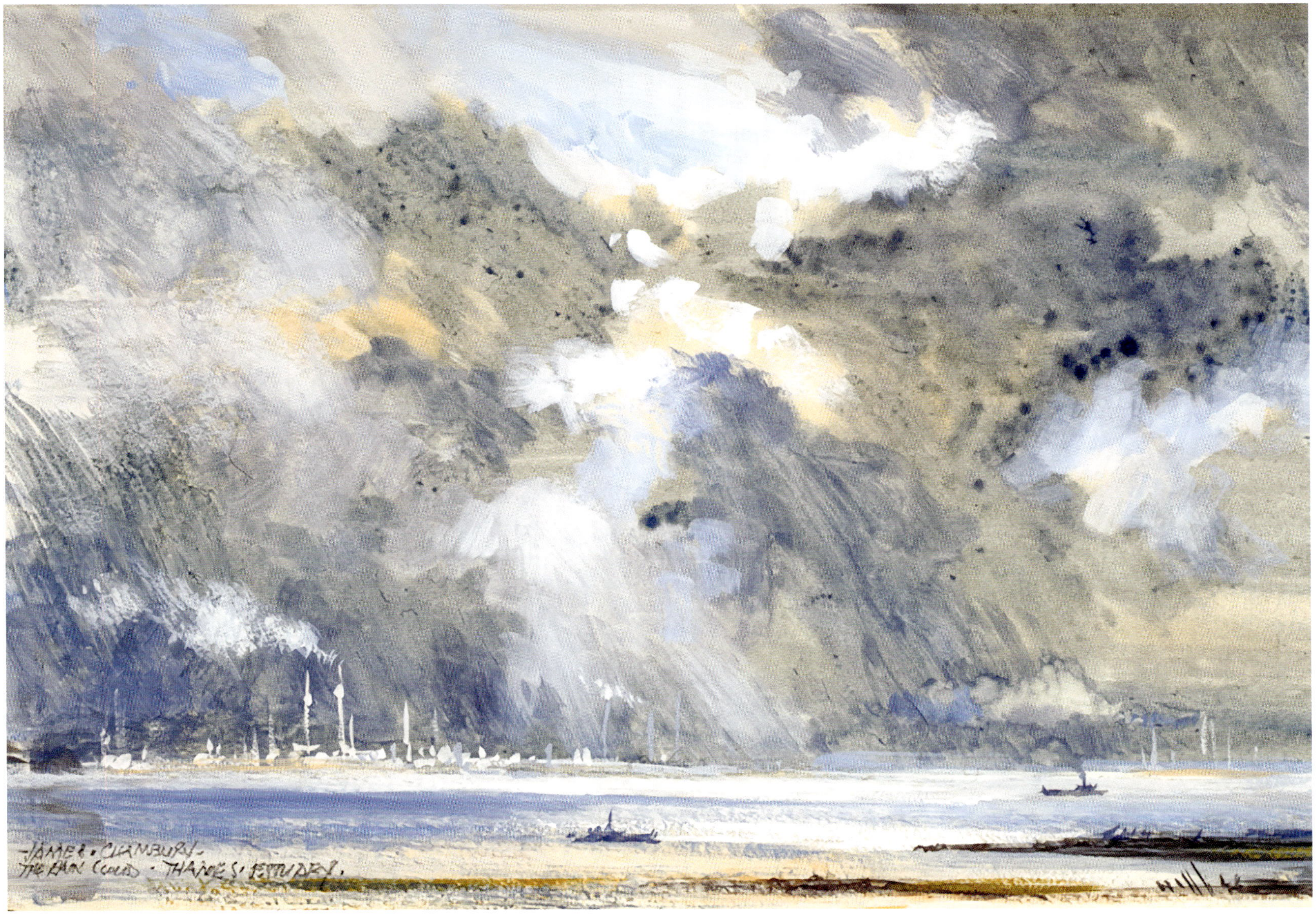

The Rain Cloud, Thames Estuary.
Watercolour

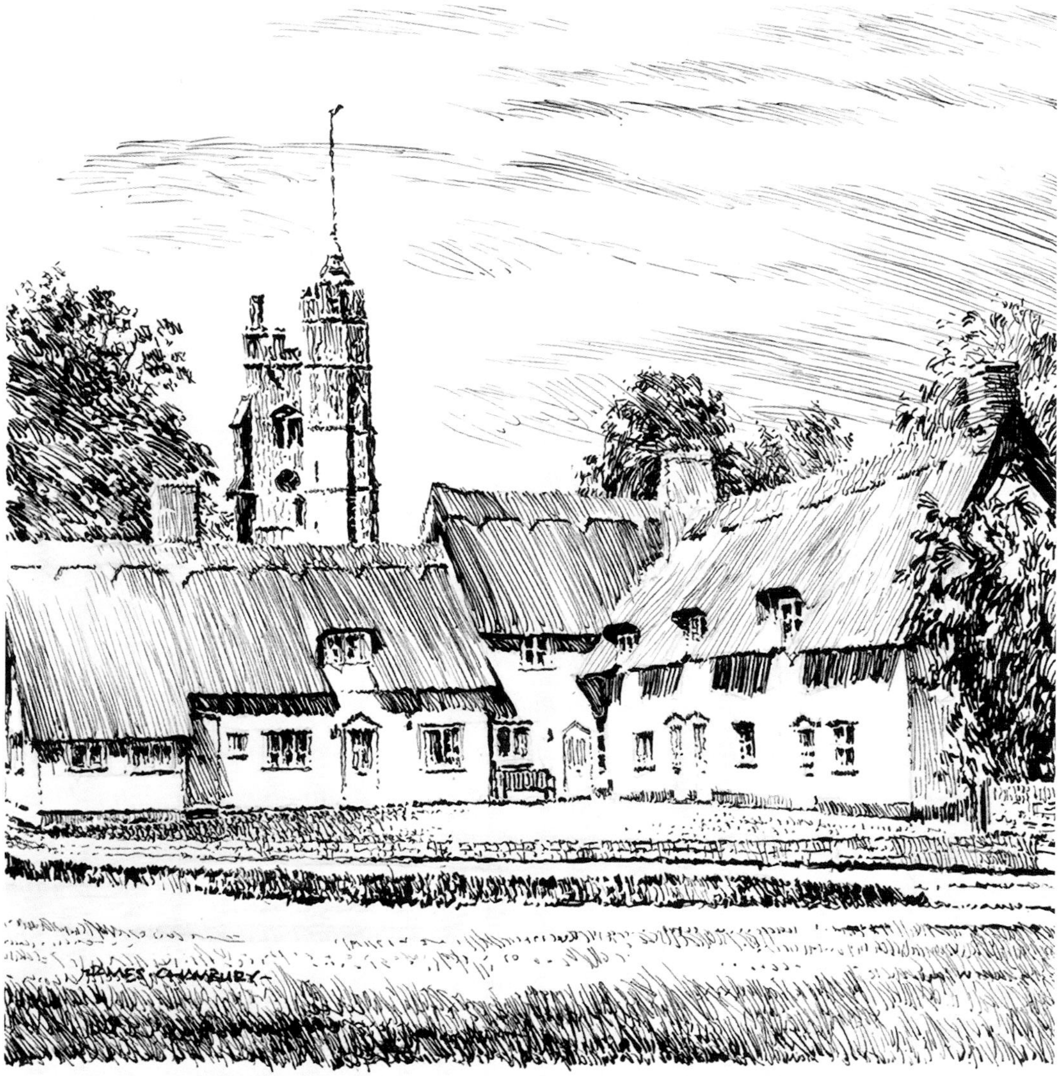

Cavendish Church and Thatched Houses, Suffolk.
Pen and ink 15x15cm

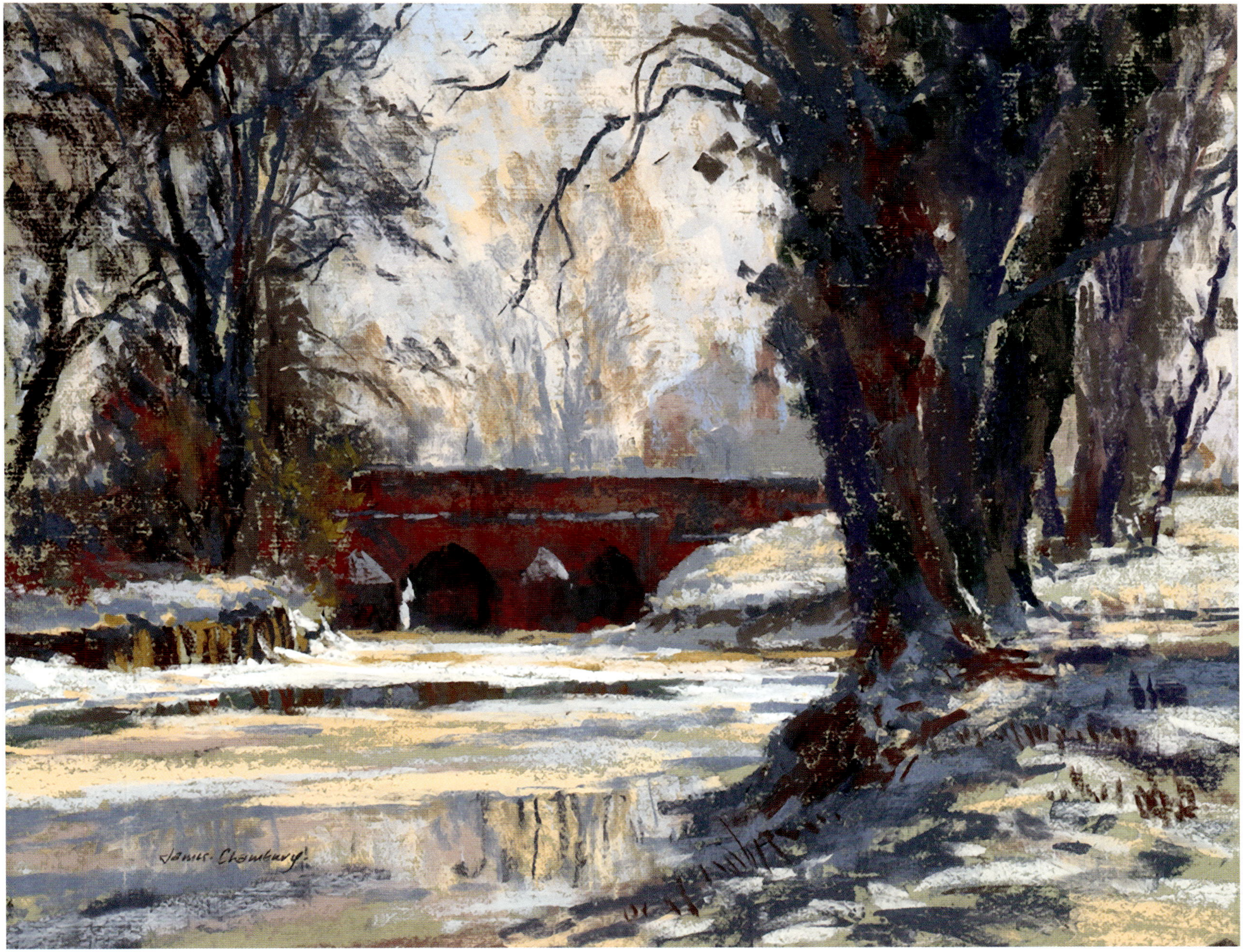

Toppesfield Bridge in the Snow.
Pastel 28x24cm

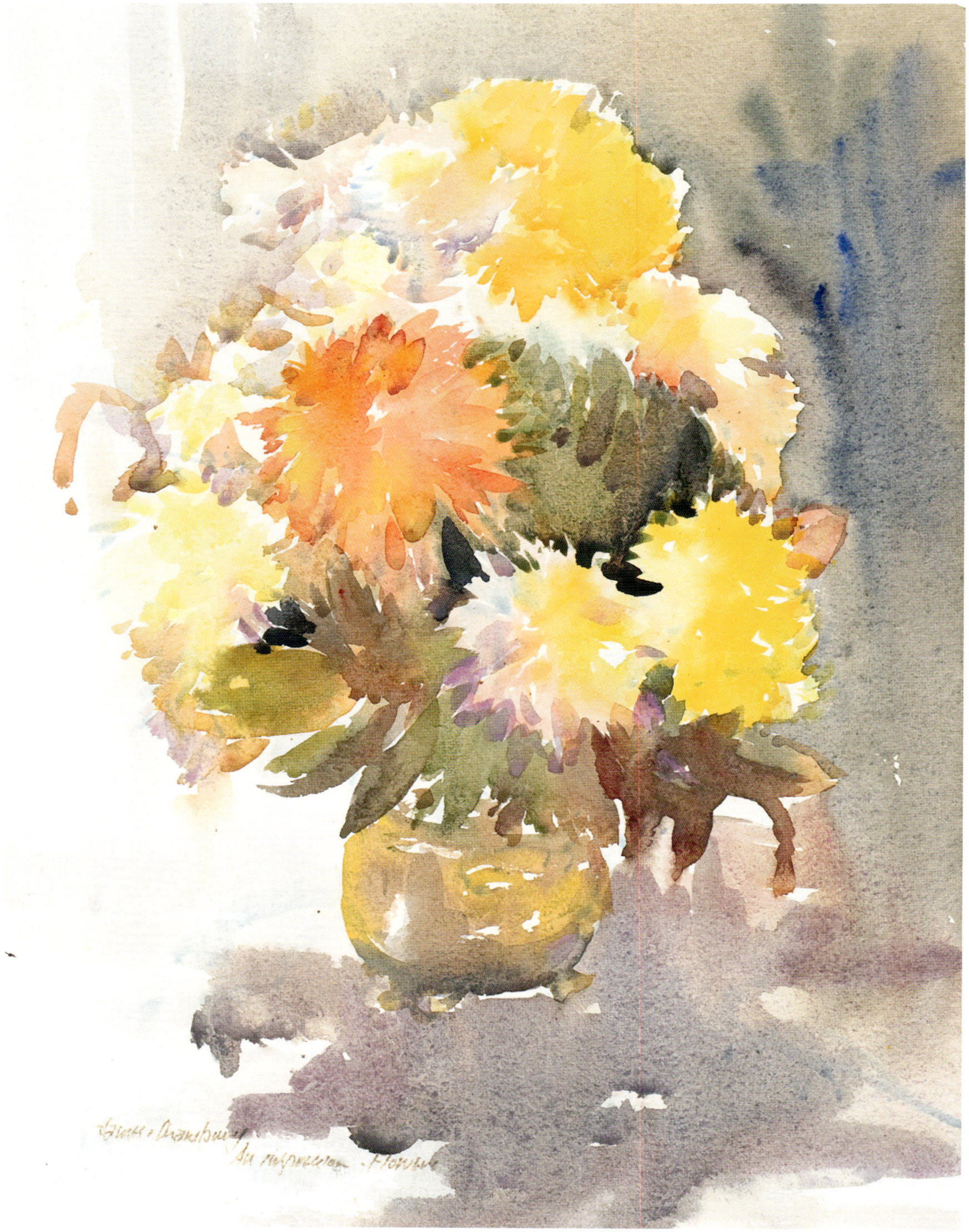

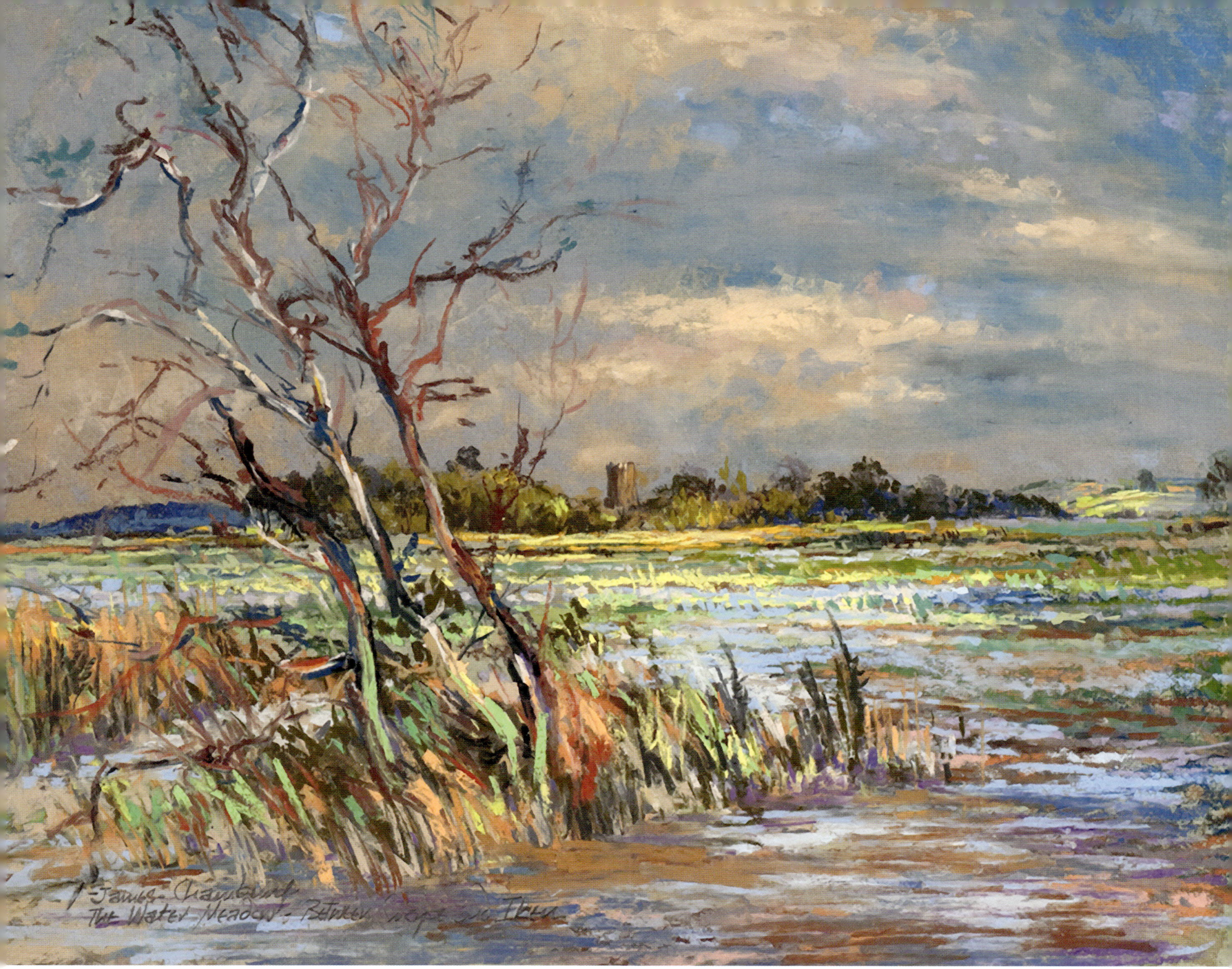

ite: An Impression – Flowers.
rcolour 25x35cm

The Water Meadow between Snape and Iken, Suffolk.
Pastel 34x27cm

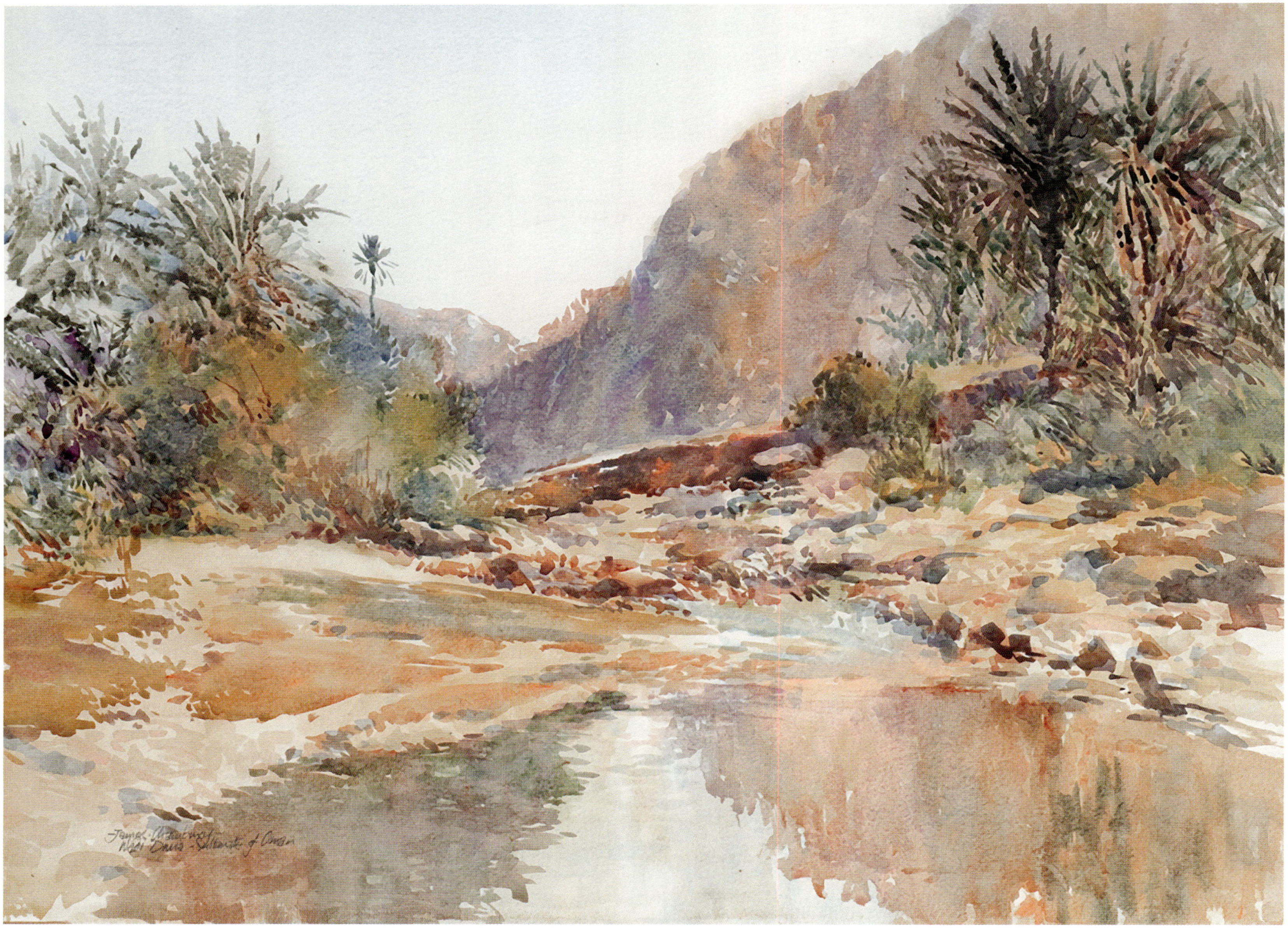

Wadi Dima, Oman.
Watercolour 54x39cm

Opposite: Muscat from the Pass, Oman.
Watercolour 34x25cm

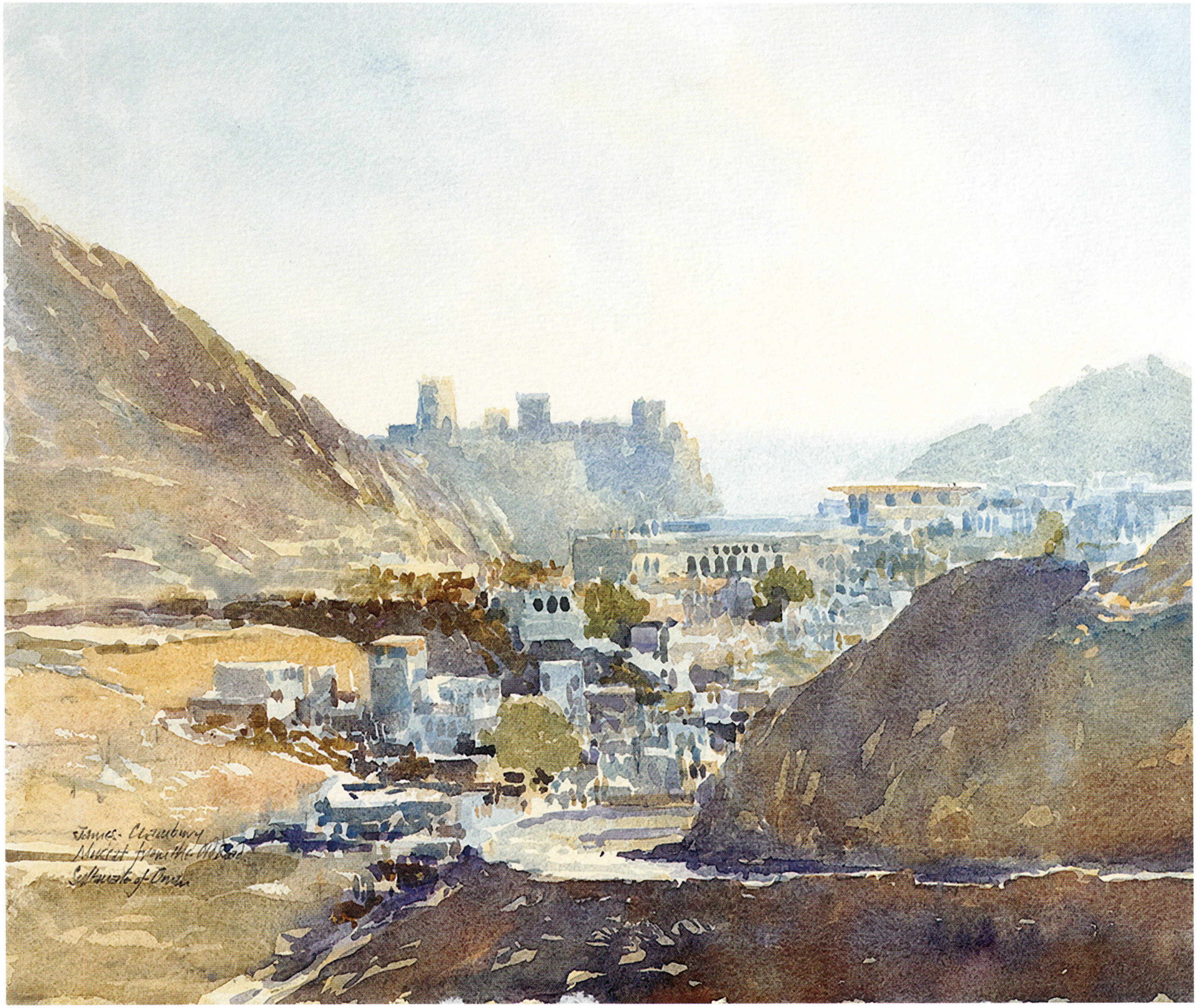
James Chambury
Muscat from the
Sultanate of Oman

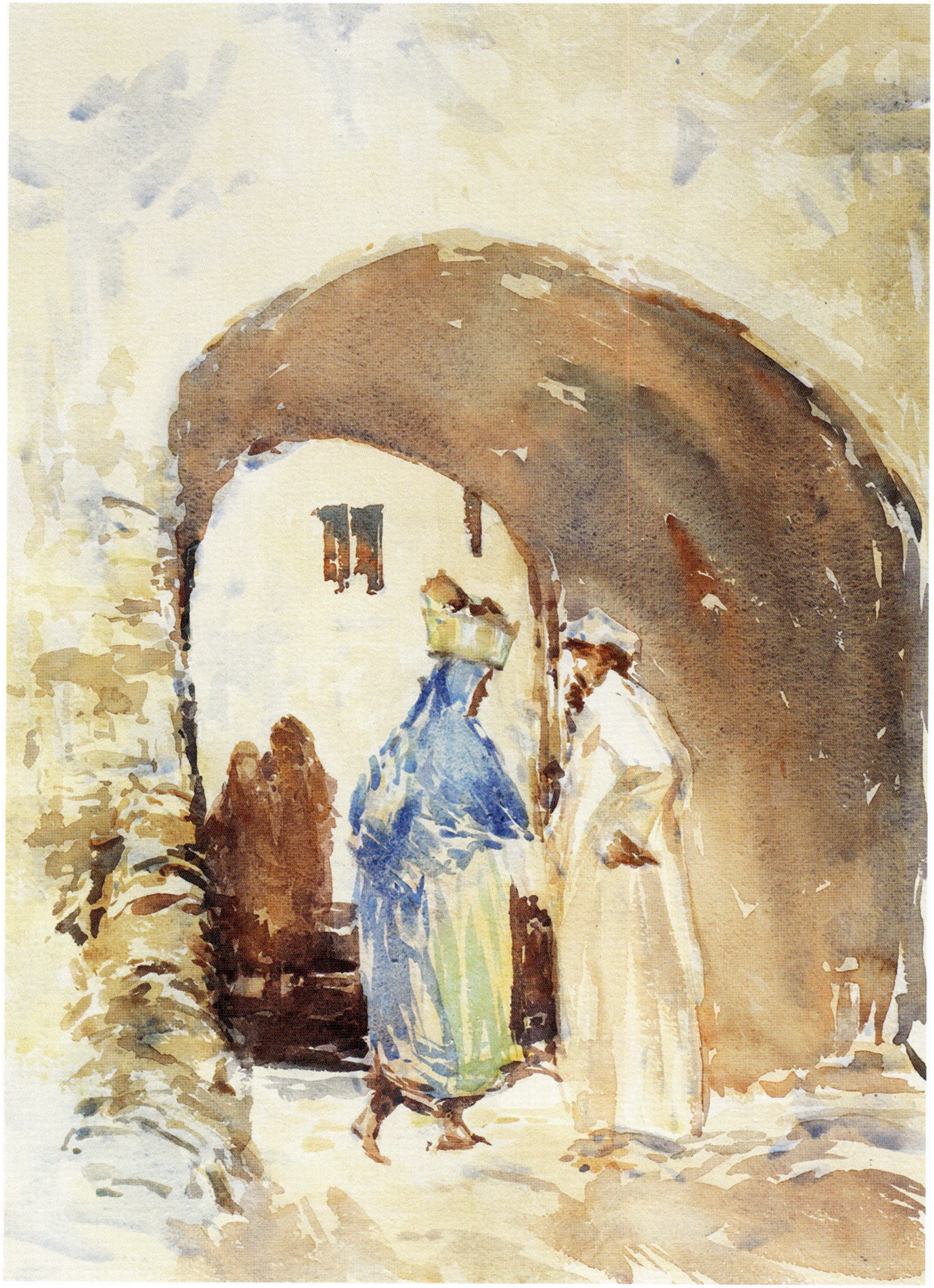

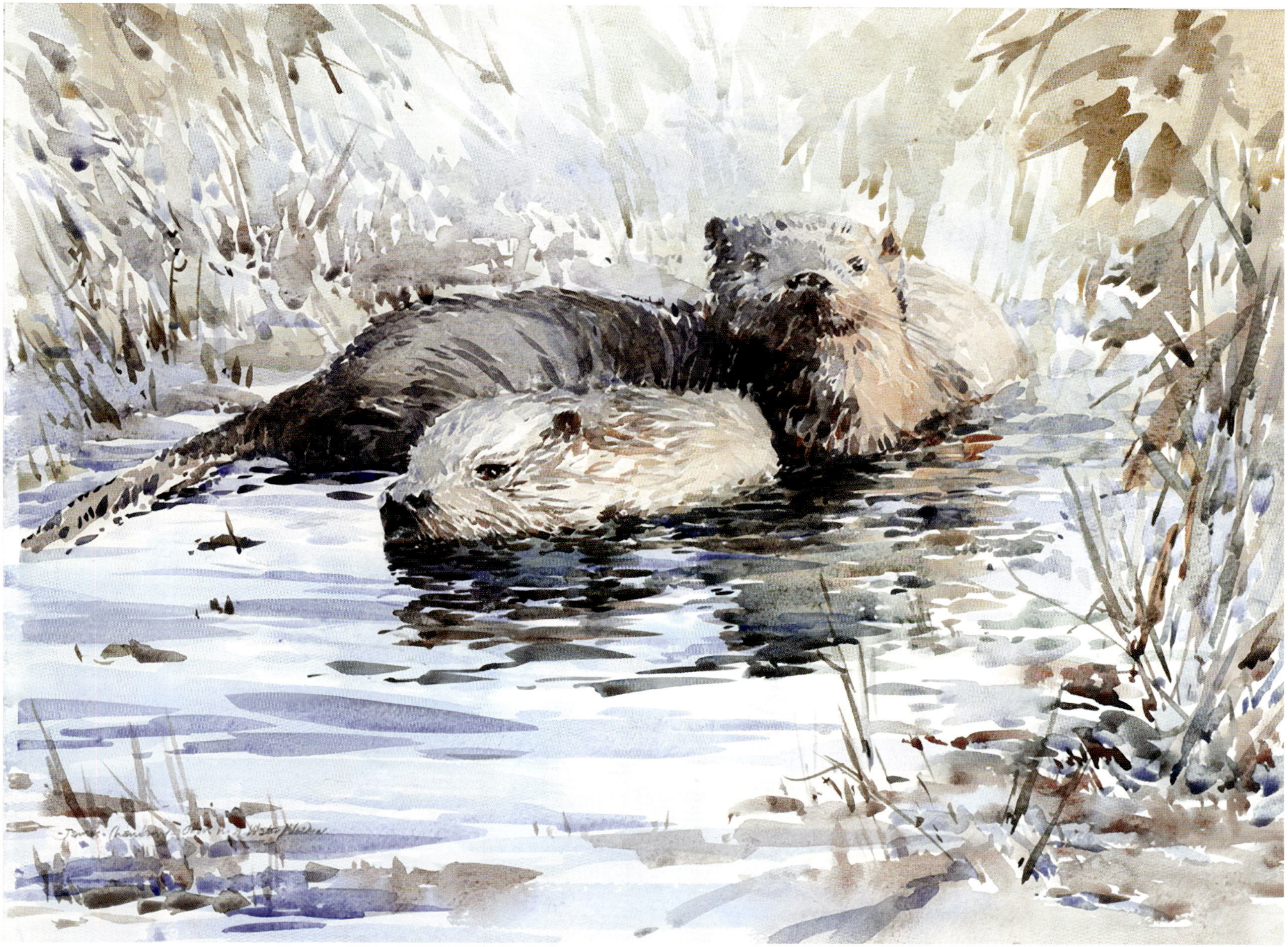

Opposite: Three Omani Figures.
Watercolour 53x35cm

Otters in a Water Meadow.
Watercolour

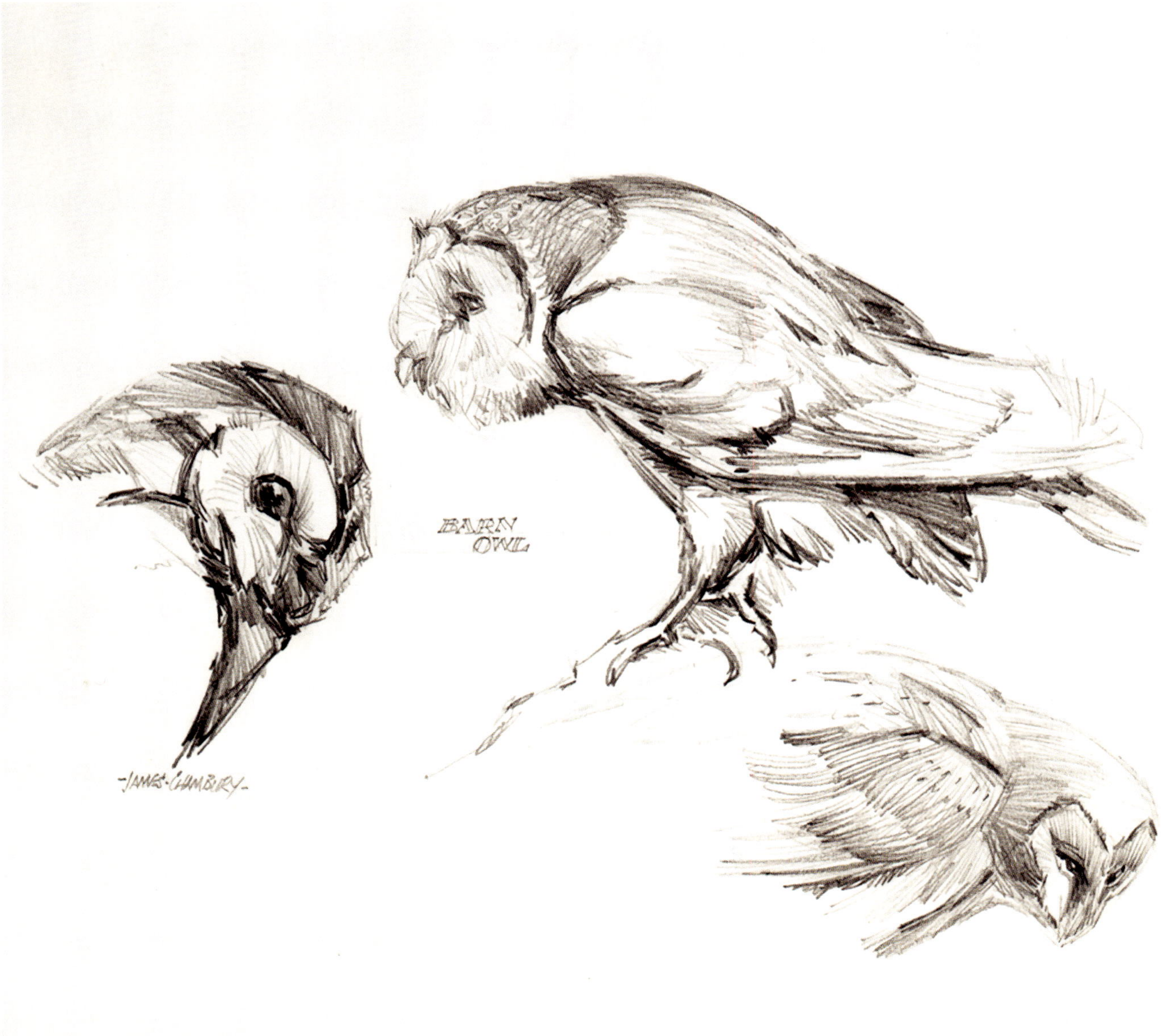

Barn Owl.
Pencil 22x18cm

Opposite: Trees in a Landscape, Dorset.
Watercolour 43x21cm

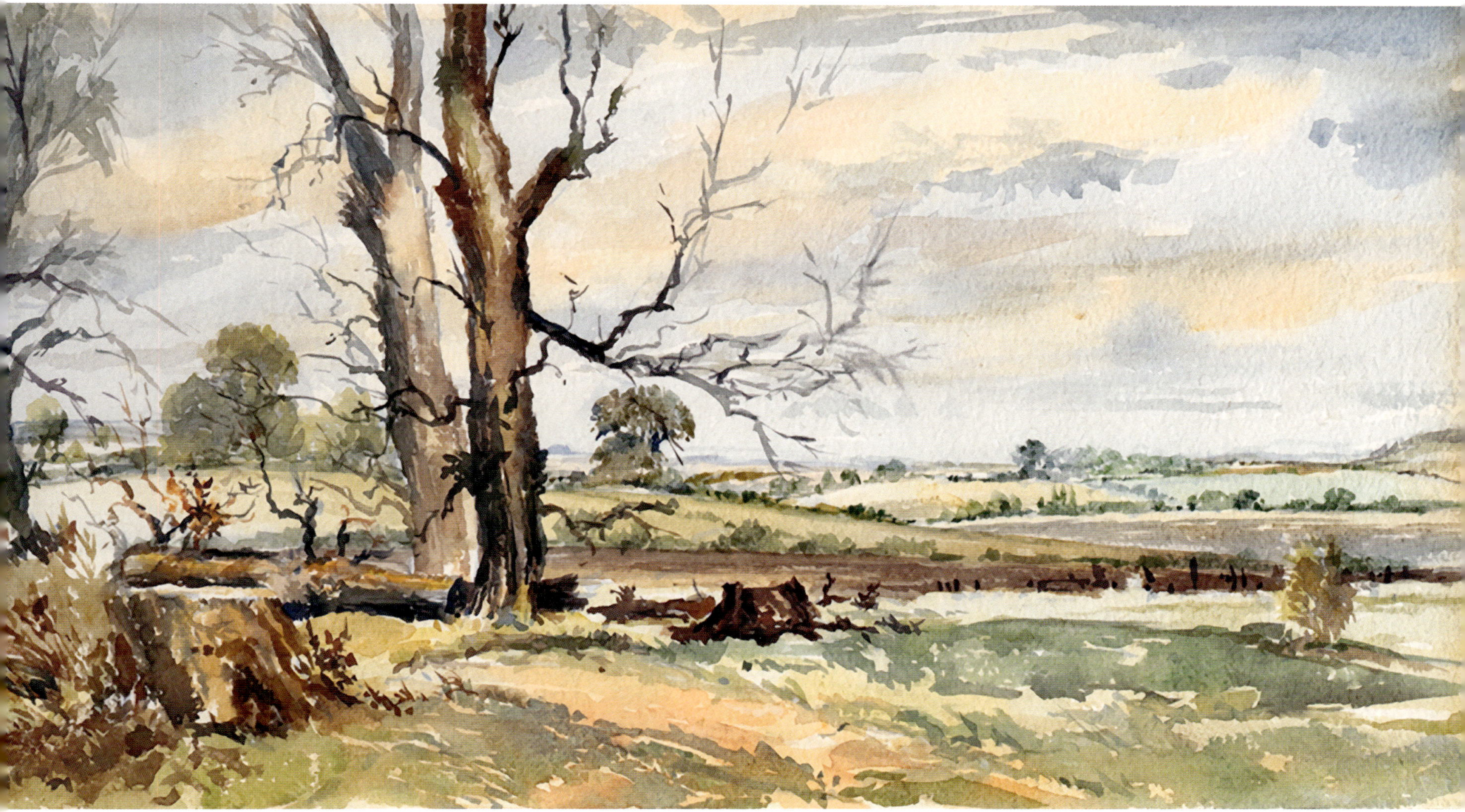

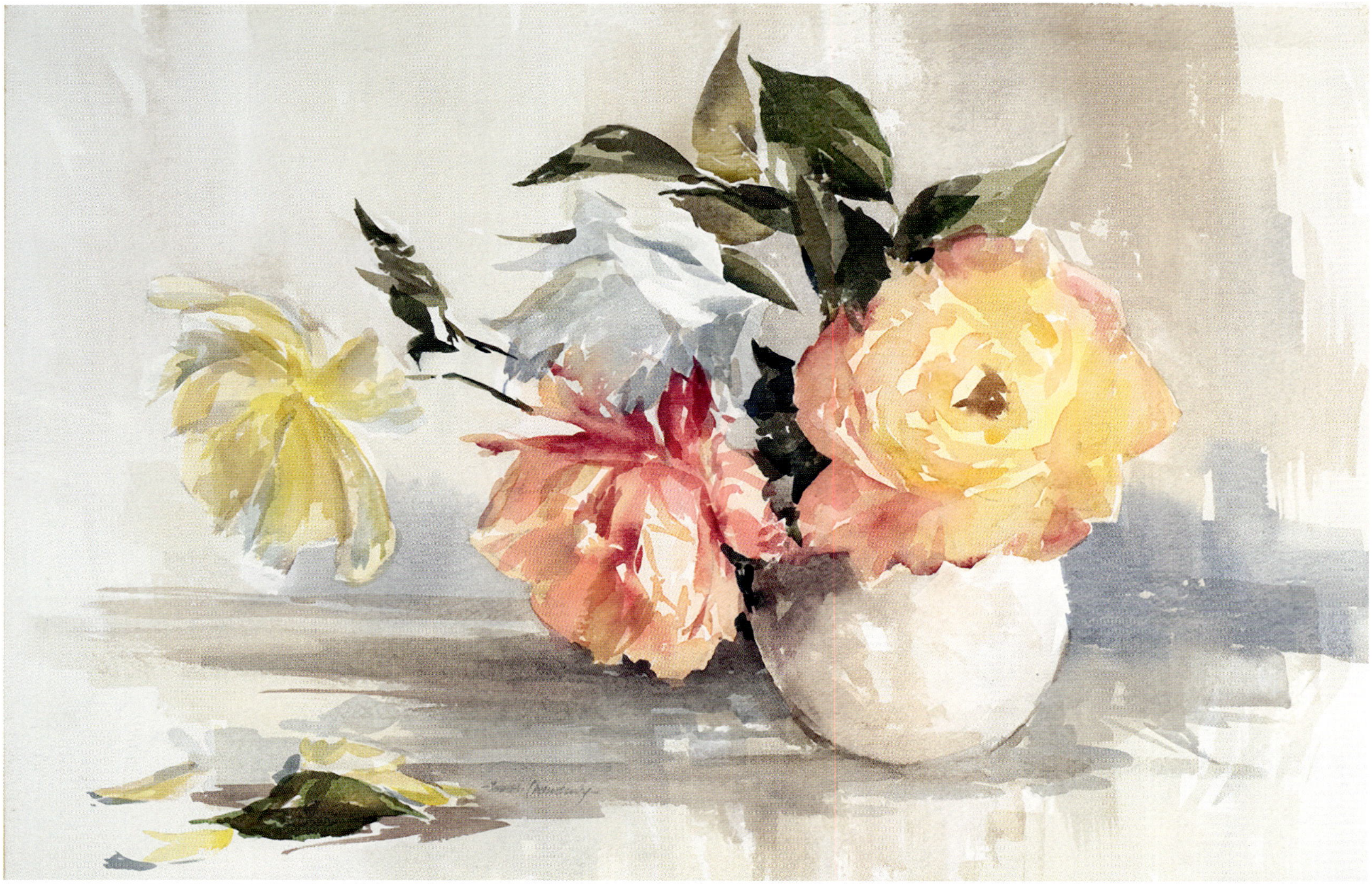

Roses in a White Bowl.
Watercolour 50x32cm

Opposite: Blakeney from Morston, Norfolk.
Pastel

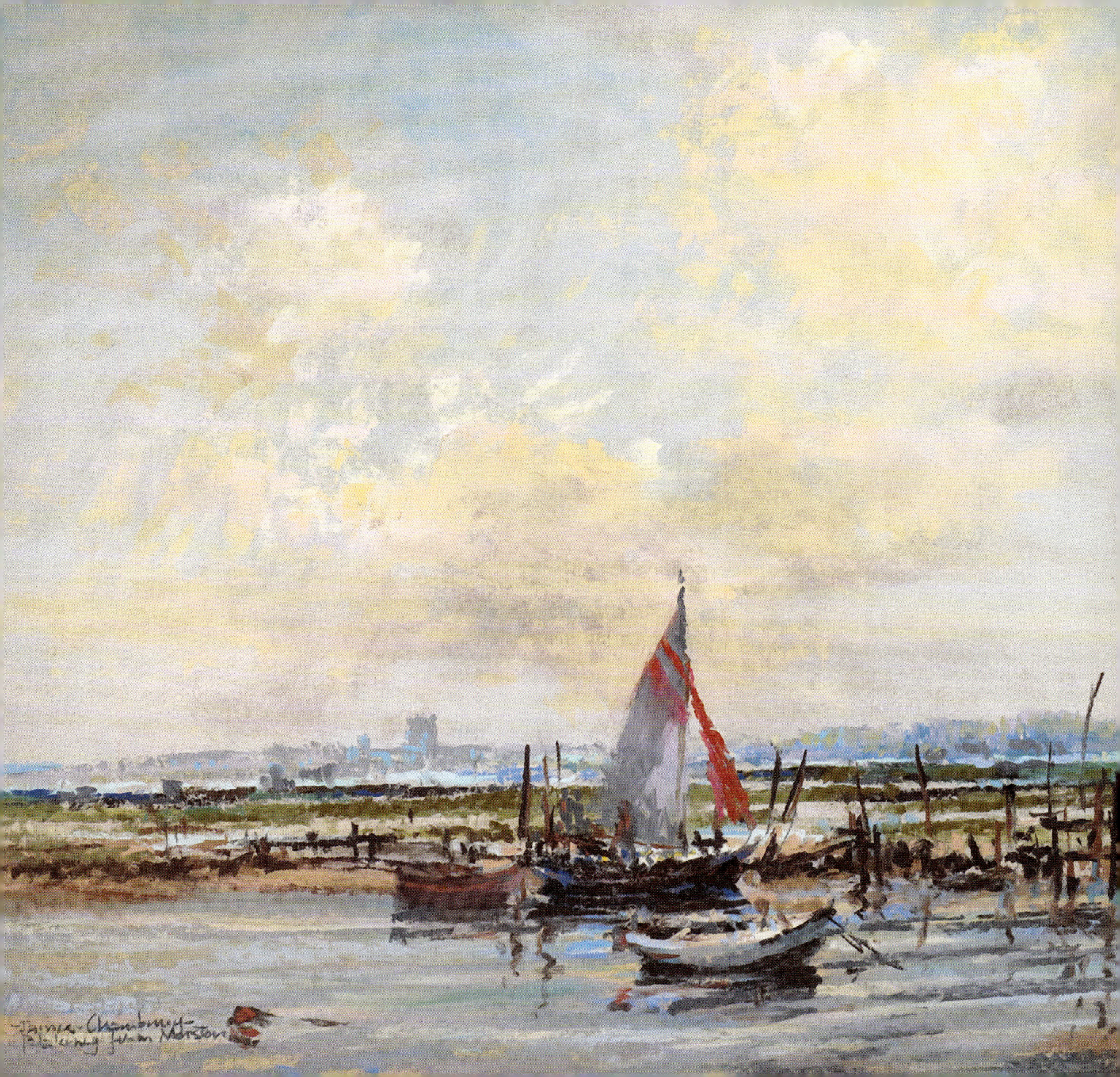

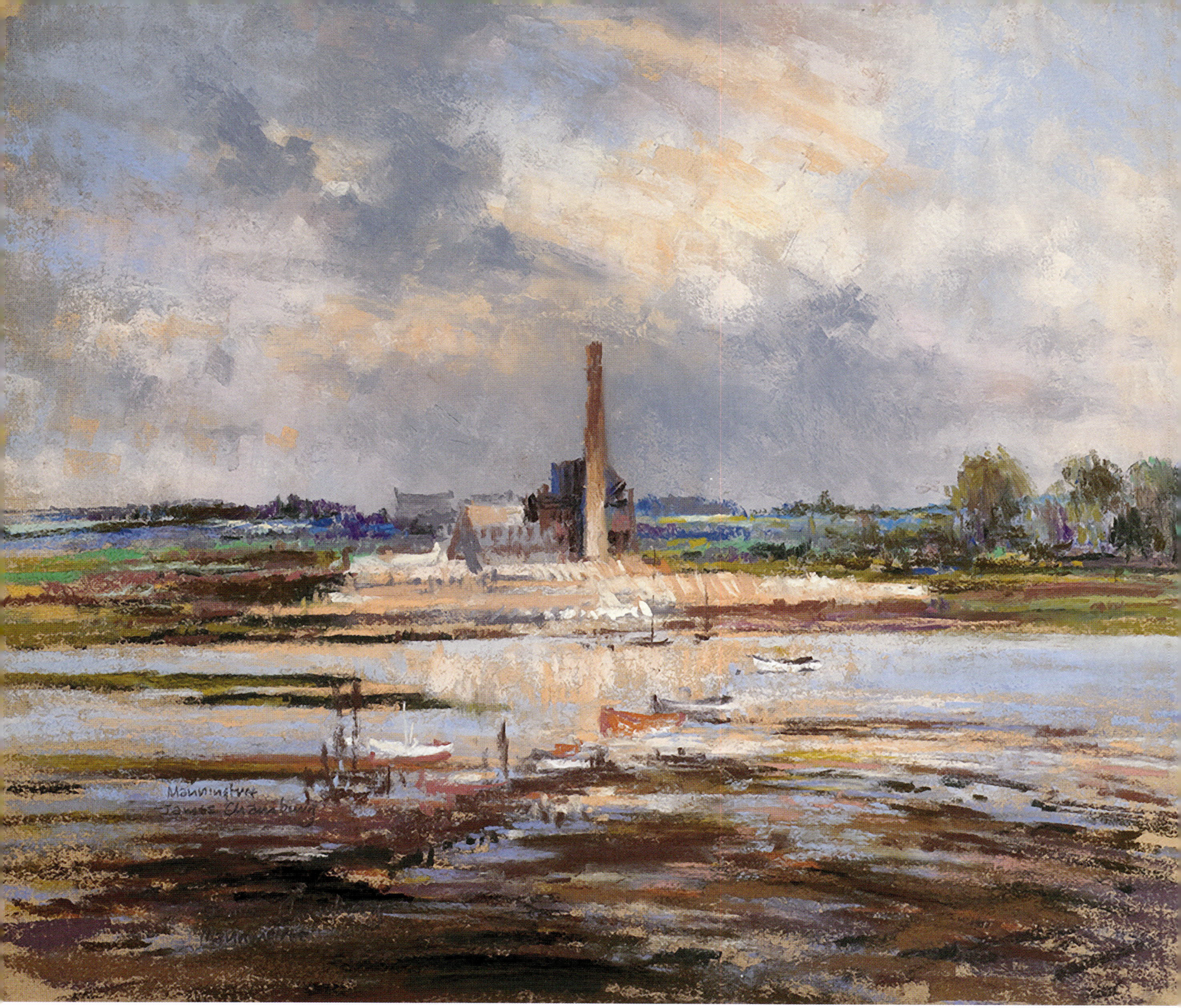
Manningtree

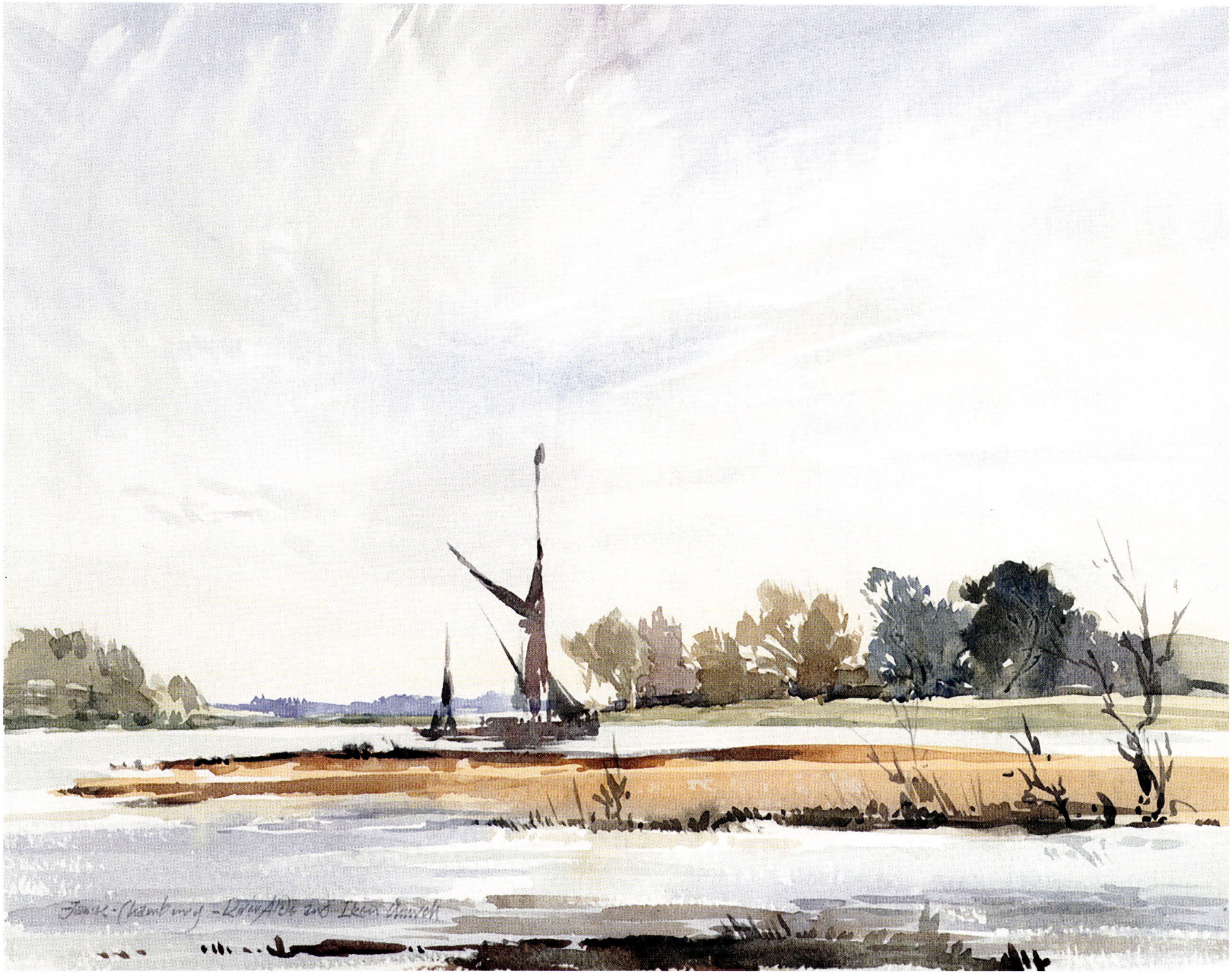

Opposite: Manningtree, Essex.
Pastel 38x29cm

River Alde and Iken Church, Suffolk.
Watercolour 35x27cm

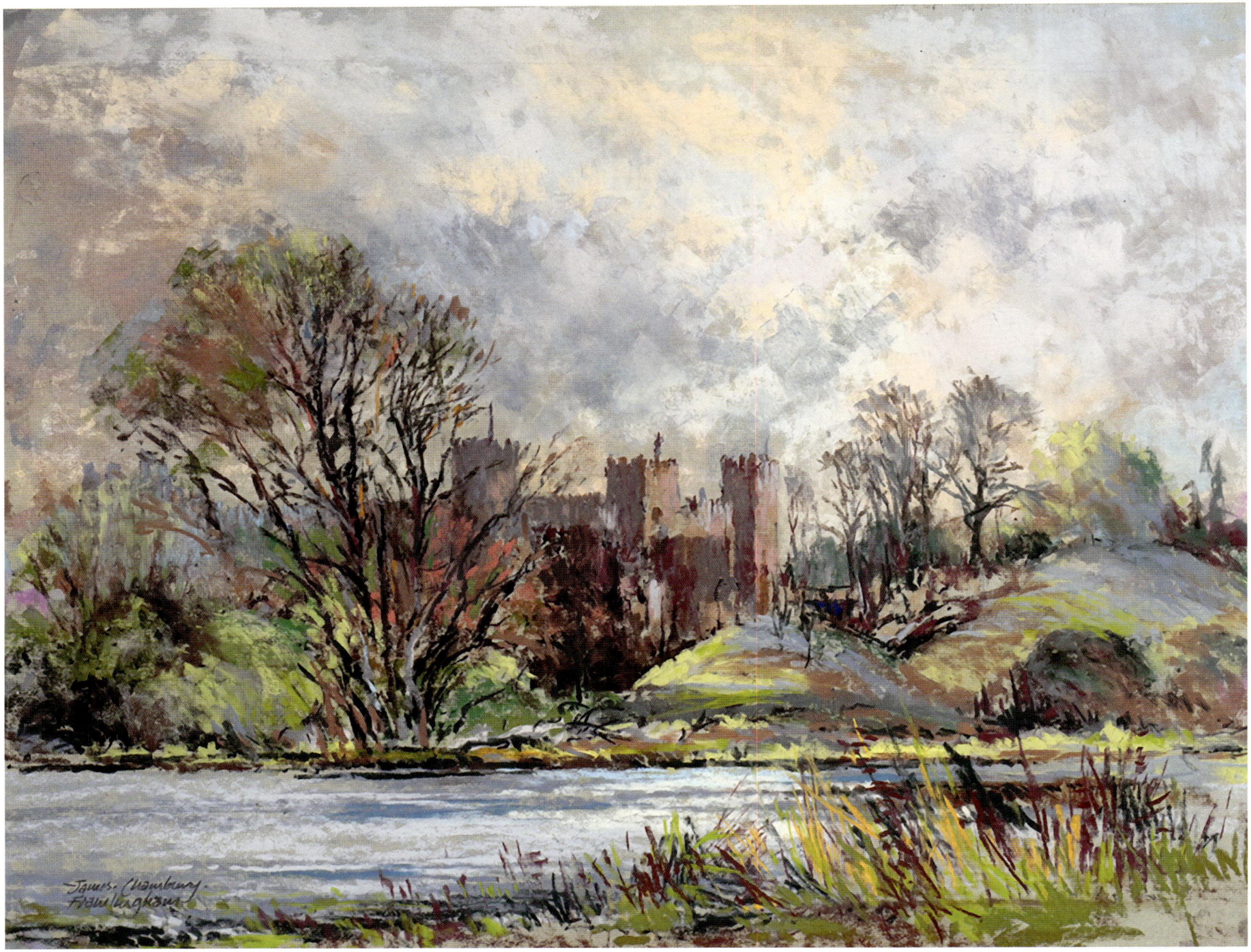

Framlingham Castle, Suffolk.
Pastel 32x24cm

Opposite: Coming Home, River Blackwater.
Pastel 62x48cm

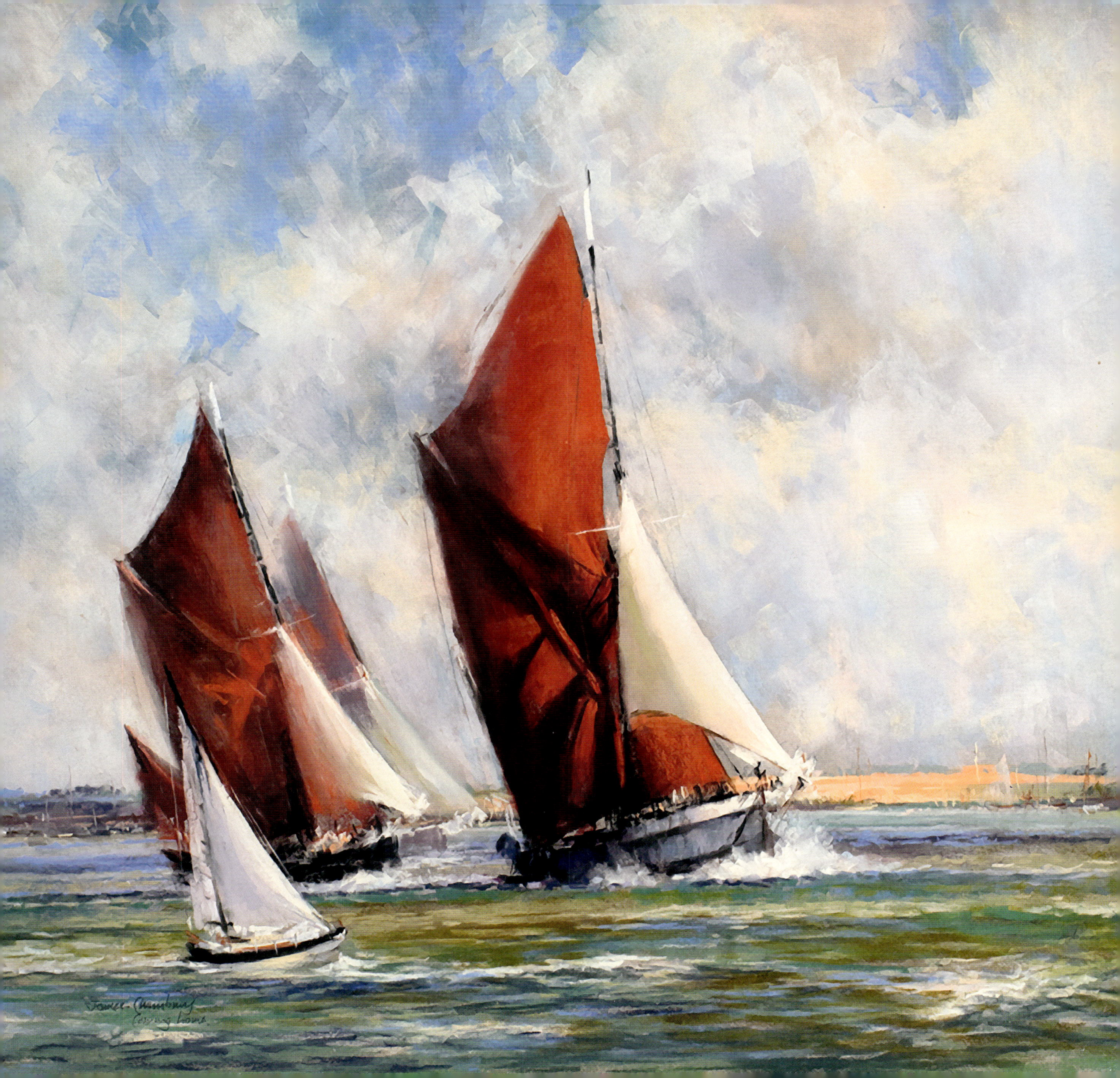

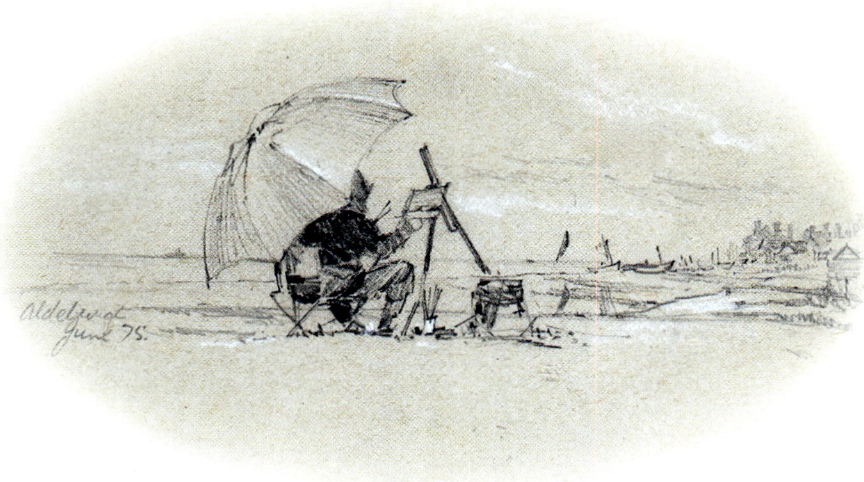
Aldeburgh
June 75.